Production Variance Analysis in SAP® Controlling

John Jordan

CW01476754

Contents

Contents

Introduction

Controlling (CO) involves the analysis of the costs of running a company, as well as, internal reporting. This helps management determine profitability and efficiency trends. The Controlling process typically begins by creating a budget or plan for the next fiscal year. The plan costs are used to create standard cost estimates, which are released at the start of the next fiscal year. Each period-end, cost center managers analyze the difference between plan costs and actual expenditure, production managers analyze production variances due to the difference between standard costs and actual production costs, and purchasing managers analyze purchase price variances due to the difference between standard cost and purchase price.

SAP provides processes and reports to assist with all phases of the Controlling process. Production variance analysis involves three main steps, which are described, in sequence, below:

1. You create a standard cost estimate to determine the expected cost to produce an assembly. The cost estimate takes the bill of materials (hierarchy of materials) and routing (series of tasks required to build the assembly), and rolls the costs up from the bottom-level purchased components to the finished product. Plan overhead is added to the assembly cost based on a percentage of either the material or labor cost.

2. Actual costs of manufacture are collected on a manufacturing order or product cost collector. Actual costs occur as component materials are moved from inventory to the production floor, as labor activities are confirmed, and during period-end overhead calculation. The total plan assembly cost becomes the cost of sales as the finished products are shipped to the customer.

3. Total variance is the difference between manufacturing order actual costs (debits) and planned costs (credits calculated at quantity of finished goods produced times standard cost estimate price). The balance on the manufacturing order is then analyzed by a period-end process called variance calculation. This process automatically analyzes why actual costs differ from planned costs, and then groups them into variance categories. These categories can be used to help analyze the reason for production variance.

It may help you understand Controlling if we use a comparison with Financial Accounting, which produces financial reports for external (legal) requirements. These reporting requirements are usually different from the requirements for analyzing company internal costs to see how efficiently the company operates. By analyzing internal manufacturing efficiency with variance analysis, a company can gain a large competitive advantage over companies either not using SAP or not utilizing the variance analysis capability provided by SAP.

This guide is useful for users, managers, and consultants alike. It explains Controlling concepts from a simple and easy-to-understand level, while also containing master data and configuration setup requirements. You can use this guide as a reference, referring to specific sections when needed. For example, during period-end processing, you may refer to the period-end variance analysis section. Or you may refer to the reporting section when setting up summarization hierarchies.

The screen shots and menu paths in this guide are taken from an SAP ERP Central Component, Release 5.0 system. Manufacturing order is used as an umbrella term for production and process orders throughout.

Structure of the Guide

Let me now familiarize you with the structure of this Essentials guide. This should help you navigate your way through it and perhaps decide which chapters to concentrate on more than others, depending on your particular requirements. Get a glimpse about the structure of this guide below:

▶ **Chapter 1**
This chapter describes the initial steps in planning for variance analysis. Sales plan quantities are converted into production plan quantities in Sales and Operations Planning and transferred to Long-Term Planning to determine work center loads and purchasing requirements. Scheduled activity requirements are transferred to Cost Center Accounting, where planned activity prices are determined.

▶ **Chapter 2**
Chapter 2 examines the requirements for creating cost estimates. Master data, such as bills of materials and routings, provide quantity information for cost estimates. Costing variant configuration provides control and price search strategy for cost estimates. I demonstrate how to create and analyze standard and preliminary cost estimates and carry out costing runs.

▶ **Chapter 3**
In this chapter you will understand how actual postings occur within Controlling by analyzing financial account postings, activity confirmations, and material movements.

▶ **Chapter 4**
Chapter 4 covers in detail the different types of variance calculations, configuration settings, and input and output variance categories. I discuss typical period-end processing transactions, and provide case scenarios to assist you when carrying out variance analysis in your system. I also cover cost center and purchase price variance analysis, and discuss how material ledger relates to variance analysis.

▶ **Chapter 5**
This chapter analyzes scrap variance in detail. I discuss how to plan scrap, analyze standard cost estimates, post actual scrap, and analyze product cost collector and production order reports.

▶ **Chapter 6**
The final chapter of this guide discusses variance reporting available in standard reports, such as summarized analysis, detailed reports, and line item reports.

Looking Ahead

After reading this guide, you will have a clear understanding of the entire cycle of variance analysis, from plan and actual postings to period-end processing and reporting. You will learn how SAP CO integrates with other modules such as Production Planning (PP) and Materials Management (MM). You will also learn configuration and master data settings to improve your present variance analysis and reporting.

The benefits of frequent variance analysis can be significant. For example, an increase in lot size variance and purchase price variance detected during analysis may indicate that actual manufacturing and purchase quantities are smaller than planned in the standard cost estimate, causing an increase in unit cost. This may lead to an investigation of manufacturing and purchase quantities, and a review of material requirements planning procedures for manufacturing. It could also lead to implementation of a new strategy of combining purchasing requirements across plants to increase purchase quantities. The trend of decreasing lot sizes would be difficult to determine by any method other than variance analysis, as described in this guide. This is only one example of the many possible scenarios of variance analysis resulting in reduced costs by early detection of trends.

This guide will allow you to take full advantage of the many benefits of variance analysis, by clearly laying out the process from start to finish and explaining in detail the different analysis and reporting options available. Readers do not need a detailed knowledge of accounting or production planning to understand the concepts and details discussed in this guide.

You can contact me at jjordan@erp-corp.com.

John Jordan

1 Initial Planning

The process of variance analysis begins much earlier than the period-end analysis of variance calculations. It actually begins in the previous fiscal year when sales, production, and cost center plans are created. This planning data assembles valuation information necessary for the creation of cost estimates for the following fiscal year. Standard cost estimates provide plan costs for the manufacture of products, and when compared with actual costs, they form the basis of variance analysis.

While there are many alternatives for entering and processing plan data in SAP, in this chapter we will follow a typical flow from Sales and Operations Planning to Long-Term Planning to Cost Center Accounting. A sales plan is entered in Sales and Operations Planning, and multiple sales scenarios are analyzed. A preferred sales plan is then converted into a production plan, which is then transferred to Long-Term Planning. Activity scheduled quantities are then be transferred from Long-Term Planning to Cost Center Accounting, where, together with cost center planning data, activity and overhead rates are calculated.

Let's begin initial planning by entering a sales plan in the Sales and Operations Planning module.

1.1 Sales and Operations Planning

You can enter the sales plan for future fiscal years directly into the Sales and Operations Planning module. The sales plan can be entered for a product group and disaggregated to lower members, or entered directly for individual materials. The production plan is determined from the sales plan, and then transferred from Sales and Operations Planning to the Long-Term Planning module. If the production plan is determined from the sales plan on a spreadsheet, instead of the Sales and Operations Planning module, it can be entered manually into Long-Term Planning.

Enter a sales plan for a material into Sales and Operations Planning with transaction MC88 or via menu path: **Logistics • Production • SOP • Planning • For Material • Change**. The data entry screen shown in Figure 1.1 is displayed.

Change Rough-Cut Plan

Material	10000		Finished Product
Plant	0021		
Version	A00	Active version	Active

SOP Plan individual material

Planning table	Un	M 03/2007	M 04/2007	M 05/2007	M 06/2007	M 07/2007	M 08/2007
Sales	EA			10.000	10.000	10.000	10.000
Production	EA		10.000	10.000	10.000	10.000	
Stock level	EA		10.000	10.000	10.000	10.000	
Target stock level	EA						
Days' supply	***			22	21	21	
Target days' supply	***						

Figure 1.1 Sales and Production Plan Entry Screen in Sales and Operations Planning

Sales plan quantities are entered in the **Sales** row, and production plan quantities are entered in the **Production** row. Figure 1.1 shows an example of the **Production** plan offset forward in time from the **Sales** plan by one month to help ensure sales plan delivery dates are met. Once the production plan is determined, it is transferred directly to Long-Term Planning with transaction MC74 or via menu path: **Logistics • Production • SOP • Planning • For Material • Transfer Material to Demand Management**. The screen shown in Figure 1.2 is displayed.

You transfer either the **Sales plan** or **Production plan**, for either an individual **material** or **PG members** (product group members), by selecting the appropriate radio button in the **Transfer strategy and period** section, and then clicking on the **Transfer now** button.

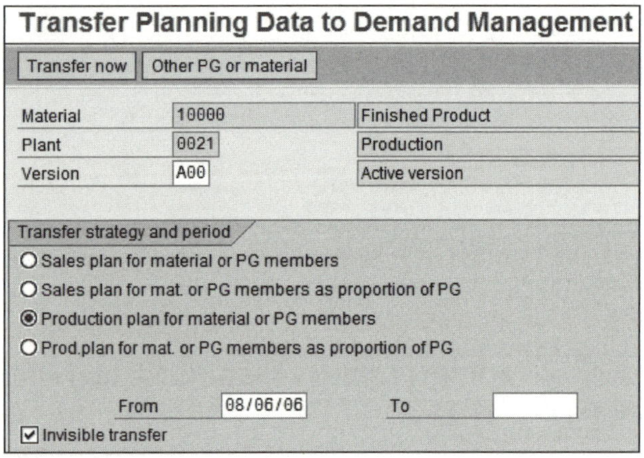

Transfer Planning Data to Demand Management

Transfer now	Other PG or material

Material	10000	Finished Product
Plant	0021	Production
Version	A00	Active version

Transfer strategy and period

○ Sales plan for material or PG members
○ Sales plan for mat. or PG members as proportion of PG
◉ Production plan for material or PG members
○ Prod.plan for mat. or PG members as proportion of PG

From 08/06/06   To

☑ Invisible transfer

Figure 1.2 Transfer Production Plan to Long-Term Planning

Now that we've converted the sales plan into a production plan and transferred the production plan to Long-Term Planning, let's start working with this information in Long-Term Planning.

1.2 Long-Term Planning

Long-Term Planning allows you to enter medium- to longer-term production plans into the system. Medium-term production plans generally involve production quantities between three months and three years into the future. Longer-term production plans can plan production quantities as far into the future as you need. The production plan represents planned independent requirements, which are used to meet the two following downstream prerequisites necessary to create cost estimates:

▶ They generate requirements for purchased items. These can be used to request vendor quotations, negotiate raw material prices, and ensure purchasing info records are current. Purchasing info records are commonly used by cost estimates to determine the estimated plan price of components.

▶ Also, planned independent requirements can be used to transfer scheduled activity requirements to cost centers. Cost center planned costs, divided by scheduled activity requirements, provide an estimate of planned activity price used by cost estimates to determine labor costs.

You can transfer the production plan from Sales and Operations Planning, as discussed in Section 1.1, or enter

it directly with transaction MD62 or via the menu path: **Logistics • Production • Production Planning • Long-Term Planning • Planned Independent Requirements • Change**. The data entry screen shown in Figure 1.3 is displayed.

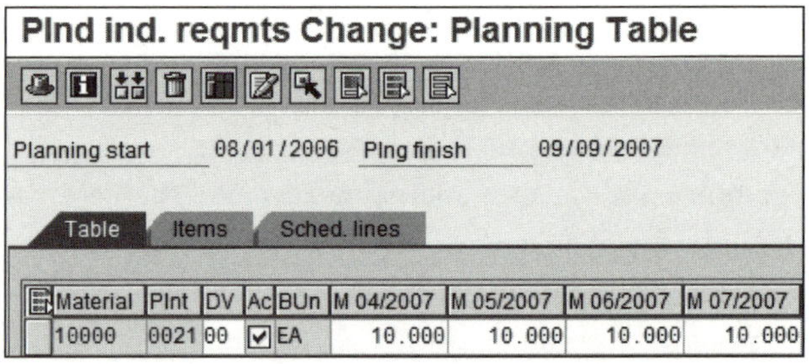

Plnd ind. reqmts Change: Planning Table

Planning start 08/01/2006   Plng finish 09/09/2007

Table	Items	Sched. lines

Material	Plnt	DV	Ac	BUn	M 04/2007	M 05/2007	M 06/2007	M 07/2007
10000	0021	00	☑	EA	10.000	10.000	10.000	10.000

Figure 1.3 Change Planned Independent Requirements in Long-Term Planning

The requirements displayed in Figure 1.3 correspond with the production plan transferred from Sales and Operations Planning shown in Figure 1.1. The requirements can be changed, or additional requirements can be entered directly in Long-Term Planning. The *version active* indicator, shown in the **Ac** column in Figure 1.3, determines if the requirements are relevant to operative Material Requirements Planning (MRP). If relevant to operative MRP, requirements will result in generation of planned orders, which can be converted to production orders for in-house production and purchase requisitions for external procurement. The system also explodes the bill of materials (BOM) for assemblies produced in-house and generates dependant requirements for material components.

Transfer Requirements to Purchasing Information System

Long-term MRP can be used to generate simulative planned orders, based on planned independent requirements. Simulative planned orders are not converted into purchase requisitions or production orders. Simulative data for external procurement can be transferred to the purchasing information system and evaluated.

This information can be used as the basis for generating vendor Request for Quotations (RFQ), negotiating raw material prices, and ensuring purchasing info records are current. Updated purchasing info records are then used by cost estimates as the basis for determining raw material purchase prices. You can transfer Long-Term Planning data to the purchasing information system with transaction MS70 or via menu path: **Logistics • Production • Production Planning • Long-Term Planning • Evaluations • Purchasing Info System • Set Up Data**. The screen shown in Figure 1.4 is displayed.

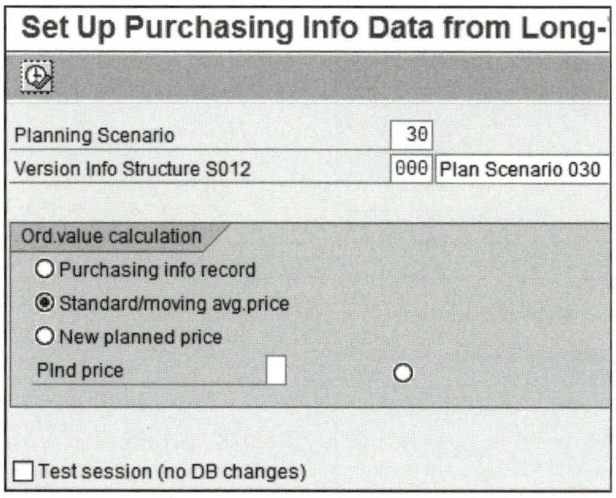

Figure 1.4 Set Up Purchasing Info Data from Long-Term Planning

The **Version Info Structure S012** field allows you to determine the receiving plan version of the purchasing plan data. If you do not enter a plan version, the system uses the **Planning Scenario** as the planning version number. You can also choose how the purchase order value is calculated, in the **Ord.value calculation** section. Complete the selection screen as follows:

1. Complete the **Planning Scenario** and **Version Info Structure S012** fields
2. Select **Standard/moving avg.price** and deselect **Test session (no DB changes)**
3. Click on the execute icon (surrounded by a dotted line in Figure 1.4) to start the transaction

Figure 1.5 shows an example of messages displayed after running transaction MS70.

The messages provide an indication of the quantity of information transferred. You can also run a report on Long-Term Planning purchasing data with transaction MCEC or via menu path: **Logistics • Production • Production Planning • Long-Term Planning • Evaluations • Purchasing Info System • Material**. The selection screen shown in Figure 1.6 is displayed.

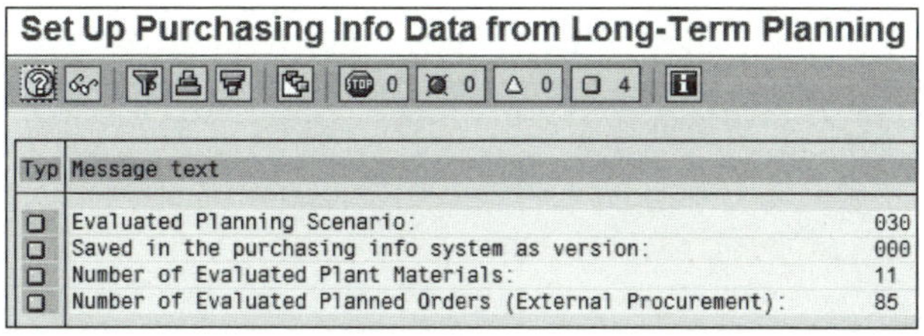

Figure 1.5 Messages After Sending Data to Purchasing Information System

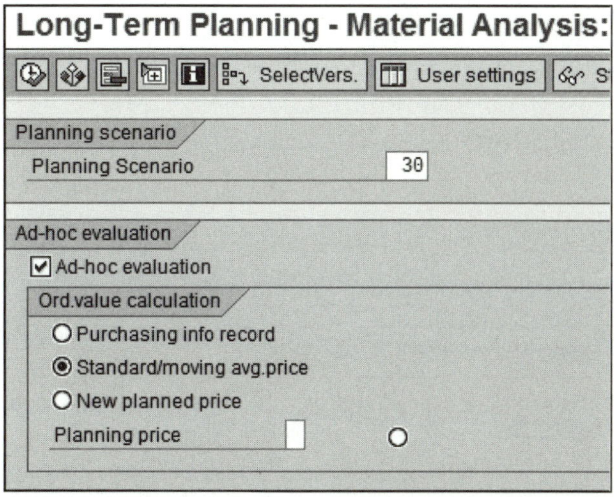

Figure 1.6 Purchasing Information System Selection Screen

The **Planning Scenario** field allows you to choose the Long-Term Planning scenario to base the analysis on. You can also choose how the purchase order value is calculated, in the **Ord.value calculation** section. Complete the selection screen as follows:

1. Complete the **Planning Scenario** field
2. Select **Ad-hoc evaluation** and **Standard/moving avg. price**
3. Press the **F8** key to start the transaction

Figure 1.7 shows an example of the data displayed.

This report provides information on future purchasing requirements. You can display purchasing requirements per period by clicking on the time series (lightning bolt) icon shown in Figure 1.7. An example of the output screen is displayed in Figure 1.8.

Click on the other (two squares) icon to toggle between purchase order value, quantity, and price. This provides useful data for obtaining vendor quotations for future requirements of purchased materials.

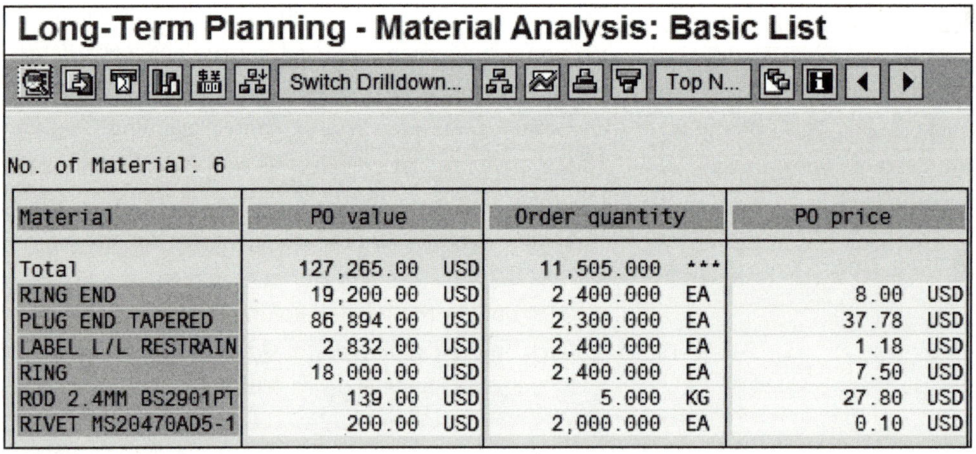

Long-Term Planning - Material Analysis: Basic List

Switch Drilldown... Top N...

No. of Material: 6

Material	PO value	Order quantity	PO price
Total	127,265.00 USD	11,505.000 ***	
RING END	19,200.00 USD	2,400.000 EA	8.00 USD
PLUG END TAPERED	86,894.00 USD	2,300.000 EA	37.78 USD
LABEL L/L RESTRAIN	2,832.00 USD	2,400.000 EA	1.18 USD
RING	18,000.00 USD	2,400.000 EA	7.50 USD
ROD 2.4MM BS2901PT	139.00 USD	5.000 KG	27.80 USD
RIVET MS20470AD5-1	200.00 USD	2,000.000 EA	0.10 USD

Figure 1.7 Purchasing Information System Data

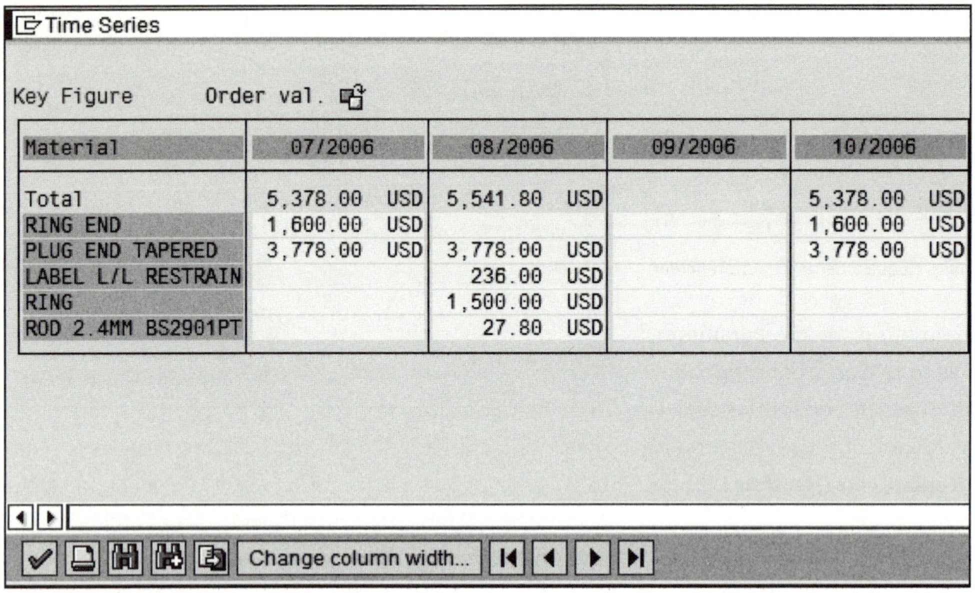

Time Series

Key Figure Order val.

Material	07/2006	08/2006	09/2006	10/2006
Total	5,378.00 USD	5,541.80 USD		5,378.00 USD
RING END	1,600.00 USD			1,600.00 USD
PLUG END TAPERED	3,778.00 USD	3,778.00 USD		3,778.00 USD
LABEL L/L RESTRAIN		236.00 USD		
RING		1,500.00 USD		
ROD 2.4MM BS2901PT		27.80 USD		

Change column width...

Figure 1.8 Time Series of Purchasing Requirements

Activated planned independent requirements are also visible in operative MRP. In addition to data transferred to the purchasing information system, the purchasing department has visibility of activated planned independent requirements through planned orders generated by operative MRP and purchase requisitions converted from the planned orders. These also can be the basis for updating purchasing info records.

Transfer Activity Quantities to Cost Center Accounting

In addition to ensuring purchasing info records are up to date, Long-Term Planning activity quantities can be transferred to Cost Center Accounting. From the production plan for products, long-term MRP generates requirements for all lower-level components and work centers. The activity requirements are then transferred to corresponding cost centers with transaction KSPP or via menu path: **Logistics • Production • Production Planning • Long-Term Planning • Environment • CO Activity Requirements • Transfer to Cost Center**. The screen shown in Figure 1.9 is displayed.

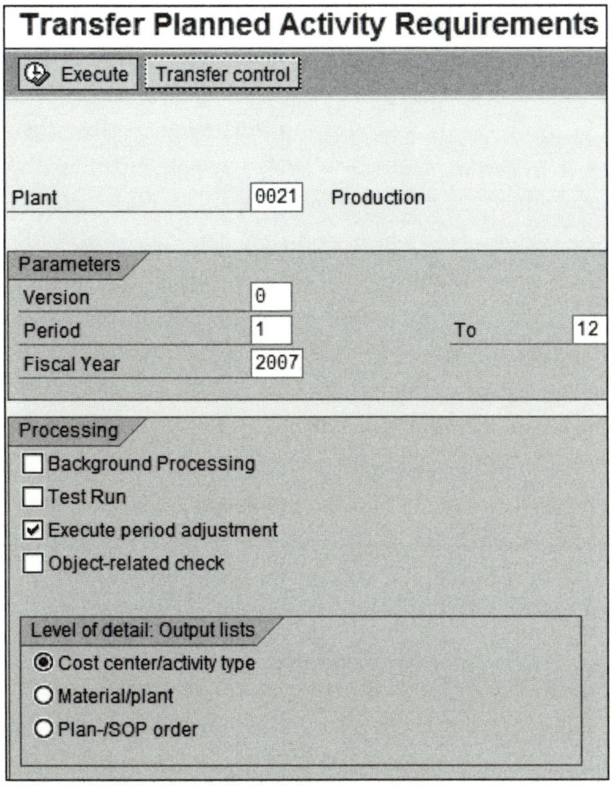

Transfer Planned Activity Requirements

⊕ Execute	Transfer control

Plant   `0021`   Production

Parameters

Version	`0`		
Period	`1`	To	`12`
Fiscal Year	`2007`		

Processing

- ☐ Background Processing
- ☐ Test Run
- ☑ Execute period adjustment
- ☐ Object-related check

Level of detail: Output lists

- ◉ Cost center/activity type
- ○ Material/plant
- ○ Plan-/SOP order

Figure 1.9 Transfer Planned Activity Requirements Selection Screen

This selection screen allows you to enter the **Parameters** of the activity quantities to send to Cost Center Accounting. Since we are interested in activity quantities sent to cost centers per activity, we will select the corresponding radio button in the **Level of detail: Output lists** section. Complete the selection screen as follows:

1. Complete the **Version**, **Period**, and **Fiscal Year** fields
2. Select the **Execute period adjustment** indicator
3. Select the **Cost center/activity type** radio button
4. Click on the **Transfer control** button

Figure 1.10 shows the next screen that is displayed.

Change View "Control: Transferring Activity

🖉 📇	New Entries	📋 📄 📄 📄 📄

CO...	Version	Version Dscrptn	Fiscal Year
`0001`	`0`	Plan/actual version	`2007`
`0001`	`2`	CO Plan Version 2	`2007`
`0001`	`3`	CO Plan Version 3	`2007`

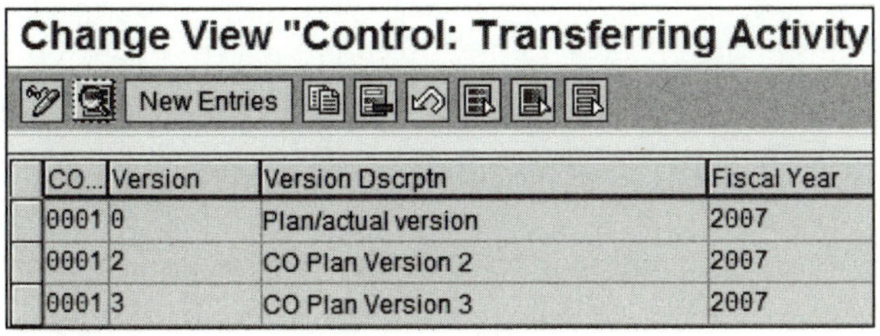

Figure 1.10 Transfer Controls for Activity Requirements

Each line in Figure 1.10 corresponds to a Controlling plan **Version**. Plan versions are used to carry out scenario testing with different cost center plans, activity prices, and any other parameter in cost center planning. You can create as many plan versions as you like, but normally only plan version 0 contains both plan and actual data. To change transfer control settings, carry out the following steps:

1. Click on **2** in the **Version** column
2. Click on the details icon (magnifying glass surrounded by a dotted line in Figure 1.10)

Figure 1.11 shows the next screen that is displayed.

Change View "Control: Transferring Activity

🖉	New Entries	📋 📄 📄 📄 📄 📄

CO Area	`0001`	Martin-Baker
Version	`2`	CO Plan Version 2
Fiscal Year	`2007`	

Transfer activity requirements from:

○ SOP	Version		
○ MRP			
◉ Long-term plng	Plnng scenario	`30`	

Scheduling leve	`1`
Last transfer	

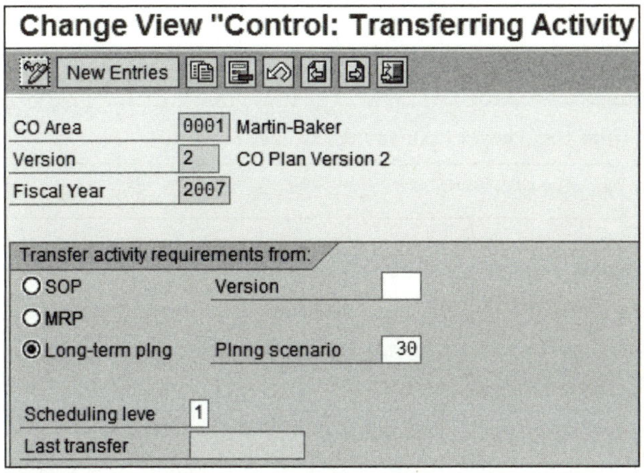

Figure 1.11 Transfer Control Definition Screen

You transfer **SOP** (Sales and Operations Planning), **MRP** or **Long-term plng** (Long-Term Planning) activity quantities to Cost Center Accounting by doing the following:

1. Choose the appropriate radio button in the **Transfer activity requirements from:** section in the screen shown in Figure 1.11
2. Press the **F3** key twice
3. Click on the **Execute** button shown in Figure 1.9 to start the transaction

You can create only one *transfer control* per *plan version*. Figure 1.12 shows an example of the resulting list of activity requirements transferred to Cost Center Accounting.

Transfer Planned Activity Requirements

Cost Ctr	ActTyp	Activity scheduled	UM
1610	RUN	1,429.749	HR
1610	SET	108.104	HR
1620	RUN	1,167.609	HR
1620	SET	52.631	HR
1650	RUN	2,919.856	HR
1650	SET	62.202	HR
1660	RUN	1,064.603	HR
1660	SET	111.246	HR
1670	MAC	487.301	HR
1670	RUN	121.685	HR
1670	SET	15.8	HR
2100	RUN	346.201	HR
2100	SET	4.750	HR
125A	RUN	3.450	HR
173A	RUN	107.250	HR
* Total		8,002.437	HR

Figure 1.12 Transfer Planned Activity Requirements

You display activity quantities per period by double-clicking on any schedule activity quantity shown in the **Activity scheduled** column. Scheduled quantities transferred to Cost Center Accounting are displayed in the planned activity price entry screen, as discussed in Section 1.3. In Long-Term Planning, we determined the component purchasing requirements and transferred them to the purchasing information system. We also determined the scheduled activity requirements and transferred them to Cost Center Accounting. The next step in initial planning is to carry out cost center primary cost planning, and then, together with scheduled quantities transferred from Long-Term Planning, calculate the planned activity rate required by cost estimates to determine activity costs.

1.3   Cost Center Planning

Cost center planning meets two requirements for variance analysis. First, primary cost planning functions as a benchmark for comparing plan costs against actual costs as they occur. This analysis provides a measure of cost center manager performance. Second, dividing the plan primary costs by the plan activity quantity provides an estimate of the planned activity rate, which is needed by cost estimates to determine labor costs.

Determining planned workload (activity quantities) of production cost centers for the following fiscal year is a desirable prerequisite for cost center planning. Activity quantities are necessary to determine variable costs such a wages and energy. Planned activity quantities are determined from work center loads resulting from the production plan, which is in turn determined from the sales plan. You can transfer scheduled activity quantities from Sales and Operations Planning, MRP, or Long-Term Planning to cost center planning. You then convert the scheduled activity quantities into planned activity quantities using plan reconciliation.

You enter the plan for primary costs by primary cost element, corresponding to a general ledger expense account. Examples are, plan payroll and depreciation costs against corresponding cost elements for each cost center.

You enter a primary cost plan for a cost center with transaction KP06 or via menu path: **Accounting • Controlling • Cost Center Accounting • Planning • Cost and Activity Inputs • Change**. A selection screen is displayed, as shown in Figure 1.13.

Change Cost Element/Activity Input Planning:

Layout	Z101-US	USD cost element planning layout
Variables		
Version	0	CO Plan V
From period	1	April
To period	12	March
Fiscal year	2007	
Cost Center	1600	Production
to		
or group		
Activity Type		
to		
or group		
Cost Element	510002	Basic Pay
to		
or group		

Figure 1.13 Cost Element Planning Selection Screen

You may see different fields, depending on the planning layout selected. You can scroll through the available planning layouts with the left and right pointing arrow icons.

Any number of planning versions can be created, for which planning data can be entered. In this example, we will use plan version 0. Actual costs post to version 0, and this is the plan version compared with actual costs during variance analysis. Complete the selection screen as follows:

1. Complete the **Version**, **From period**, **To period**, and **Fiscal year** fields

2. Leave the **Activity Type** field blank to plan for activity-independent costs

3. Click on the overview (mountain range and sun, seen in Figure 1.13) icon to display the screen shown in Figure 1.14

Change Cost Element/Activity Input Plan

Version	0		Plan/actual ve
Period	1	To	12
Fiscal Year	2007		
Cost Center	1600		Production

Costs				
Cost element	Plan fix costs in OC	Dis...	Plan var. costs OC	Dis..
510002	283,683.76	2	0.00	2

Figure 1.14 Cost Element Planning Screen for Cost Centers

This screen allows you to enter cost center plan fixed costs per **Cost element**. These are activity-independent costs, because we did not enter an activity in the **Activity Type** field in the screen shown in Figure 1.13. To carry out primary cost planning, do the following:

1. Enter the plan cost in the **Plan fix costs in OC** column

2. Click on the period screen (graph) icon to plan costs at an individual period level, if necessary

3. Save your work

If an activity type is entered in the selection screen shown in Figure 1.13, both fixed and variable costs can be planned in the screen shown in Figure 1.14.

There are several reports available to view planning data. One such report can be viewed with transaction KSBL or via menu path: **Accounting • Controlling • Cost Center Accounting • Information System • Reports for Cost Center Accounting • Planning Reports • Cost Centers: Planning Overview**. A selection screen is displayed, as shown in Figure 1.15.

Planning Report: Initial Screen

Execute | Execute Multiple

Cost Center	1600

Report parameters			
Fiscal Year	2007		
Period	1	To	12
Version	0		
☑ Output in ALV grid			

Figure 1.15 Cost Center Planning Report Selection Screen

This selection screen allows you to make entries in the **Report parameters** section to determine the values in the output screen. Complete the selection screen as follows:

1. Complete the **Cost Center**, **Fiscal Year**, **Period**, and **Version** fields

2. Ensure that the **Output in ALV grid** indicator is selected

3. Click on the **Execute** button to start the transaction

Figure 1.16 shows an example of the data displayed.

Cost Centers: Planning Report

Cost element/description		Σ Value report curr.
500335	Indirect Prod Mats	5,000.00
506105	Cons Stores Safety	1,000.00
506109	Consumables - Misc	600.00
510002	Basic Pay Monthly	283,683.76
510004	Overtime at 1.5	4,792.12
541000	PR Tax Employer	24,174.68
541100	Workers Compensat...	4,989.02
546000	Health/Dental	56,104.44
547000	Life/Disability	5,048.20
625132	Accom. & Sub.	4,000.00
635243	Trade Publications	300.00
645101	Depr Land & Buidings	115.36
645120	Depr Plant Machinery	75,492.42
645130	Depr Furniture & Fix	6,422.48
645140	Depr Computers	362.70
660060	Education & Training	5,000.00
Primary Costs	▪	**477,085.18**
Activity-Independent Costs	▪▪	**477,085.18**
Debit	▪▪▪	**477,085.18**
Under/Over-Absorbed Overhead	▪▪▪▪	**477,085.18**

Figure 1.16 Cost Center Planning Overview Report

This screen displays a summary view of planned primary costs for a cost center.

After primary costs have been planned for the next fiscal year, you can calculate and enter activity rates. If primary cost planning is carried out in SAP, the system can automatically calculate the activity rate. Most companies calculate and enter planned activity rates manually, at least for the first couple of years after implementation. There are usually more pressing concerns during this time, such as fine-tuning master data converted from a legacy system, compared to setting up automatic activity rate calculation.

To enter planned activity prices for a cost center, use transaction KP26 or menu path: **Accounting • Controlling • Cost Center Accounting • Planning • Activity Output/Prices • Change**. A selection screen is displayed, as shown in Figure 1.17.

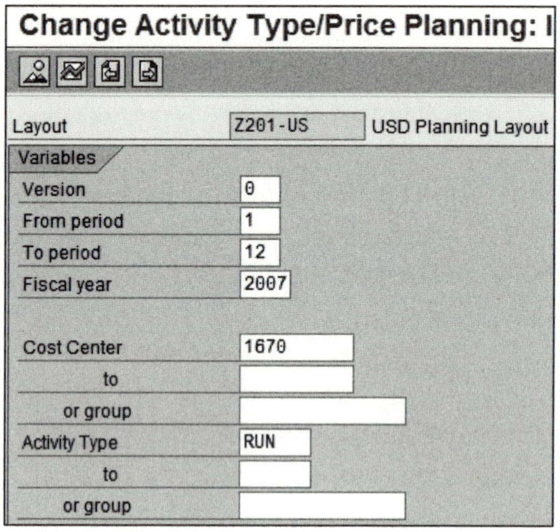

Figure 1.17   Plan Activity Price Selection Screen

This selection screen allows you to enter the plan version, time period, cost center, and activity type you wish to plan. Complete the selection screen as follows:

1. Complete the **Version**, **From period**, **To period**, and **Fiscal year** fields
2. Complete the **Cost Center** and **Activity Type** fields
3. Click on the overview icon to display the screen shown in Figure 1.18

In this screen you can enter plan activity quantity, capacity quantity, and plan fixed and variable activity prices. To do this, follow these three steps:

1. Complete the **Plan activity** and **Capacity** quantity fields
2. Complete **Fixed USD** and/or **Var USD** activity price fields
3. Save your work

Plan activity quantity, entered in the second column in Figure 1.18, is required to automatically calculate the plan activity price. Another, less well known benefit of entering the plan activity quantity is it appears at the bottom of the standard cost center report S_ALR_87013611—Cost Centers: Actual/Plan/Variance. You can then compare plan and actual activity quantities in the cost center report to analyze production and cost center variance.

Act. Sched. (scheduled activity quantity), the last column in Figure 1.18 was previously transferred from Sales and Operations Planning, MRP, or Long-Term Planning, as discussed at the end of Section 1.2. This field cannot be adjusted manually. You can use it to overwrite the plan activity quantity, the second column in Figure 1.18, with transaction KPSI or via menu path: **Accounting • Controlling • Cost Center Accounting • Planning • Plan-**

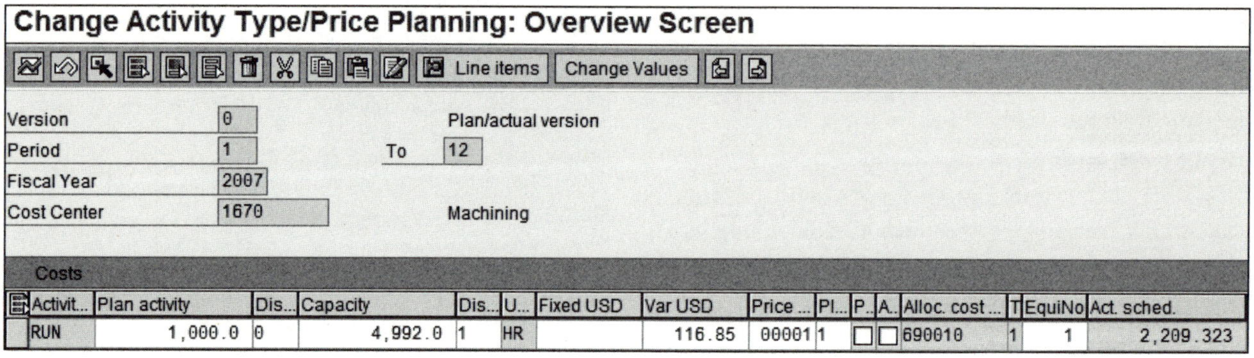

Figure 1.18   Plan Activity Price Entry Screen

ning Aids • Plan Reconciliation. A selection screen is displayed, as shown in Figure 1.19.

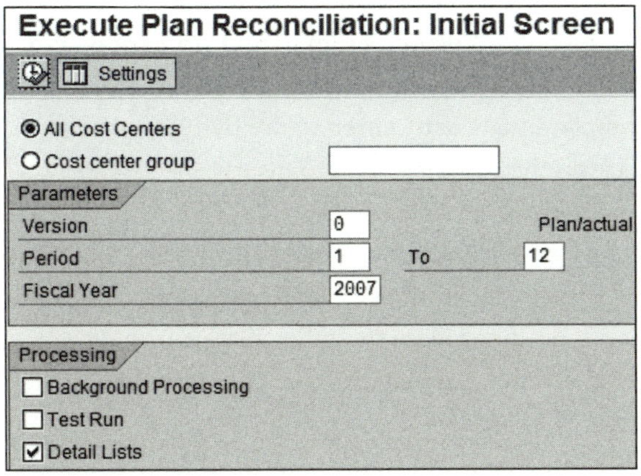

Execute Plan Reconciliation: Initial Screen

Settings

- ⦿ All Cost Centers
- ○ Cost center group [   ]

Parameters

Version	0		Plan/actual
Period	1	To	12
Fiscal Year	2007		

Processing

- ☐ Background Processing
- ☐ Test Run
- ☑ Detail Lists

Figure 1.19 Execute Plan Reconciliation Screen

This selection screen allows you to enter the **Parameters** to choose which cost centers and periods are to be updated with the scheduled activity quantity from Long-Term Planning. Complete the selection screen as follows:

1. Select either the **All Cost Centers** or **Cost center group** radio button
2. Complete the **Version**, **Period**, and **Fiscal Year** fields
3. Ensure that the **Test Run** indicator is deselected and the **Details Lists** indicator is selected
4. Click on the execute icon (surrounded by a dotted line in Figure 1.19) to start the transaction

Figure 1.20 shows an example of the data displayed.

OTy	Object	AUn	Pln actvty	New PlnAcv	Actv diff.
ATY	1610/RUN	HR	4,000.0	6,657.820	2,657.820
ATY	1610/SET	HR	0.0	671.682	671.682
ATY	1620/RUN	HR	2,500.0	17,056.014	14,556.014
ATY	1620/SET	HR	0.0	1,161.867	1,161.867
ATY	1650/FAE	HR	0.0	1,817.960	1,817.960
ATY	1650/RUN	HR	11,000.0	57,352.511	46,352.511
ATY	1650/SET	HR	0.0	456.539	456.539
ATY	1660/FAE	HR	0.0	24.360	24.360
ATY	1660/RUN	HR	3,500.0	7,509.271	4,009.271
ATY	1660/SET	HR	0.0	936.768	936.768
ATY	1670/FAE	HR	0.0	62.4	62.4
ATY	1670/MAC	HR	2,500.0	13,085.993	10,585.993
ATY	1670/RUN	HR	1,000.0	2,209.323	1,209.323
ATY	1670/SET	HR	0.0	548.936	548.936
ATY	2100/RUN	HR	4,500.0	1,161.934	3,338.066-
ATY	2100/SET	HR	0.0	7.0	7.0
ATY	2500/RUN	HR	1,800.0	1,800.0	0.0
ATY	2600/RUN	HR	2,000.0	2,000.0	0.0

Figure 1.20 Plan Reconciliation List

The **Pln activity** (plan activity) column in Figure 1.20 corresponds to the second column in Figure 1.18. The **New PlnAcv** (new plan activity) column in Figure 1.20 corresponds to the last column in Figure 1.18. The **Actv diff.** (activity difference) column in Figure 1.20 is the difference between the two previous columns.

When you execute plan reconciliation, the plan activity manually entered in the second column in Figure 1.18 is automatically overwritten with the scheduled activity from the last column in Figure 1.18.

1.4 Summary

This chapter covered the initial planning steps required for variance analysis. We created a sales plan, which was converted into a production plan in Sales and Operations Planning. The production plan was then transferred to Long-Term Planning. Purchasing requirements were analyzed, and purchasing info records that contained quotations for all purchased components were created. Work center loads were transferred to Cost Center Accounting.

Cost center activity quantities transferred from Long-Term Planning, together with primary cost planning, allowed the calculation of planned activity prices.

In Chapter 2 we will continue with our discussion of the cost planning process by examining additional prerequisites necessary to create cost estimates, including logistics master data and costing variant configuration. We'll then create and analyze standard and preliminary cost estimates.

2 Cost Estimates

Now that we've planned activity prices and updated purchasing info records for components with the latest vendor quotations, the next step in preparing for variance analysis is the creation and processing of cost estimates. These provide a plan of how much it will cost to procure components and produce assemblies and finished goods. Standard cost estimates are typically created several weeks before the start of the next fiscal year. System messages are analyzed and corrective actions are taken. For instance, there may be missing purchasing info records or activity prices, which need to be entered in the system.

After corrections are made and error messages are eliminated, standard cost estimates are typically released on the first day of the fiscal year. Releasing standard cost estimates updates inventory valuation, and new material standard prices become the benchmark for all production and purchasing activities over the next twelve months.

Some companies with rapidly changing and developing products create and release standard cost estimates more frequently to keep pace with the changes. Otherwise variances would become so large toward the end of the fiscal year that they would provide no assistance during variance analysis. I'll discuss this further in Section 2.5.

We will look at logistics master data, e.g., bills of material and routings, in this chapter. These structures provide quantity information, which, together with the price information from Chapter 1, allows cost estimates to determine the price of assemblies.

We'll look at how overhead is allocated to products, and we'll see how the costing variant instructs the system which prices, bills of material, and routings to use. Finally we'll create standard and preliminary cost estimates and see how they assemble and present price information.

2.1 Master Data

Master data is information that stays relatively constant over long periods of time, such as purchasing info records, which contain vendor information (such as the business name) that usually doesn't change. In comparison to master data, transactional data is posted often, resulting in frequent updates to general ledger accounts and cost center balances.

Logistics master data provides information on how materials are procured and manufactured. This section provides an overview of the master data fields most relevant to variance analysis.

Even though master data is relatively stable, companies that want to remain competitive in rapidly changing environments constantly assess whether it's more cost effective to manufacture assemblies in-house, procure externally, or outsource. Changing methods of procurement can produce large effects on variance calculation and require constant master data and purchasing information maintenance. This may also influence the frequency of price updates with standard cost estimates.

Material Master

Material masters contain all the information required to manage a material. Information is stored in views, each corresponding to a department or area of business responsibility. Views conveniently group information together for users in different departments, e.g., sales and purchasing. The two views of particular interest during variance analysis are MRP and Costing. These views are plant-specific, so plants can have different values for fields in these views.

You can view or change material master views with transaction MM02 or menu path: **Logistics • Production • Master Data • Material Master • Material • Change •**

Immediately. Click the **MRP 2** tab to display the screen shown in Figure 2.1.

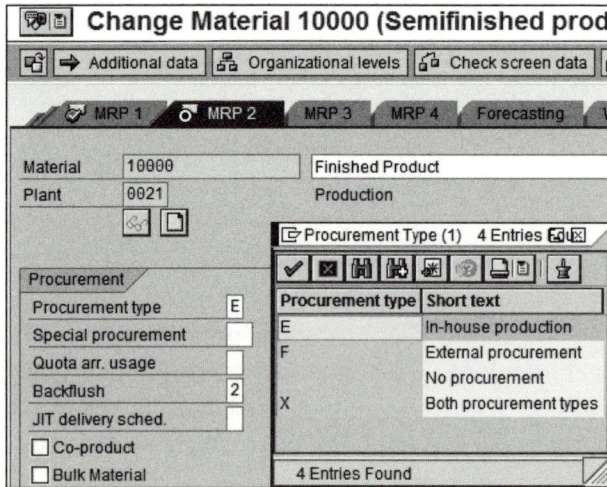

Figure 2.1 Material Master MRP 2 View

To display a list of possible entries for the **Procurement type** field, proceed as follows:

1. Left click in the **Procurement type** field
2. Press the **F1** key or right click and choose **Possible Entries**

A list of possible procurement types is displayed as shown on the right in Figure 2.1. The procurement type defines how the material is procured. Usually it is either manufactured in-house or purchased externally. An **In-house production** setting means the system will search for a BOM and routing. An **External procurement** setting results in the system searching for purchasing information.

The **Special procurement** field found immediately below the **Procurement type** field in Figure 2.1 is used to more closely define the procurement type. For example, it may indicate if the item is produced in another plant and transferred to the plant you are looking at.

Now let's look at the Costing views and fields relevant to variance analysis. In the screen shown in Figure 2.1, scroll to the right and click on the **Costing 1** tab (not shown). The screen shown in Figure 2.2 is displayed.

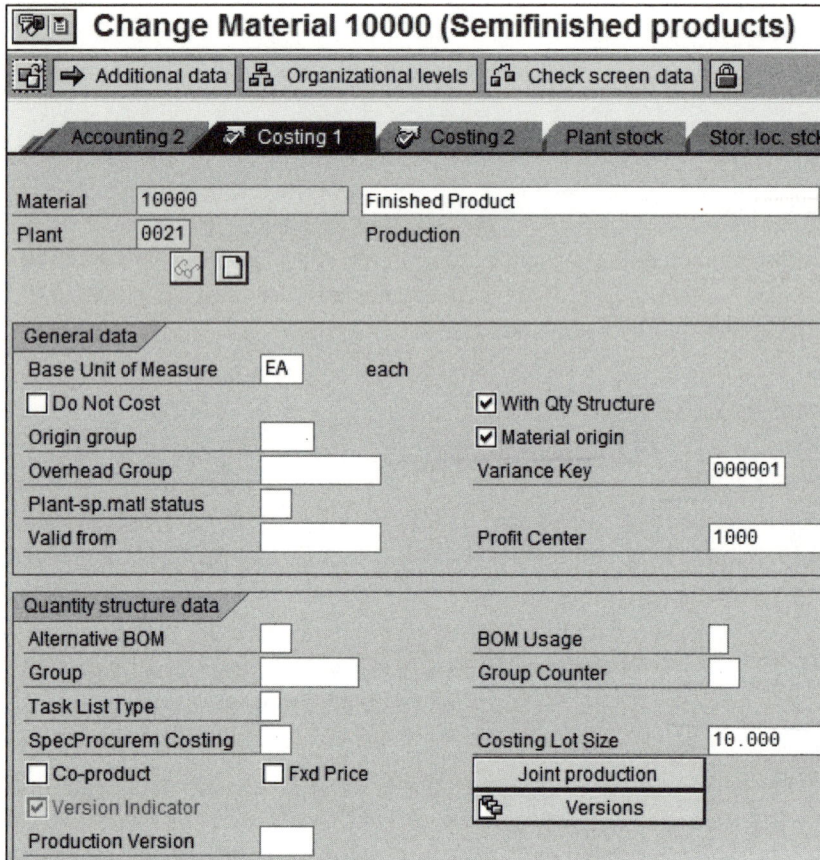

Figure 2.2 Material Master Costing 1 View

A field of particular relevance to variance analysis is the **Variance Key** field. Variances are only calculated on production orders or product cost collectors containing a variance key. This key is defaulted from the **Costing 1** view when production orders or product cost collectors are created. The variance key also determines if the value of scrap is subtracted from actual costs before variances are determined.

Another field relevant to variance analysis is **Costing Lot Size**. When a standard cost estimate is created, it uses this value in the **Costing 1** view by default. The costing lot size should be set as close as possible to actual procurement lot size. Unfavorable variances may result if a production order is created for a quantity less than the costing lot size. Setup time is time needed to prepare equipment and machinery for production of assemblies, and it is generally the same regardless of quantity produced. Setup time spread over a smaller production quantity increases the unit cost. This also applies to exter-

nally procured items, since vendors usually quote higher prices for smaller quantities.

There are two **Costing** tabs, because you would need to scroll down to see all the costing fields on one tab. Now let's inspect the **Costing 2** fields. Click on the **Costing 2** tab (see Figure 2.2) to get to the screen shown in Figure 2.3.

The **Cost Estimate** fields in the **Standard Cost Estimate** section are updated when a standard cost estimate is marked and released. The **Future Planned price** field is populated when a cost estimate is marked. The **Current Planned price** and **Standard price** fields are overwritten when subsequently releasing a cost estimate. The **Previous Planned price** field contains the value of the previously released standard cost estimate. Cost estimate fields in the material master cannot be manually changed.

You can manually update the **Planned price 1**, **2**, and **3** fields in the **Planned prices** section of the screen shown in Figure 2.3 with estimated purchase prices.

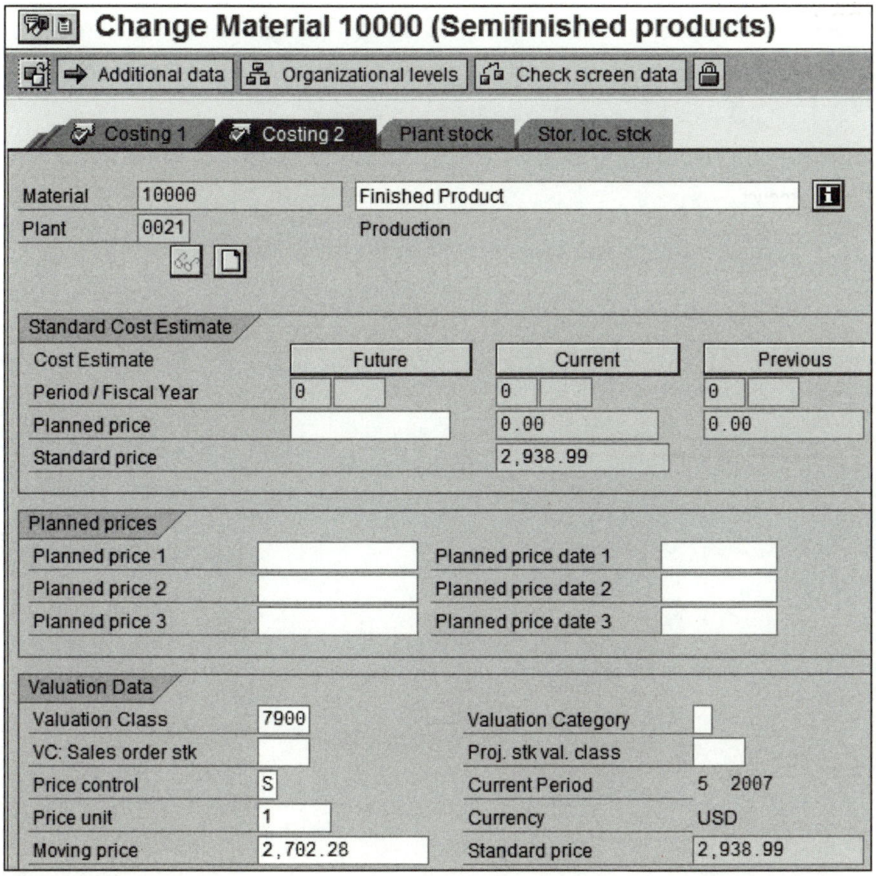

Change Material 10000 (Semifinished products)

⟹ Additional data   Organizational levels   Check screen data

| Costing 1 | Costing 2 | Plant stock | Stor. loc. stck |

| Material | 10000 | Finished Product |
| Plant | 0021 | Production |

Standard Cost Estimate

Cost Estimate	Future	Current	Previous
Period / Fiscal Year	0	0	0
Planned price		0.00	0.00
Standard price		2,938.99	

Planned prices

Planned price 1		Planned price date 1	
Planned price 2		Planned price date 2	
Planned price 3		Planned price date 3	

Valuation Data

Valuation Class	7900	Valuation Category	
VC: Sales order stk		Proj. stk val. class	
Price control	S	Current Period	5 2007
Price unit	1	Currency	USD
Moving price	2,702.28	Standard price	2,938.99

Figure 2.3 Material Master Costing 2 View

A standard cost estimate usually retrieves planned prices from these fields if no vendor quotations or purchasing info records exist for purchased items. This is useful when creating cost estimates before vendor quotations are received, early in the lifecycle of a new or modified product.

The **Valuation Class** field in the **Valuation Data** section of Figure 2.3 determines which general ledger accounts are updated as a result of inventory movement or settlement. The **Price control** field indicates whether inventory is valuated at standard (S) or moving average (V) price.

After material masters are created and fields are populated correctly, you use them to create a bill of material, as discussed in the next section.

Bill of Material

The bill of material (BOM) is a structured hierarchy of components necessary to build an assembly. BOMs, together with purchasing info records or vendor quotations, provide cost estimates with the information necessary to calculate material costs of products. You can view or change BOMs with transaction CS02 or menu path: **Logistics • Production • Master Data • Bills of Material • Bill of Material • Material BOM • Change**. An example of a BOM is shown in Figure 2.4. You can also refer to the SAP training course guide related to Product Cost Planning for additional information on this.

The BOM determines which materials are costed. Each BOM item contains many fields and indicators. The most relevant to variance analysis are the *quantity* field and *relevancy to costing* indicator. The BOM item quantity multiplied by the material standard price provides planned material costs. Deselecting the relevancy to costing indicator allows you to exclude the cost of some BOM items, e.g., bulk materials. Bulk materials are expensed directly to a cost center, so the cost is already included in the cost estimate via overhead or activity rates.

A cost estimate created for the top-level finished good selects materials at the lowest level in the BOM first. In Figure 2.4, all materials with material type **ROH** (raw materials) are costed first, and then **HALB** (subassemblies), and finally **FERT** (finished goods). Material costs are rolled up from raw materials through subassemblies to the finished good.

Material masters and BOMs provide cost estimates with material and assembly prices and quantities. To determine labor and activity standard quantities, we need to consider routings.

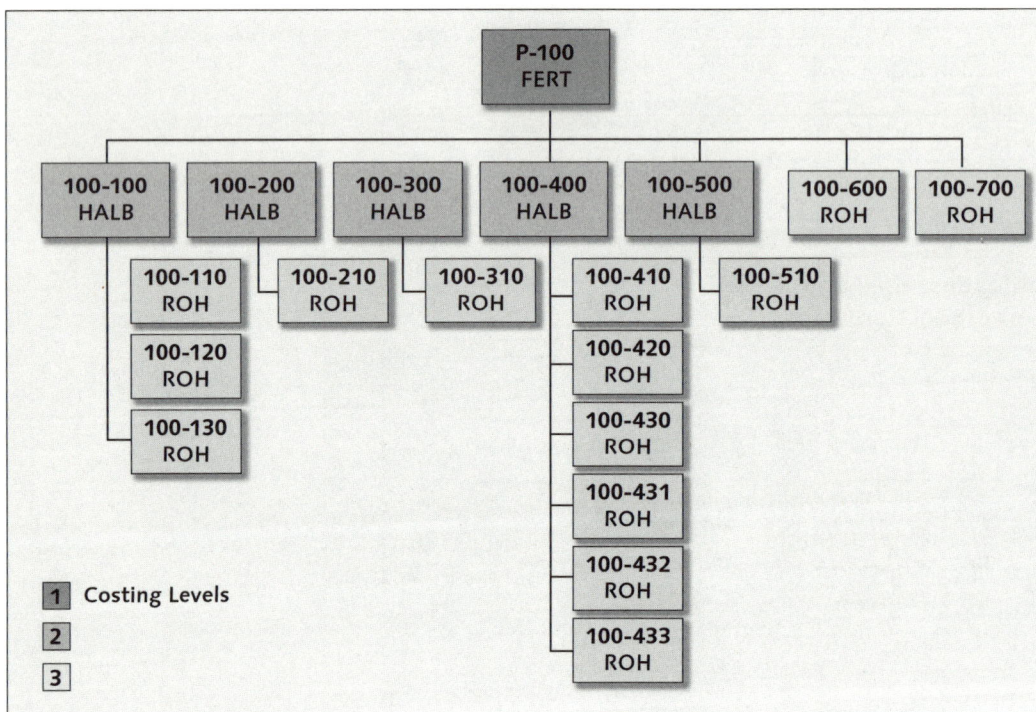

Figure 2.4 Example of a BOM

Routing

A routing is a list of tasks containing standard activity times required to perform operations to build an assembly. Routings, together with planned activity prices, provide cost estimates with the information necessary to calculate labor costs of products. You can view or change routings with transaction CA02 or via menu path: **Logistics • Production • Master Data • Routings • Routings • Standard Routings • Change**. An example of a routing is shown in Figure 2.5 (Source: SAP training course guide: AC505 - Product Cost Planning).

Each operation in the routing contains many fields and indicators. The most relevant to variance analysis are the *standard value* field and *relevancy to costing* indicator. The standard value indicates how long it normally takes to perform the task. The standard value multiplied by the planned activity rate provides planned labor costs. The calculation can be modified by a performance efficiency rate and formula. Labor costs are rolled up from subassemblies to the finished good.

You can include overhead costs in the planned activity rate. Dedicated overhead activity types can also be used to include overhead costs. The manufacturing order or product cost collector is debited, and the cost center is credited at the time of activity confirmation. Overhead can also be included in the standard price with costing sheets, as described in Section 2.2.

After BOMs and routings are created, you need to create product cost collectors if you are using Product Cost by Period. Product cost collectors contain information relating to which BOM and routing the cost estimate should access, since there may be many alternative methods of manufacture. Product cost collectors also, as the name suggests, collect costs.

Product Cost Collector

A product cost collector collects actual costs during the production of a material. Product Cost Collectors are necessary for repetitive manufacturing and optional for order-related manufacturing. Repetitive manufacturing eliminates the need for production or process orders in manufacturing environments with production lines and long production runs. It reduces the work involved in production control and simplifies confirmations and goods receipt postings.

Several advantages result from using product cost collectors. Period-end closing and reporting performance is improved, since there are fewer cost objects than in Product Cost by Order. Also, variance analysis is carried out for a product instead of a manufacturing order. It's usually more useful for managers to know how efficiently different products are manufactured, compared to the efficiency of a particular manufacturing order.

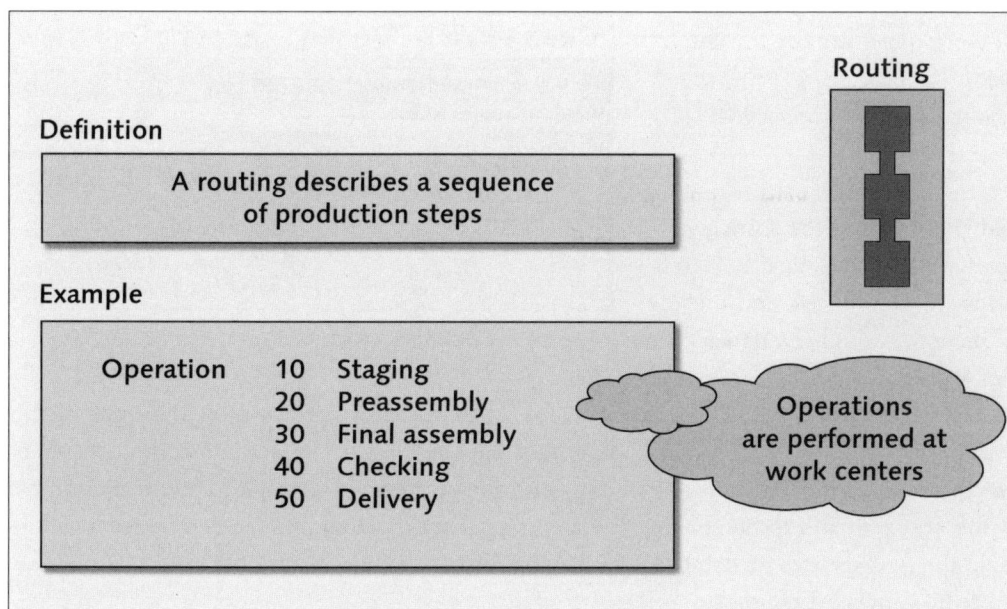

Figure 2.5 Example of a Routing

You can create, change, or view product cost collectors with transaction KKF6N or via menu path: **Accounting • Controlling • Product Cost Controlling • Cost Object Controlling • Product Cost by Period • Master Data • Product Cost Collector • Edit**. A selection screen is displayed, as shown in Figure 2.6.

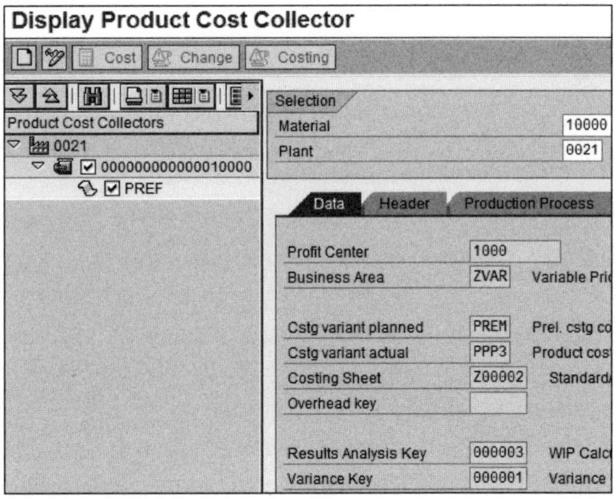

Figure 2.6 Display Product Cost Collector

A product cost collector contains all the information needed to manufacture a product. This includes fields relevant to variance analysis. To display these fields, proceed as follows:

1. Fill in the relevant information into the **Material** and **Plant** fields
2. Select the Production Version indicator on the left (**PREF** in this example)
3. Press Enter to display details of the product cost collector

The **Cstg variant planned** field contains the costing variant used to create the preliminary cost estimate. I'll discuss costing variants further in Section 2.4, and preliminary cost estimates in Section 2.6. The **Variance Key** shown at the bottom of Figure 2.6 defaults from the material master Costing 1 view when the product cost collector is created.

With master data now created and setup correctly, the structure is in place for the cost estimate to determine material and labor costs. In the next section, I'll describe how to include overhead costs in the cost estimate.

2.2 Overhead Costs

In addition to material and labor costs, overhead costs usually need to be included as a component of the finished product standard price. Overhead costs may include costs such as building lease, insurance, and general office staff not directly involved in the production process. You can either increase the planned activity price to include overhead, or you can create separate overhead activity types as discussed in Section 2.1.3. Advantages of this method of overhead allocation include real-time posting during activity confirmation, and no configuration requirement. A disadvantage of dedicated overhead activity types is increased production data setup required in work centers and routings, and possibly increased maintenance during activity confirmations.

Costing sheets offer more flexibility in allocating overhead across individual products or product groups. Also, less production data maintenance is required. Configuration is required, however, as explained in the following sections.

Let's inspect the configuration of a costing sheet to see how it works. To view configuration settings, use transaction KZS2 or menu path: **IMG • Controlling • Product Cost Controlling • Product Cost Planning • Basic Settings for Material Costing • Overhead • Define Costing Sheets**. The screen shown in Figure 2.7 is displayed.

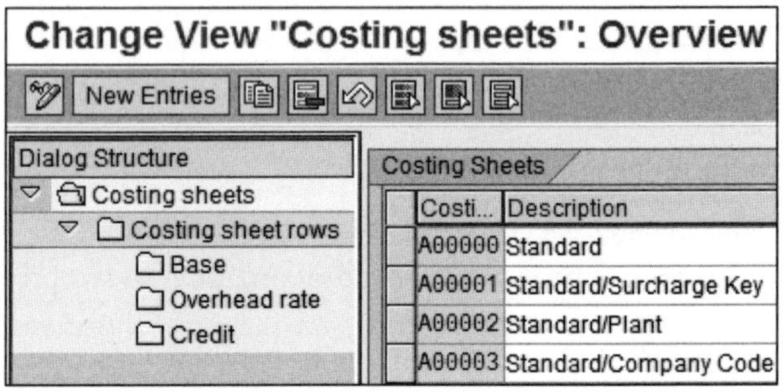

Figure 2.7 Costing Sheet Overview Screen

Available costing sheets are listed on the right of this overview screen. You can use existing costing sheets or copy one and create your own. Let's choose an example of a costing sheet and examine the components via the following steps:

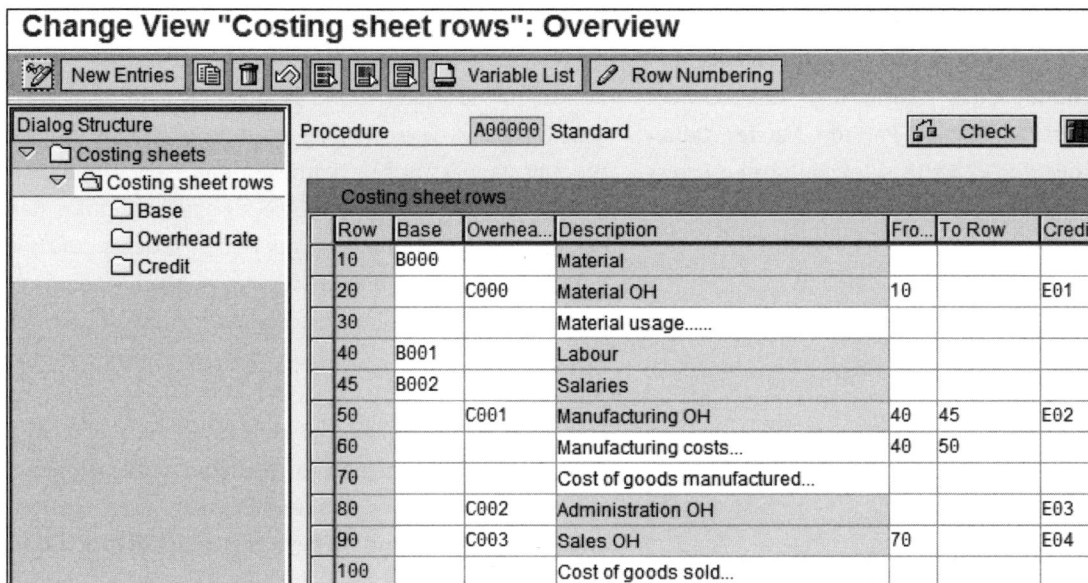

Figure 2.8 Costing Sheet Rows Overview

1. Select the first costing sheet (**A00000** in this example)
2. Double-click on **Costing sheet rows** on the left

The screen shown in Figure 2.8 is displayed.

The three costing sheet components, **Base**, **Overhead rate**, and **Credit**, are listed on the left of the screen, while costing sheet details are displayed on the right.

A base is a group of cost elements to which overhead is applied. Each cost element identifies unique cost types within a cost estimate, such as raw material or machining labor costs. These costs, identified by the base, are then multiplied by an overhead rate to determine the overhead value in the cost estimate.

When overhead is calculated during period-end processing (discussed in Chapter 4), the manufacturing order or product cost collector receives a debit, and a cost center receives a credit with the calculated overhead value. Now let's examine each costing sheet component in detail.

Calculation Base

You can combine cost elements in base rows. For example, you can calculate material overhead on a base consisting of cost element postings when raw materials are goods issued from inventory to a production order.

To see how cost elements are entered in a base, select any row with an entry in the **Base** column in the screen shown in Figure 2.8, and double-click on **Base** at the left of the screen and you will get to the screen shown in Figure 2.9.

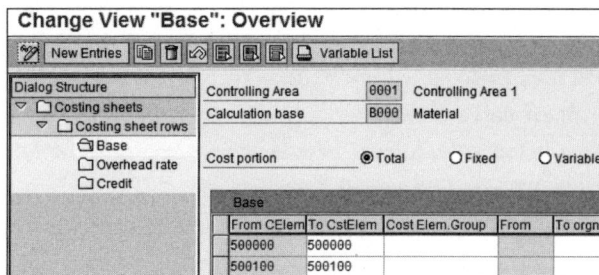

Figure 2.9 Calculation Base Overview

You can enter individual cost elements or ranges in the **From CElem** and **To CstElem** columns. Your also have the option of entering a cost center group in the **Cost Elem. Group** column. You can subdivide within cost elements by entering origin groups in the **To orgn** column, and also in the material master Costing 1 view. You can also divide the calculation base into **Fixed** and **Variable** costs if necessary by selecting the appropriate radio button. Now that we've discussed how bases work, let's examine the next cost sheet component, the overhead rate.

Overhead Rate

The overhead rate is a percentage factor applied to the value of the calculation base (group of cost elements). To see how percentage rates are entered in a calculation rate, select any row with an entry in the **Overhea...** (overhead rate) column shown in Figure 2.8 and double-click on **Overhead rate** at the left of the screen. The screen shown in Figure 2.10 is displayed.

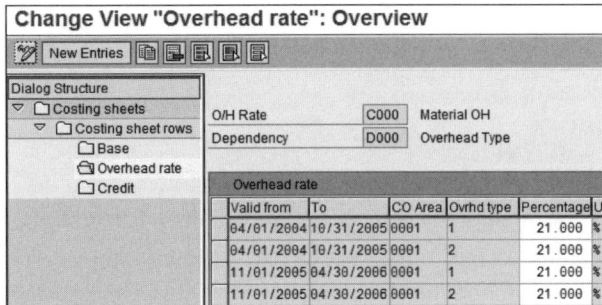

Figure 2.10 Overhead Rate Overview

The **Dependency** field allows the same overhead rate to be applied to all materials within a plant or company code. Other dependencies are available, allowing different rates to be applied per order type or overhead key. Overhead keys can be entered per individual manufacturing order or product cost collector. This provides a high level of control and flexibility, but also increased setup and maintenance requirements.

Overhead rates are date-dependant, allowing different rates to be entered per fiscal year or even fiscal period, if required. Before utilizing this functionality at its most detailed level, be sure the maintenance effort required is offset by any increased accuracy of overhead allocation.

Now that we've looked at bases and the overhead rate, let's examine the final costing sheet component, the credit key.

Credit Key

You assign a credit key in the **Credit** column shown in Figure 2.8, to each row with an entry in the **Overhea...** (overhead rate) column. During overhead allocation, a manufacturing order or product cost collector is debited, and a cost center is credited. The credit key defines which cost center receives the credit. To display how a cost center is entered in a credit key, select any row with an entry in the **Credit** column shown in Figure 2.8, and double-

click on **Credit** at the left of the screen. The screen shown in Figure 2.11 is displayed.

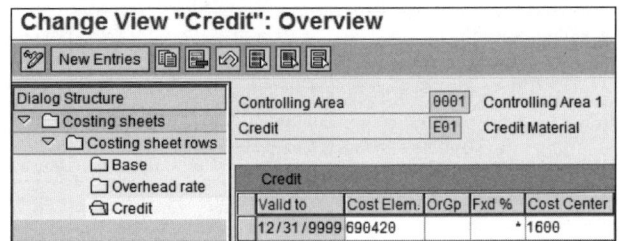

Figure 2.11 Credit Overview

Enter the cost center to receive the overhead credit in the **Cost Center** (last) column. A secondary cost element is also a required entry in the **Cost Elem.** column. The secondary cost element identifies the *plan* overhead cost in the cost estimate and the *actual* overhead debit in manufacturing order and product cost collector cost reports. It also identifies the overhead credit to the cost center in cost center reports. See Chapter 6 for more information on reporting in SAP CO.

Now that we've completed master data and costing sheet creation and maintenance, structures are in place for the cost estimate to determine material, labor, and overhead costs. The next step is to instruct the cost estimate on how to group costs together for the *Cost component view* in the cost estimate. This complements the basic *Itemization* view, or a simple listing of items in the cost estimate. The most common cost components are materials, labor, and overhead. You can create you own cost components with the procedure described in the following section.

2.3 Cost Components

The cost component split allows a cost estimate to group costs of similar types of components, such as material, labor, and overhead. Analysis of cost components such as material, labor, and overhead over time or across a range of products can assist in Profitability Analysis. Cost components increasing over time may result in an effort to reduce material, labor, or overhead costs. Comparison of cost components across products can influence marketing decisions. A manufacturing company may decide to focus on products that require less labor and overhead,

22

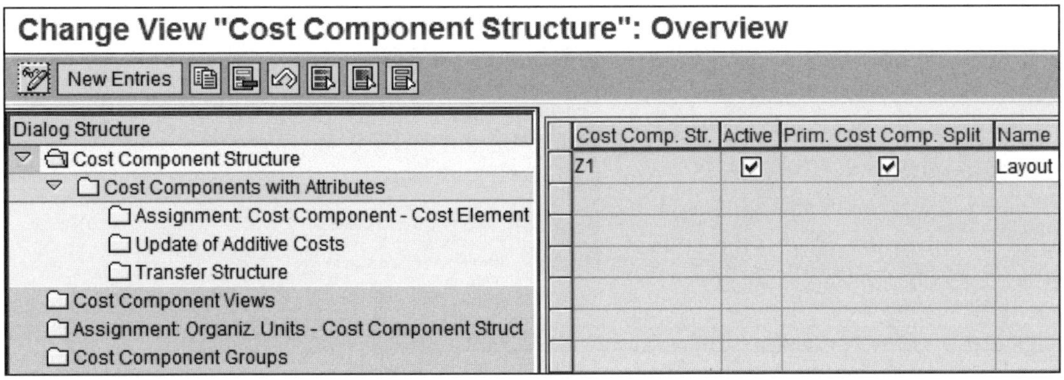

Change View "Cost Component Structure": Overview

New Entries

Dialog Structure
- ▽ Cost Component Structure
  - ▽ Cost Components with Attributes
    - Assignment: Cost Component - Cost Element
    - Update of Additive Costs
    - Transfer Structure
  - Cost Component Views
  - Assignment: Organiz. Units - Cost Component Struct
  - Cost Component Groups

Cost Comp. Str.	Active	Prim. Cost Comp. Split	Name
Z1	☑	☑	Layout

Figure 2.12 Cost Component Structure Overview

or a company may be interested in analyzing the results of efforts to reduce labor and overhead costs.

All individual costs are identified by cost elements. Primary cost elements correspond to general ledger accounts, which identify costs such as material consumed from inventory or external processing costs. Secondary cost elements identify labor, overhead, or process costs allocated to production orders or product cost collectors from cost centers. Cost components group similar types of cost elements together.

Cost components only consider component material costs, which are rolled up through the BOM. Value added by activities at subassemblies are also grouped together by cost element and rolled upward through the BOM to the higher-level cost estimate.

Let's look at the configuration of a cost component structure to see how cost components are rolled up by cost element. To view cost component structure configu-

ration settings use transaction OKTZ or menu path: **IMG • Controlling • Product Cost Controlling • Product Cost Planning • Basic Settings for Material Costing • Define Cost Component Structure**. The screen shown in Figure 2.12 is displayed.

Available cost component structures are listed on the right of this overview screen. You can use existing cost component structures or copy one and create your own. Let's choose the cost component structure shown in Figure 2.12 and examine the components with the following steps:

1. Select cost component structure **Z1**
2. Double-click on **Cost Components with Attributes**

The screen shown in Figure 2.13 is displayed.

Available cost components are listed on the right of the overview screen. You can use existing cost components or copy one and create your own. Let's choose the

Change View "Cost Components with Attributes": Overview

New Entries

Dialog Structure
- ▽ Cost Component Structure
  - ▽ Cost Components with Attributes
    - Assignment: Cost Component - Cost Element
    - Update of Additive Costs
    - Transfer Structure
  - Cost Component Views
  - Assignment: Organiz. Units - Cost Component Struct
  - Cost Component Groups

Cost Comp. Str.	Cost Co...	Name of Cost Comp.
Z1	1	Semi-finished goods
Z1	2	Set-Up
Z1	3	Labour
Z1	4	Machine
Z1	5	Component materials
Z1	6	Material Overhead
Z1	7	Labor Overhead
Z1	8	Quality Overhead
Z1	9	External Processing

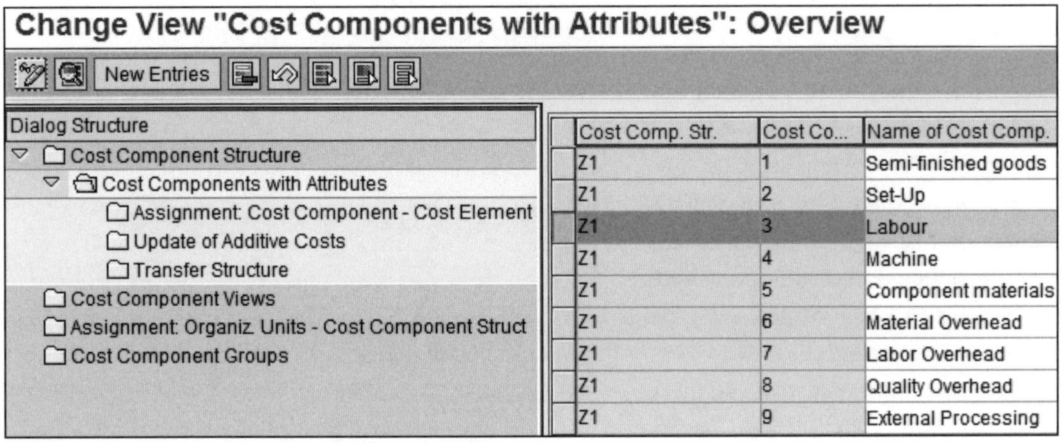

Figure 2.13 Cost Components with Attributes Overview

Change View "Assignment: Cost Component - Cost Element Interval": Over

C...	Ch...	From cost ...	Origin group	To cost ele...	Cost...	Name
Z1	CAUK	620230		620230	3	Labour
Z1	CAUK	690010		690010	3	Labour

Dialog Structure
- Cost Component Structure
  - Cost Components with Attributes
    - Assignment: Cost Component - Cost Element
    - Update of Additive Costs
    - Transfer Structure
  - Cost Component Views
  - Assignment: Organiz. Units - Cost Component Struct
  - Cost Component Groups

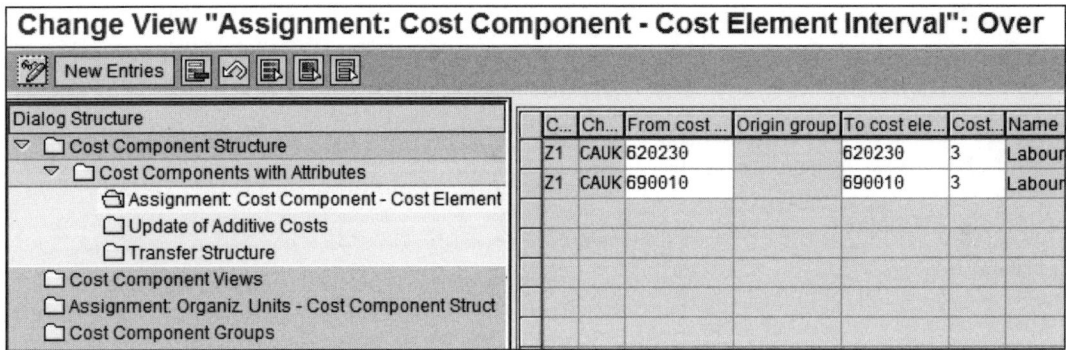

Figure 2.14 Cost Element Assignment Overview

Labour cost component and examine the components via the following steps:

1. Select the **Labour** cost component (shown as selected)
2. Double-click on **Assignment: Cost Component— Cost Element**

The English spelling of the word labor (labour) is used since this example is based on a UK company.

The screen shown in Figure 2.14 is then displayed.

Individual cost elements or cost element ranges are assigned to cost components in the **From cost...** (From cost element) and **To cost ele...** (To cost element) columns.

With master data, costing sheet, and cost component setup completed, we have nearly finished the necessary preparations needed for creating a cost estimate. The one remaining step required is to set up the costing variant, which is described in detail in Section 2.4.

2.4 Costing Variant

The costing variant contains information on how a cost estimate calculates the standard price. For example, it determines if the purchasing info record price is used for purchased materials or if an estimated price is manually entered in the **Planned price 1** field of the material master Costing 2 view. Only the standard cost estimate adjusts inventory values. In this section, we'll explore how the costing variant determines the standard price.

Let's inspect the configuration of a costing variant to gain an understanding of how it works. To view costing variant configuration settings, use transaction OKKN or

menu path: **IMG • Controlling • Product Cost Controlling • Product Cost Planning • Material Cost Estimate with Quantity Structure • Define Costing Variants**. The screen shown in Figure 2.15 is displayed.

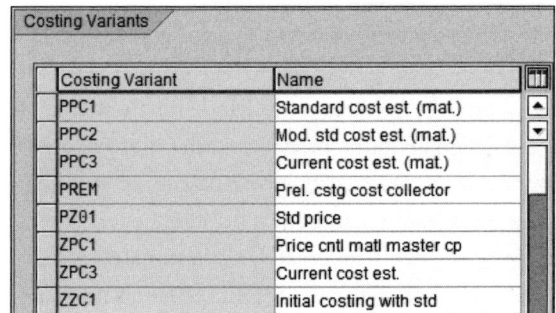

Costing Variants

Costing Variant	Name
PPC1	Standard cost est. (mat.)
PPC2	Mod. std cost est. (mat.)
PPC3	Current cost est. (mat.)
PREM	Prel. cstg cost collector
PZ01	Std price
ZPC1	Price cntl matl master cp
ZPC3	Current cost est.
ZZC1	Initial costing with std

Figure 2.15 Costing Variant Selection Screen

A list of available costing variants is presented in the **Costing Variant** column. Let's examine the first costing variant, **PPC1** in this example, by double-clicking on it. The screen shown in Figure 2.16 is displayed.

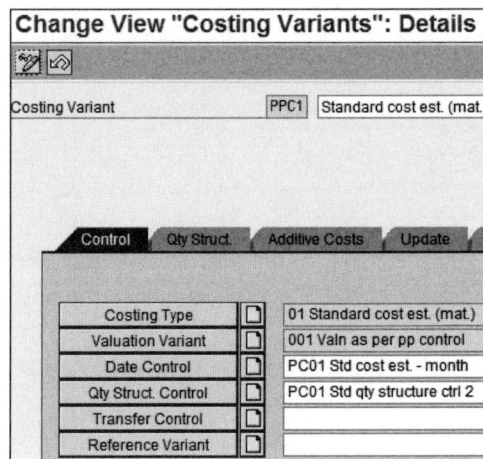

Change View "Costing Variants": Details

Costing Variant   PPC1   Standard cost est. (mat.)

Control | Qty Struct. | Additive Costs | Update

Costing Type	01 Standard cost est. (mat.)
Valuation Variant	001 Valn as per pp control
Date Control	PC01 Std cost est. - month
Qty Struct. Control	PC01 Std qty structure ctrl 2
Transfer Control	
Reference Variant	

Figure 2.16 Costing Variant PPC1 Details Screen

The costing variant components are shown as buttons on the left. **Costing Type** and **Valuation Variant** are particularly relevant to variance analysis, and we'll now discuss why. Click on the **Costing Type** button to display the screen shown in Figure 2.17.

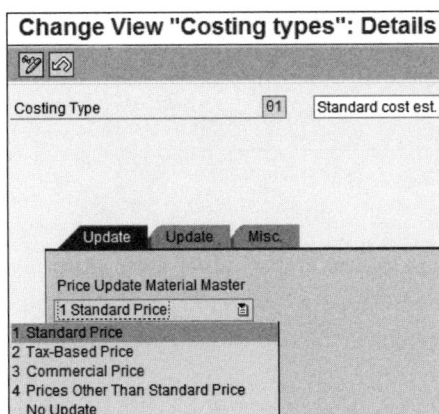

Figure 2.17 Costing Type Details Screen

The costing type determines if the cost estimate is able to update the standard price in the material master. There are many reasons for also requiring cost estimates that can't update the material master. A product development department may need to create cost estimates, which should not be able to update the standard price, while developing a new product. By using costing variants that do not include **Costing Type 01**, you can allow users the ability to create cost estimates that cannot update the standard price.

In variance analysis, we are particularly interested in costing variants that can update the material master standard price. This is because the standard price is used as the benchmark for all production and purchasing activities, and it is the basis for calculating total variance, as discussed in Chapter 4. Click on the **Valuation Variant** button to display the screen shown in Figure 2.18.

The valuation variant allows different search strategies for materials, activity types, subcontracting, and external processing. The material search strategy, shown in the **Material Val.** tab in Figure 2.18, indicates that the cost estimate first searches for purchasing info records containing the material price, due to the **L Price from Purchasing Info Record** entry next to **Priority 1**. L, 4 and 3 are the keys of the strategy sequence, while the text following the keys is the description. If unsuccessful, it will

then search for an entry in the **Planned Price 1** field in the material master Costing 2 view. If still unsuccessful, an error message will be issued, which must be corrected before the cost estimate can be released.

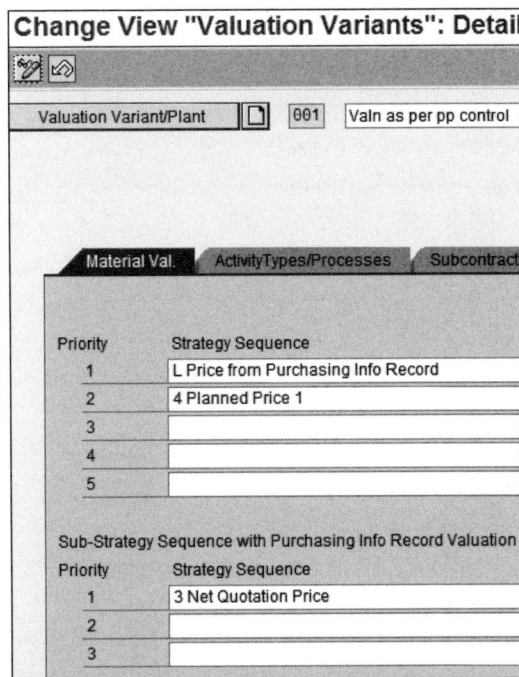

Figure 2.18 Valuation Variant Details Screen

Similarly, you can enter search strategies for **Activity-Types/Processes**, **Subcontracting**, and **Ext. Processing** (not shown) by clicking on the corresponding tab shown in Figure 2.18.

Now that preparations are complete, we're ready to create a standard cost estimate. In Section 2.5, I'll demonstrate how to create and analyze cost estimates.

2.5 Standard Cost Estimate

The standard cost estimate is involved in variance analysis because it is used for stock valuation. When a production or process order delivers product to inventory, it receives a credit based on the standard price. Total variance is the difference between actual costs debited to the order and costs credited to the order due to deliveries to stock.

Let's now create a standard cost estimate. Then, in the following subsections, we'll mark and release the cost estimate and mass-process cost estimates with a costing run.

Create Standard Cost Estimate

The standard cost estimate is usually created with costing variant PPC1. This is the only cost estimate that can be used to update the standard price in the material master. Let's create a standard cost estimate and analyze the results. You create a standard cost estimate with transaction CK11N or menu path: **Accounting • Controlling • Product Cost Controlling • Product Cost Planning • Material Costing • Cost Estimate with Quantity Structure • Create**. A selection screen is displayed, as shown in Figure 2.19.

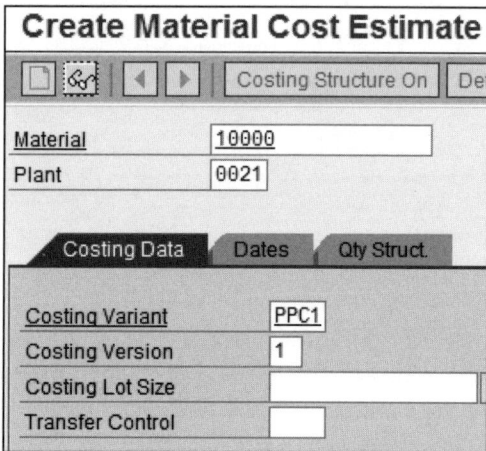

Figure 2.19 Create Standard Cost Estimate Selection Screen

In the selection screen, you enter the essential data needed to create a cost estimate: **Material**, **Plant**, and **Costing Variant**. You can also create different **Costing Versions**, which is useful for scenario analysis. You normally only release **Costing Version 1** cost estimates. If you leave the **Costing Lot Size** field blank, the cost estimate retrieves the costing lot size from the corresponding field in the material master Costing 1 view.

If you leave the **Transfer Control** field blank, the cost estimate searches for an entry next to the **Transfer Control** button in the costing variant shown in Figure 2.16. Create the cost estimate with the following steps:

1. Complete the **Material**, **Plant**, and **Costing Variant** fields
2. Press Enter or click on the **Dates** tab

The screen shown in Figure 2.20 is displayed.

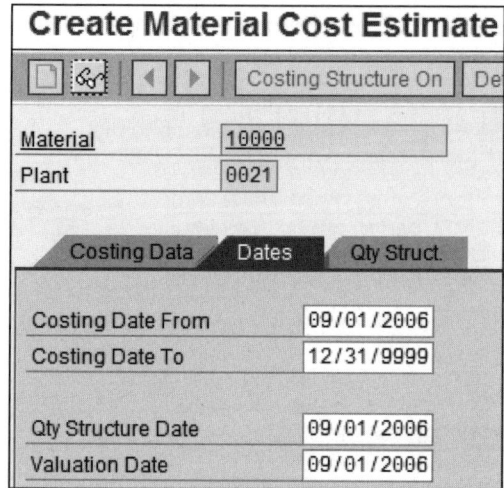

Figure 2.20 Create Standard Cost Estimate Dates Tab

Four default dates appear, based on the **Date Control** component of the costing variant shown in Figure 2.16. These are described in some detail below:

► **Costing Date From**
This field determines the validity start date of the cost estimate. The cost estimate cannot be marked and released, i.e., used to adjust inventory valuation, until the start date has been reached. The start date can be changed to a previous date, and the cost estimate can be created. However, a standard cost estimate cannot be saved, marked, or released with a start date in the past.

► **Costing Date To**
This field determines the validity finish date of the cost estimate. Variance calculation requires a standard cost estimate that is valid for the entire fiscal year. This date is typically set to the maximum possible date.

► **Quantity Structure Date**
This field determines which BOM and routing are selected for the cost estimate. Since these can change over time, it is useful to be able to select a particular BOM or routing by date.

► **Valuation Date**
This field determines which material and activity prices are selected for the cost estimate. Purchasing info records can contain different vendor-quoted prices for different dates.

Create Material Cost Estimate with Quantity Structure

Costing Structure	E...	Total val...	C...	Quan...	U
▽ 📊 Finished Pr 🔲		19,677.60 USD		10.000 EA	▲
▽ 📊 MAIN/TL 🔲		1,086.96 USD		10.000 EA	▼
▽ 📊 TUB 🔲		871.02 USD		10.000 EA	
📊 / 🔲		385.70 USD		70.000 FT	
▽ 📊 LINI 🔲		171.76 USD		20.000 EA	
📊 / 🔲		54.84 USD		12.000 FT	
▽ 📊 ATTENL 🔲		1,443.68 USD		10.000 EA	
📊 COV 🔲		30.40 USD		10.000 EA	
▽ 📊 TUB 🔲		140.54 USD		10.000 EA	
📊 (🔲		.51.25 USD		3.330 M	
📊 STE 🔲		850.00 USD		10.000 EA	
📊 PIN 🔲		195.00 USD		20.000 EA	
📊 ROL 🔲		180.00 USD		20.000 EA	
📊 PIN 🔲		0.50 USD		10.000 EA	
▽ 📊 ATTENL 🔲		1,443.68 USD		10.000 EA	
📊 COV 🔲		30.40 USD		10.000 EA	
▽ 📊 TUB 🔲		140.54 USD		10.000 EA	
📊 (🔲		51.25 USD		3.330 M	

Material   10000   Finished Product
Plant   0021

Costing Data | Dates | Qty Struct. | Valuation | History | Costs

Costs Based On   1 Costing Lot Size   10.000   EA

Cost Component View	Total Costs	Fixed Costs	Variable	Currency
Cost of goods manufactured	19,677.60	0.00	19,677.60	USD
Cost of goods sold	19,677.60	0.00	19,677.60	USD
Sales and administration c...	0.00	0.00	0.00	USD
Inventory (commercial)	0.00	0.00	0.00	USD
Inventory (tax-based)	0.00	0.00	0.00	USD

1 Cost of goods manufactured   Partner

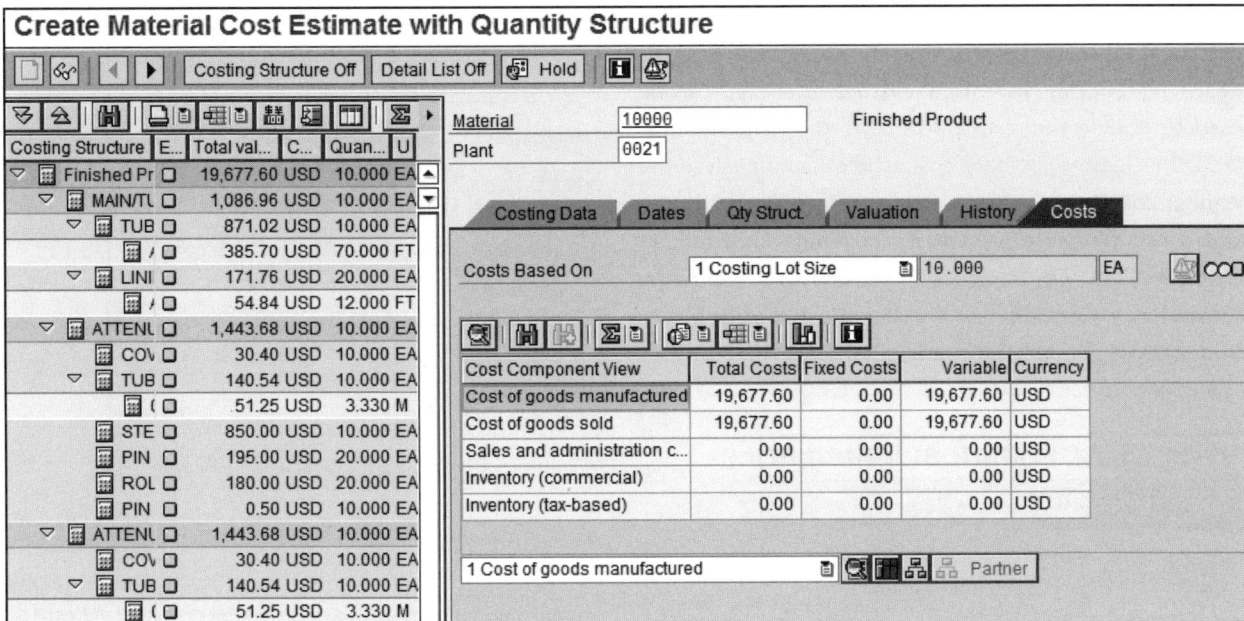

Figure 2.21 Create Standard Cost Estimate Results Screen

Likewise, different activity prices can be planned per period. It can be useful to, for instance, hold the valuation date constant, while changing the quantity structure date to isolate the cost effect of changing the structure of a BOM.

Press Enter to create the cost estimate, which is displayed in Figure 2.21.

A costed multilevel BOM is displayed at the left of the screen. Even though we initially created a cost estimate for material 10000 shown in Figure 2.19, cost estimates are also created for all underlying components and sub-assemblies. Cost estimates are indicated by the cost esti-mate (calculator) icons in the costed BOM. Double-click-ing on any cost estimate in the multilevel costed BOM causes the information on the right of the screen to cor-respond to the individual cost estimate.

The **Costs Based On** field indicates the quantity the costs *displayed* are based on. The costs are always *calcu-lated* based on the costing lot size. The entry in the **Costs Based On** field defaults to **Costing Lot Size**. Purchas-ing or manufacturing in quantities that are different to the costing lot size can cause variances, since it is usually more efficient to purchase or manufacture items in larger quantities and less efficient to do so in smaller quantities.

To *display* costs based on a quantity of one (but still *calcu-lated* based on the costing lot size), click on the **Costing Lot Size** text shown in Figure 2.21. The screen shown in Figure 2.22 is displayed.

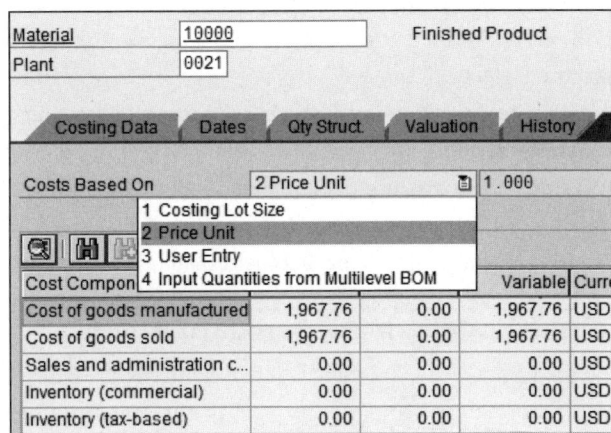

Material   10000   Finished Product
Plant   0021

Costing Data | Dates | Qty Struct. | Valuation | History

Costs Based On   2 Price Unit   1.000

        1 Costing Lot Size
        2 Price Unit
        3 User Entry
Cost Compon 4 Input Quantities from Multilevel BOM

Cost Compon...			Variable	Curr
Cost of goods manufactured	1,967.76	0.00	1,967.76	USD
Cost of goods sold	1,967.76	0.00	1,967.76	USD
Sales and administration c...	0.00	0.00	0.00	USD
Inventory (commercial)	0.00	0.00	0.00	USD
Inventory (tax-based)	0.00	0.00	0.00	USD

Figure 2.22 Change Cost Basis to Unit Entry

Click on **Price Unit** and inspect the quantity displayed in the field to right of the text. If the price unit is 1.000, the cost estimate costs displayed are now based on a quan-tity of one. Otherwise, click on **User Entry** and manually enter the quantity.

Now that we've created a standard cost estimate, the next steps are to mark and release the cost estimate. During the release step, inventory revaluation occurs if there is stock.

Mark and Release

After a standard cost estimate is saved without errors, it can be marked with transaction CK24 or via menu path: **Accounting • Controlling • Product Cost Controlling • Product Cost Planning • Material Costing • Price Update**. A selection screen is displayed, as shown in Figure 2.23.

Price Update: Mark Standard Price

🔄 ⚒ 📇 📋 ⅋⅋ Release ⅋⅋ Other Prices	⚔ Log	

Posting Period/Fiscal Year	5 2007
Company Code	
Plant	0021
Material	1000

Figure 2.23 Mark Standard Cost Estimate Selection Screen

You mark and release cost estimates with this same selection screen. Mark a cost estimate by taking the following steps:

1. Complete the **Posting Period/Fiscal Year**, **Plant**, and **Material** fields
2. Click on the execute (clock) icon

The screen shown in Figure 2.24 is displayed.

Price Update: Mark Standard Price

Ex...	Material	Plant	Costing Status	Fut. plnd price	Standard price
☐	10000	0021	VO	1,974.36	2,938.99

Figure 2.24 Mark Standard Cost Estimate Results Screen

A green traffic light icon, together with costing status **VO**, indicates the standard cost estimate was successfully marked. There are no inventory revaluations or account postings during marking. The proposed standard price is copied to the **Future Cost Estimate** column of the material master **Costing 2** view, as shown in Figure 2.25.

⊙ Costing 1	⊙ Costing 2	Plant stock	Stor. loc. stck

Material	10000	Finished Product	
Plant	0021	Production	

Standard Cost Estimate

Cost Estimate		Future		Current	
Period / Fiscal Year	5	2007		0	
Planned price	1,974.36			0.00	
Standard price				2,938.99	

Figure 2.25 Marked Cost Estimate in Future Column

You can create and mark standard cost estimates many times before release. Within the same fiscal period, new standard cost estimates overwrite existing cost estimates. If you do not want a standard cost estimate to be overwritten, create it with a different **Costing Version**, as we saw in Figure 2.19. It may not be possible to release cost estimates created with different costing versions, though. They are for reference only.

After you have successfully marked a cost estimate, check that the proposed standard price is correct. To release it, click on the **Release** button Figure 2.23, and then the execute icon. The screen shown in Figure 2.26 is displayed.

Price Update: Release Standard Price

Ex...	Material	Plant	Costing Status	Standard pri...	Price unit	Currency	Document Number
☐	10000	0021	FR	1,974.36	1	USD	3000009280

Figure 2.26 Release Standard Cost Estimate Results Screen

A green traffic light icon, together with costing status **FR** in the **Costing Status** column, indicates the standard cost estimate was successfully released. You can display the price change document by clicking on the underlined document number in the **Document Number** column. If there is valuated stock, inventory will be revalued, and a financial account posting will occur during release. The **Future Standard price** is moved to the **Current Planned price** and **Standard price** fields of the material master **Costing 2** view, as shown in Figure 2.27.

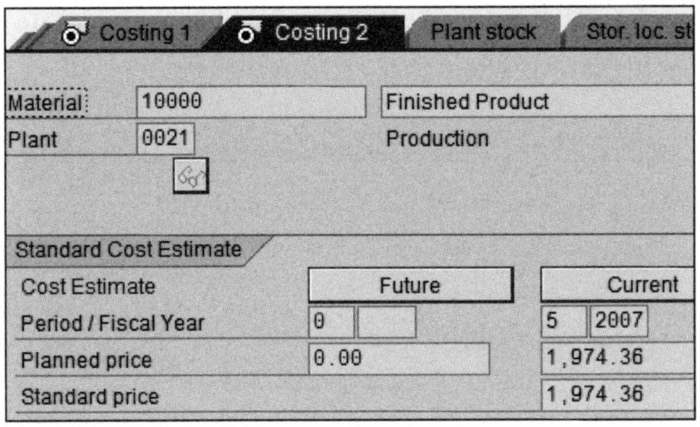

Figure 2.27 Released Cost Estimate in Current Column

Standard cost estimates can be released only once per fiscal period. As a rule, you should try to release cost estimates less frequently—say, once every 12 months. This provides greater visibility to purchase price and production variances. Releasing cost estimates more frequently reduces variances, though inventory revaluation postings increase. Industries with rapidly moving purchase prices or short product development times may need to release cost estimates more frequently.

I've shown you how to create, mark, and release individual standard cost estimates. When it's time to create, mark, and release many cost estimates, such as at the start of a fiscal year, you can create a costing run to process a large number of cost estimates.

Costing Run

A costing run can create, mark and release a large number of cost estimates, e.g., all materials in a plant or company code. The costing run should be started well in advance of the required release date, since master data errors may need to be corrected, such as missing purchasing info record prices. Differences between proposed and existing standard prices may also need to be analyzed and approved before release.

There are several steps involved in processing a costing run. Let's follow the first steps in detail, starting with creating a costing run. You can create a costing run with transaction CK40N or via menu path: **Accounting • Controlling • Product Cost Controlling • Product Cost Planning • Material Costing • Costing Run • Edit Costing Run**. A selection screen is displayed, as shown in Figure 2.28.

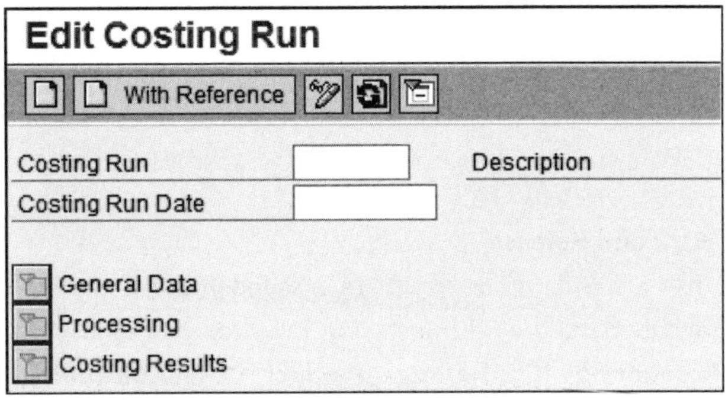

Figure 2.28 Edit Costing Run Initial Screen

To create a new costing run, click on the create (new page) icon. The screen shown in Figure 2.29 is displayed.

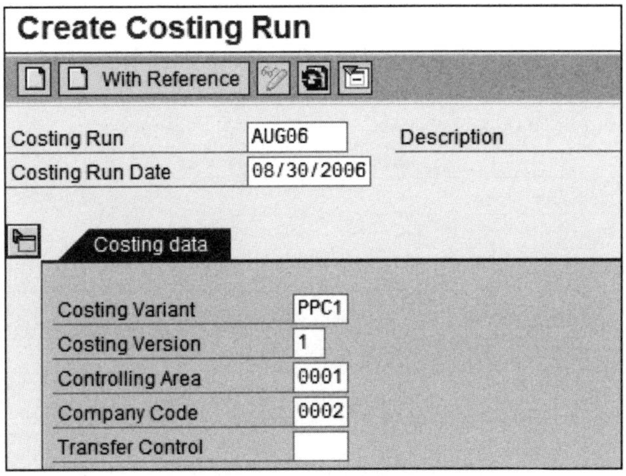

Figure 2.29 Create Costing Run Entry Screen

Enter the required information in the selection screen. You can use the entries shown in Figure 2.29 as an example. Then save your entries to display the screen shown in Figure 2.30.

The **Edit Costing Run** screen allows you to carry out and record the results of all the costing run steps in one screen. The costing run steps are listed in the **Flow Step** column. When first displaying this screen, ensure the dates shown in the **Dates** tab are correct. To carry out the first costing run step, click on the icon shown in the **Parameter** column of the **Selection** row. The screen shown in Figure 2.31 is displayed.

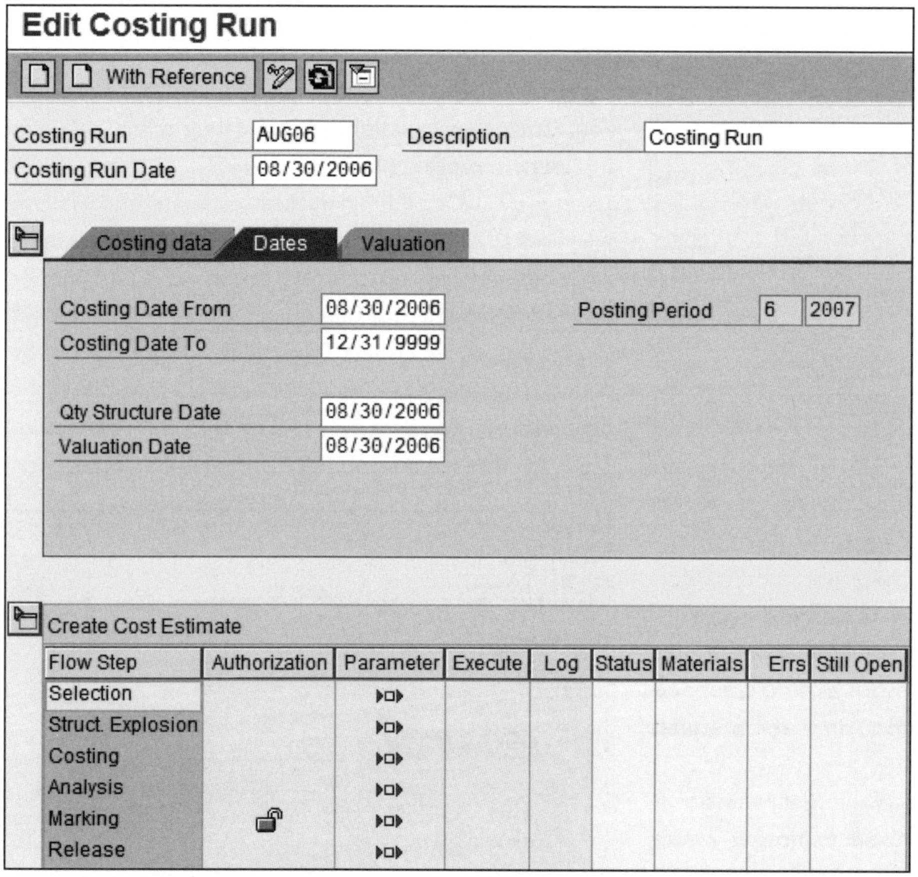

Edit Costing Run

With Reference

Costing Run	AUG06
Costing Run Date	08/30/2006

Description: Costing Run

Costing data | **Dates** | **Valuation**

Costing Date From	08/30/2006
Costing Date To	12/31/9999
Qty Structure Date	08/30/2006
Valuation Date	08/30/2006

Posting Period 6 2007

Create Cost Estimate

Flow Step	Authorization	Parameter	Execute	Log	Status	Materials	Errs	Still Open
Selection		▶☐▶						
Struct. Explosion		▶☐▶						
Costing		▶☐▶						
Analysis		▶☐▶						
Marking	🔓	▶☐▶						
Release		▶☐▶						

Figure 2.30 Edit Costing Run Dates Tab

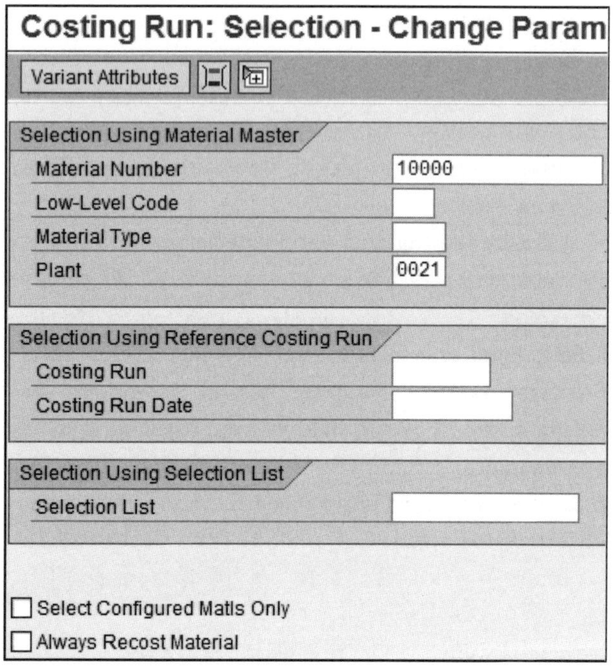

Costing Run: Selection - Change Param

Variant Attributes

Selection Using Material Master

Material Number	10000
Low-Level Code	
Material Type	
Plant	0021

Selection Using Reference Costing Run

Costing Run	
Costing Run Date	

Selection Using Selection List

Selection List	

☐ Select Configured Matls Only
☐ Always Recost Material

Figure 2.31 Change Costing Run Selection Parameters

There are many options available for using selection criteria. I'll follow a simple example to demonstrate the process. Complete the **Material Number** and **Plant** fields, and save your entries. The screen shown in Figure 2.32 is displayed.

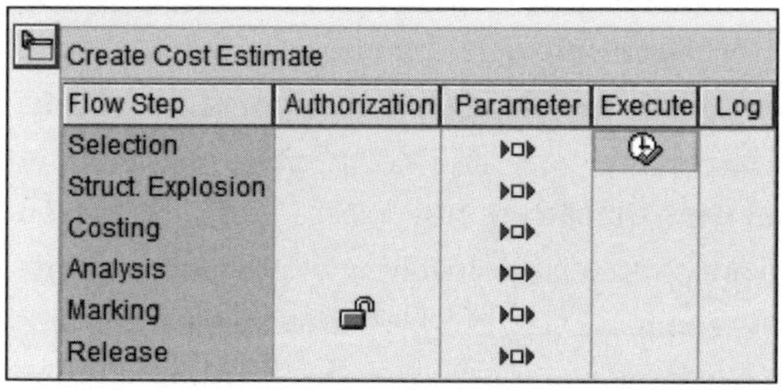

Create Cost Estimate

Flow Step	Authorization	Parameter	Execute	Log
Selection		▶☐▶	🕀	
Struct. Explosion		▶☐▶		
Costing		▶☐▶		
Analysis		▶☐▶		
Marking	🔓	▶☐▶		
Release		▶☐▶		

Figure 2.32 Selection Step Parameters Saved

The icon in the **Execute** column of the **Selection** row indicates selection parameters have been saved. Click on this icon to complete the selection step. The screen shown in Figure 2.33 is displayed.

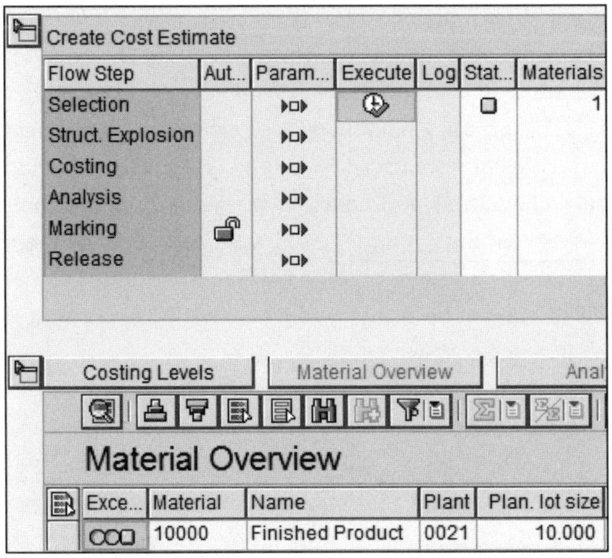

Figure 2.33 Selection Step Completed

The green traffic light icon in the **Selection** row indicates that the selection step was successfully completed. The materials selected in this step are shown in the **Material Overview** section of the screen.

Follow the same procedure to complete the remaining steps of the costing run. In the **Struct. Explosion** (structural explosion) step, all materials contained at lower levels in BOMs selected in the **Selection** step are selected. In the **Costing** step, cost estimates are created for all selected materials, starting with the lowest-level materials. The **Analysis** step allows a detailed comparison of the proposed and existing standard prices. The **Marking** step updates the **Future planned price** field in the material master Costing 2 view. The final **Release** step updates the **Current Planned price** and **Standard price** fields in the material master Costing 2 view. During the release step, inventory is revaluated, and accounting documents are posted.

Completing the costing run release step means you have almost completed preparations for variance analysis. There's one more step required if you are using product cost collectors. You must carry out a mass-processing of preliminary cost estimates, as described in the following section. Preliminary cost estimates are used to valuate work in process and scrap, and you may receive error messages during period-end processing if you don't create new preliminary cost estimates following a costing run.

2.6 Preliminary Cost Estimate

The preliminary cost estimate is involved with production, variance calculation, and valuating scrap variances and work in process (WIP).

Let's create a preliminary cost estimate and analyze the results. You can create a preliminary cost estimate for a product cost collector with transaction KKF6N or via menu path: **Accounting • Controlling • Product Cost Controlling • Cost Object Controlling • Product Cost by Period • Master Data • Product Cost Collector • Edit**. The screen shown in Figure 2.34 is displayed.

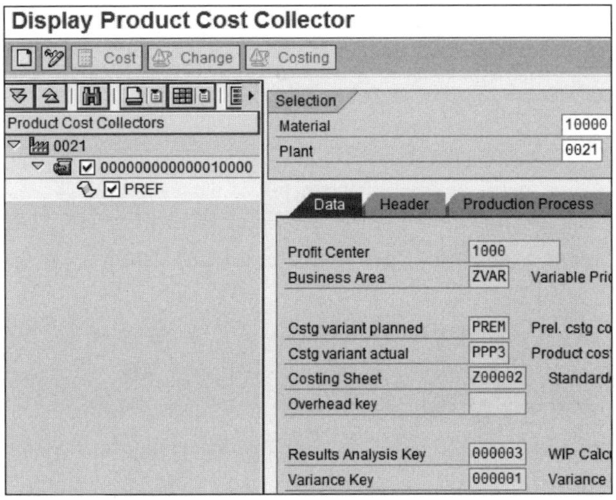

Figure 2.34 Display Product Cost Collector

You can create individual preliminary cost estimates from this product cost collector screen. To create a preliminary cost estimate for a product cost collector, carry out the following steps:

1. Complete the **Material** and **Plant** fields
2. Select the Production Version indicator (**PREF** in this example)
3. Press Enter to display the details of the product cost collector
4. Click on the display/change (pencil) icon to allow edits
5. Click on the **Cost** button to create the cost estimate
6. Click on the **Header** tab to display the **Cost Estimate** button

The screen shown in Figure 2.35 is displayed.

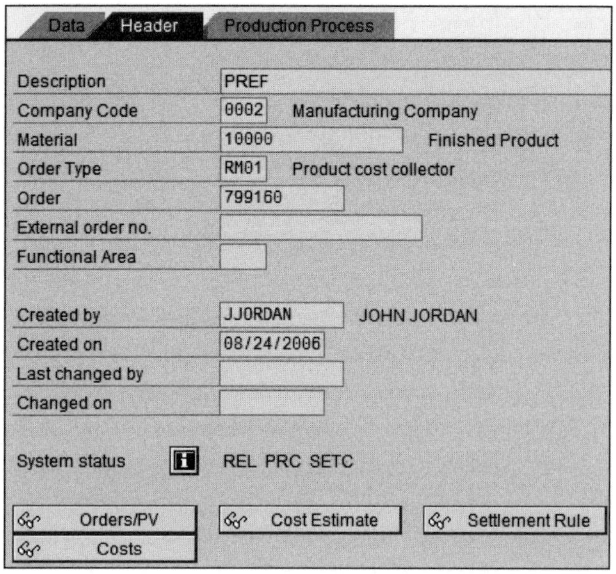

Figure 2.35 Product Cost Collector Header Tab

Click on the **Cost Estimate** button to display the most recent preliminary cost estimate, which is shown in Figure 2.36.

The preliminary cost estimate looks similar to the standard cost estimate we saw in Section 2.5.1. The two important differences, however, are the number of preliminary cost estimates possible per material, and transfer control. I'll now discuss these two differences in the following subsections.

Production Process

There can be only one standard cost estimate per material, though there can be many preliminary cost estimates. This is because preliminary cost estimates for product cost collectors are usually based on a production version controlling level. A production version is a unique combination of BOM, routing, and work center. Since there can be many different methods of manufacturing a material, there can be many production versions, and hence, preliminary cost estimates.

From SAP R/3 release 4.5A on, product cost collectors are created with reference to a production process. A production process describes the way a material is produced, i.e., which quantity structure is used. The quantity structure is taken from the production version, which is noted during the production process. The production process is determined by the following characteristics: material, production plant, and production version. One production process can be created for each production version.

Transfer Control

Preliminary cost estimates for product cost collectors use transfer control. Transfer control requires a top-level cost estimate to use recently created standard cost estimates for all lower-level materials. The quickest way to create

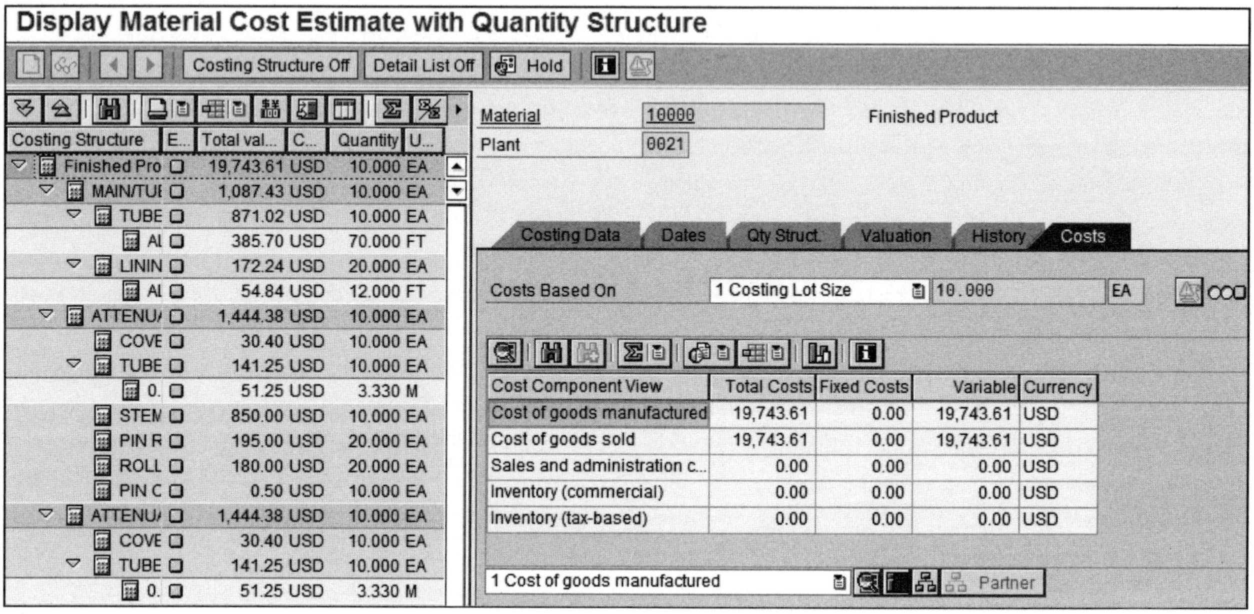

Figure 2.36 Preliminary Cost Estimate for Product Cost Collector

many standard cost estimates is within a costing run, as discussed in Section 2.5.

Let's examine transfer control in greater detail, since it is important in order to create preliminary cost estimates for product cost collectors without errors. In the preliminary cost estimate shown in Figure 2.36, click on the **Costing Data** tab to display the screen shown in Figure 2.37.

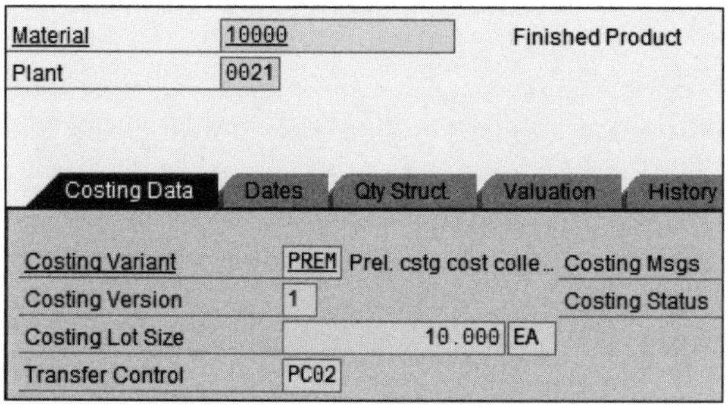

Figure 2.37 Preliminary Cost Estimate Costing Data Tab

In Figure 2.37, notice that the **Transfer Control** for the preliminary cost estimate is **PC02**. Double-click on the underlined text, **PREM** in the **Costing Variant** field, to display the screen shown in Figure 2.38.

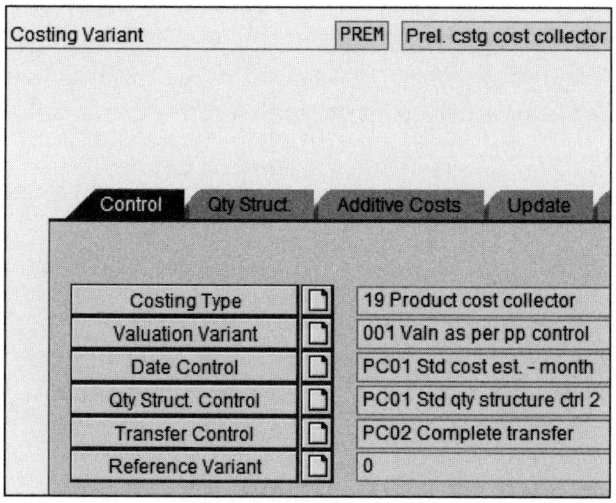

Figure 2.38 Costing Variant PREM Details Screen

This screen shows the components of costing variant **PREM**. Click on the **Transfer Control** button shown in Figure 2.38 to display the screen shown in Figure 2.39.

Figure 2.39 shows the **Strategy Seq.** (strategy sequence) that **Transfer Control PC02** uses to search for

existing cost estimates within a **Single-Plant**. The three following points refer to each of the three search strategies in turn, shown in Figure 2.39:

▶ A marked standard cost estimate with a start date within the current fiscal year, indicated by the selection in the **Fiscal Year** column. When a standard cost estimate is marked, it appears in the Future standard cost estimate column of the material master **Costing 2** view.

▶ A released standard cost estimate with a start date within the current fiscal period. When a standard cost is released, it moves from the Future standard cost estimate to the Current standard cost estimate column of the material master **Costing 2** view.

▶ A previously released cost estimate with a start date within the current fiscal period. When a standard cost estimate is released, the cost estimate it replaces moves to the Previous standard cost estimate column in the material master **Costing 2** view.

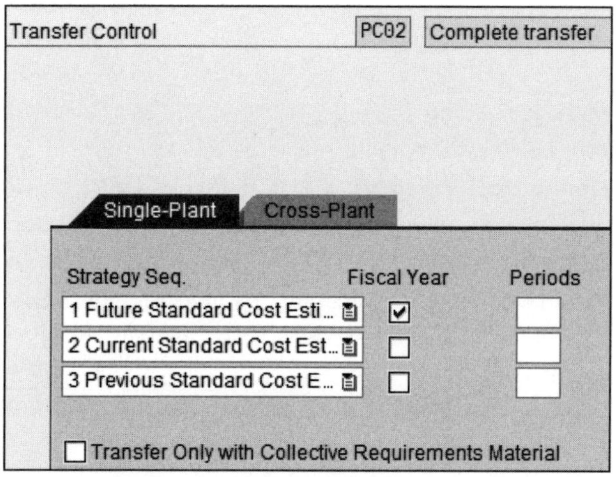

Figure 2.39 Transfer Control PC02 Details

Preliminary cost estimates created in the same period that standard cost estimates are released for lower-level materials use the standard cost estimates. This is based on the second transfer control strategy sequence shown in Figure 2.39. To demonstrate this, in the cost estimate shown in Figure 2.36, double-click on the second cost estimate on the left side of the screen, immediately below the highlighted **Finished Product**. The right side of the cost estimate screen now refers to the second cost estimate. Click on the **Costing Data** tab to display the screen shown in Figure 2.40.

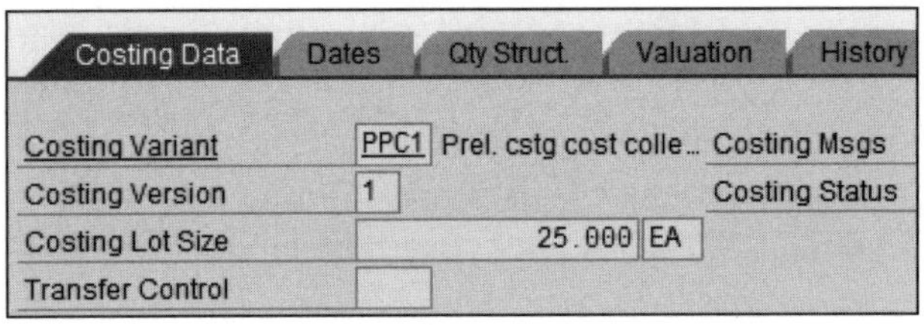

Figure 2.40 Lower-Level Cost Estimate Costing Data Tab

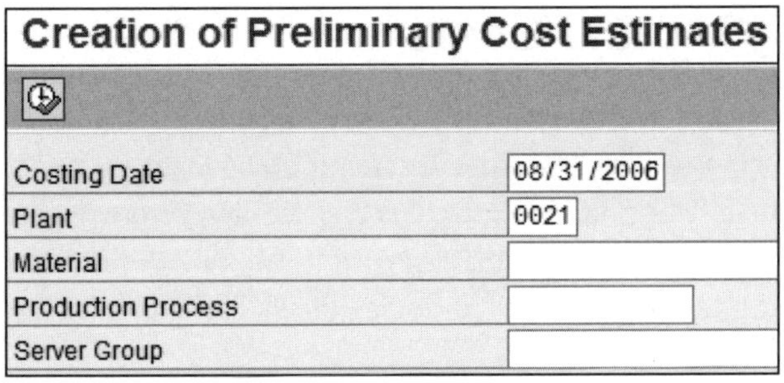

Figure 2.41 Preliminary Costing for Product Cost Collectors

Notice the lower-level cost estimate was previously created with costing variant **PPC1**. To find out when the standard cost estimate was created, click on the **History** tab.

We've now created individual preliminary cost estimates and examined how they access existing standard cost estimates at lower levels in the BOM. Since preliminary cost estimates are normally used to valuate WIP and scrap during period-end processing in Product Cost by Period, you need to mass-create preliminary cost estimates immediately following a costing run. In the next section I'll explain how to mass-process preliminary cost estimates.

Mass-Processing

You can create multiple preliminary cost estimates for product cost collectors with transaction MF30 or via menu path: **Accounting • Controlling • Product Cost Controlling • Cost Object Controlling • Product Cost by Period • Planning • Preliminary Costing for Product Cost Collectors**. A selection screen is displayed, as shown in Figure 2.41.

The selection screen allows you to enter a range or list of materials or production processes. To mass-create preliminary cost estimates, complete the selection fields as required, and press the execute icon to run the transaction. The resulting screen displays a list of messages that should be analyzed. Errors should be resolved where necessary.

2.7 Summary

In this chapter we continued with our preparations for creating cost estimates by creating Logistics master data and setting up costing sheets for overhead allocation. Configuration settings for the costing variant were examined, and standard and preliminary cost estimates were created and analyzed. We've now completed planning for variance analysis. In Chapter 3 we will examine how and when actual cost postings occur.

3 Actual Costs

In Chapter 2 we created cost estimates, which provide the basis for plan and target costs. Since variance analysis involves comparing target and actual costs, in this chapter I'll discuss how actual cost postings occur.

Actual costs debit a product cost collector or manufacturing order during business transactions such as general ledger account postings, inventory goods movements, internal activity allocations, and overhead calculation. These transactions can be divided into two groups, based on the posting origin. Postings to CO from *external* business transactions are identified as primary costs. Business transactions *within* CO result in secondary costs. I'll now discuss primary and secondary costs in more detail.

3.1 Primary Costs

When goods are issued from inventory, a general ledger balance sheet account is credited and a profit and loss consumption account is debited automatically. A primary cost element with the same number and identifier as the inventory consumption account is usually created in Controlling.

Postings to general ledger accounts with a primary cost element also generate a parallel posting to a Controlling cost object. Since components are issued to a production order, the system automatically chooses the production order or attached product cost collector as the cost object. The debit value is calculated by multiplying the standard price by the component quantity issued from inventory. Figure 3.1 shows account postings when components with a value of 100 are issued from inventory to a production order.

External costs are also incurred when external services, such as those supplied by a contracting workshop, are purchased. External services may be required for specialized activities, or if workload exceeds internal work center capacity. In this case an external services expense account is debited, and the goods receipt/invoice receipt (GR/IR) clearing account is credited. There is usually a corresponding primary cost element corresponding to the expense account, so the production order receives a corresponding debit.

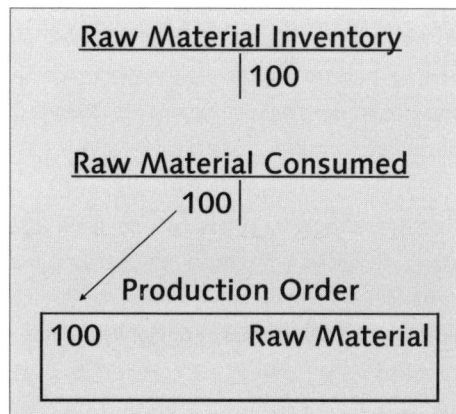

Figure 3.1 Goods Issue Debits to Production Order

3.2 Secondary Costs

When production order activities are confirmed, the production order or product cost collector is debited, and the cost center is credited. There are no corresponding postings to financial accounts during activity confirmation.

A production cost center receives debits due to primary costs such as payroll and electricity. Many products can be manufactured at a work center, with labor and facilities paid for by the cost center. Confirmation of labor and overhead activities allocates these primary costs across many products. Figure 3.2 shows an overview of labor allocation postings from a cost center to the production order.

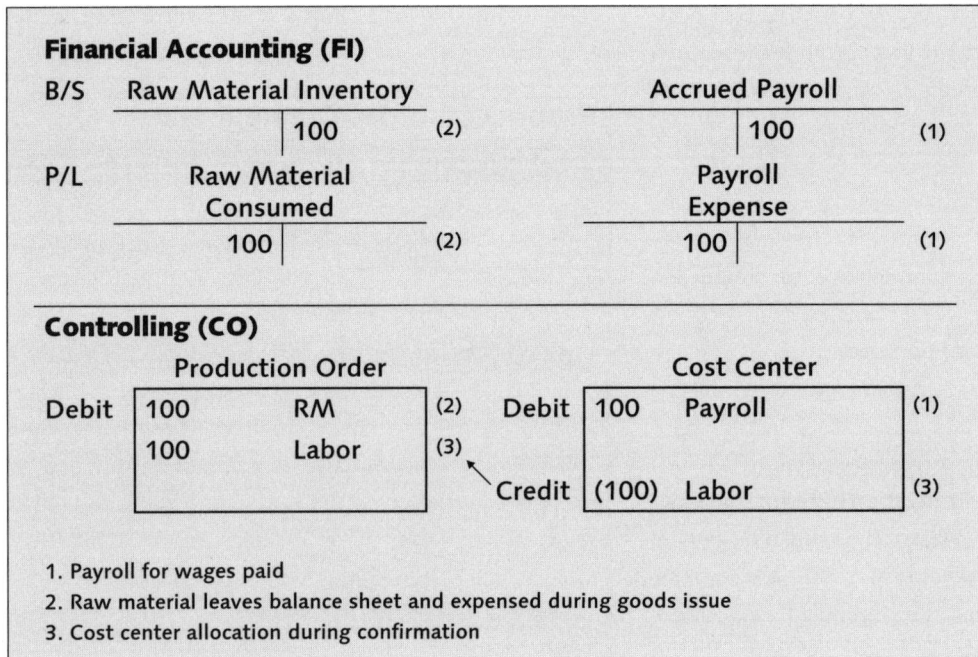

Figure 3.2 Production Cost Center Allocation During Confirmation

Overhead calculation allocates overhead costs across products from cost centers in a similar way. Overhead costs are distributed at the end of the month during overhead calculation, as we will discuss in detail in Chapter 4.

Now that I've explained how product cost collectors are debited with primary and secondary costs, in the following section I'll describe how primary and secondary credits occur.

3.3 Credits

As finished goods are delivered from a manufacturing order into inventory, an inventory balance sheet account is debited, and a profit and loss production output account is credited. Since there is a primary cost element corresponding to the production output account, a controlling cost object is also credited. The finished goods are delivered from a production order, so the system automatically chooses the production order or product cost collector to receive the primary credit. The credit value is calculated by multiplying the standard price by the finished goods quantity delivered to inventory. Figure 3.3 shows an example of a production order cost report with

primary and secondary debits, and a primary credit for delivery to inventory.

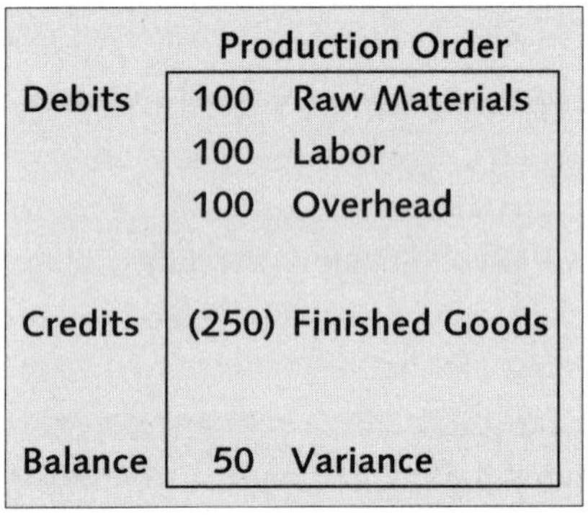

Figure 3.3 Production Order Delivery Credits

Total variance is the order **Balance**, or the difference between total **Debits** and **Credits**. Variance calculation at period-end divides the variance into categories, based on the source of the variance. This assists in determining corrective action during variance analysis.

At period-end, the production order receives a secondary credit equal to the variance during settlement, resulting in a zero balance. This results in total product cost collector and manufacturing order costs posting to financial accounting and profitability analysis.

Now that I've presented an overview of actual cost postings, let's examine transactions that result in these postings. I'll create a production order, carry out activity confirmations, and then analyze the postings.

3.4 Post Actual Costs

The first step in posting actual costs is to create and release a production order. We'll then carry out a confirmation, which is when actual postings occur.

Create Production Order

You create a production order with transaction CO01 or via menu path: **Logistics • Production • Production Control • Order • Create • With Material**. A selection screen is displayed, as shown in Figure 3.4.

Production Order Create: Initial Screen

Material	10000
Production plant	0021	Production
Planning plant	
Order type	PP01
Order	

Figure 3.4 Create Production Order

Production orders are usually created based on a material, which is also linked to BOMs and routings for assemblies. All relevant linked information is copied to the production order as you create it with the following steps:

1. Complete the **Material**, **Production plant**, and **Order type** fields
2. Press Enter to display the screen shown in Figure 3.5

Let's look at a basic example of the process of creating a production order, by following these steps:

1. Complete the **Total Qty** and **Finish BasicDates** fields
2. Click on the release (green flag) icon to release the production order
3. Save the production order

During creation, BOM and routing data are copied to the production order. You need to release the production

order before any costs can be posted in relation to the production order.

Production order Create: Header

Order		
Material	10000	Finished Product
Status		

General | Assignment | Goods receipt | Control data

Quantities

Total Qty	1	EA	Scrap portion
Delivered	0.000		ExpectYieldVar

Dates

	BasicDates		Scheduled	
Finish	09/08/2006	00:00		00:00
Start		00:00		00:00
Release				

Scheduling

Type	2 Backwards	Floats
Reduction		Sched
Note	No scheduling note	Floa
		Floa
		Rele
Priority		

Figure 3.5 Create Production Order Header Screen

Confirm Activities

Now that the production order is released, we can carry out an activity confirmation. During activity confirmation, the activity quantity performed is entered in the system. The actual activity quantity is multiplied by the plan activity price to calculate the activity value. The product cost collector is debited, and the production cost center is credited with the calculated value.

It is common practice to generate goods issues automatically during activity confirmation. This is known as backflushing. You can also make Logistics settings to generate automatic goods receipts during activity confirmation. Backflushing and automatic goods receipts are common practice, because less manual entry of inventory transactions is required. Since all components required to make the assembly are listed in the BOM, it's relatively simple to transfer this information to the produc-

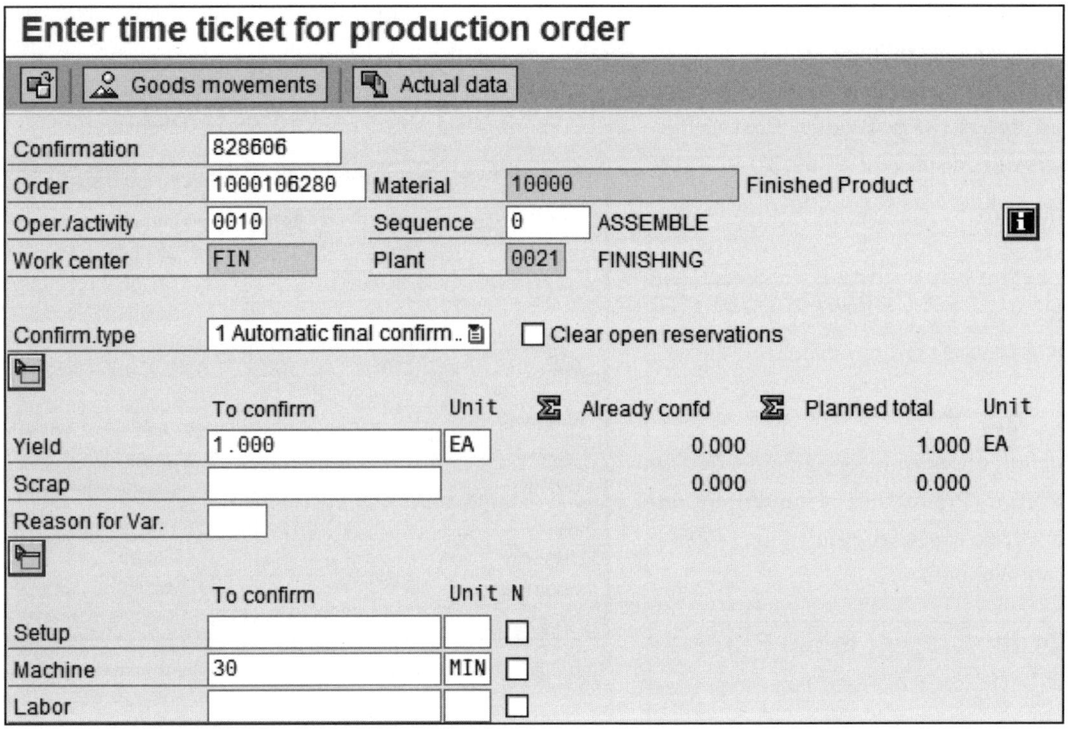

Enter time ticket for production order

| 🖳 | 👤 Goods movements | 🔍 Actual data |

Confirmation	828606			
Order	1000106280	Material	10000	Finished Product
Oper./activity	0010	Sequence	0	ASSEMBLE
Work center	FIN	Plant	0021	FINISHING

Confirm.type   1 Automatic final confirm.. 📋   ☐ Clear open reservations

	To confirm	Unit	Σ Already confd	Σ Planned total	Unit
Yield	1.000	EA	0.000	1.000	EA
Scrap			0.000	0.000	
Reason for Var.					

	To confirm	Unit	N
Setup			☐
Machine	30	MIN	☐
Labor			☐

Figure 3.6 Enter Time Ticket Activity Confirmation

tion order and issue the components automatically from inventory during activity confirmation. It's also relatively easy to carry out automatic goods receipt during final confirmation, since the system already has all the information required.

You confirm activities per operation with transaction CO11N (time ticket) or CO19 (time event), or via menu path: **Logistics • Production • Production Control • Confirmation • Enter • For Operation**. A selection screen is displayed, for a time ticket confirmation in this example, as shown in Figure 3.6.

You carry out a time ticket confirmation per *operation*, so you need to enter the operation number. You also enter the operation yield, if any. If this is the final operation and automatic goods receipt is activated, a goods receipt will occur while saving the confirmation, based on the yield quantity. Activity quantities are entered in the relevant activity field at the bottom of the screen. To complete the activity confirmation, carry out the following steps, as seen in Figure 3.6:

1. Complete the **Order** and **Oper./activity** fields
2. Complete **Yield** and **Machine** fields (in this example)
3. Save the confirmation

After you enter your data, press Enter before saving to default expected activity and component quantities into the relevant fields. If you manually change the default quantities, you are introducing a variance, since the default quantities are the expected quantities.

In the screen shown in Figure 3.6, click on the **Goods movements** button before saving to display plan component goods issues quantities. The components and quantities are copied to the confirmation automatically from the production order.

Now that we've examined how actual costs are posted, you'll need to report on actual costs during a period. During variance analysis, you may need to analyze actual costs posted to a product cost collector because actual costs are greater than expected. In Section 3.5, I'll demonstrate how to report actual cost postings. I also discuss cost reporting in more detail in Chapter 6.

3.5 Report Actual Costs

You can report on actual costs posted during the period by displaying a detailed analysis of the product cost collector for the period with transaction KKBC_PKO or via menu path: **Accounting • Controlling • Product Cost Controlling • Cost Object Controlling • Product Cost by Period • Information System • Reports for Product Cost by Period • Detailed Reports • For Product Cost Collectors**. A selection screen is displayed, as shown in Figure 3.7. Use transaction KKBC_ORD for production/process orders.

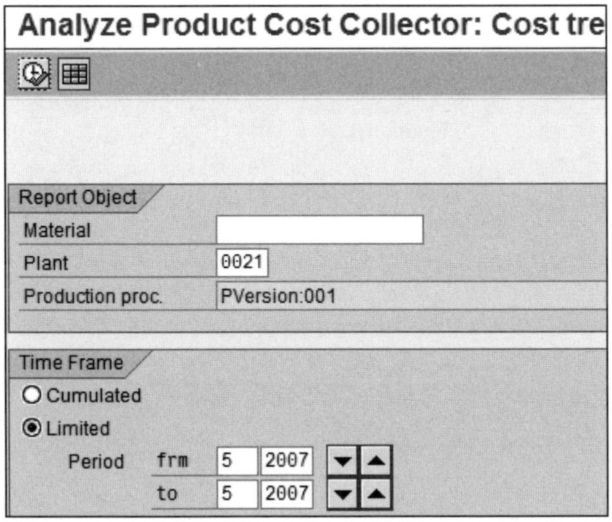

Analyze Product Cost Collector: Cost tre

Report Object	
Material	
Plant	0021
Production proc.	PVersion:001

Time Frame
○ Cumulated
● Limited
Period frm 5 2007 ▼ ▲
to 5 2007 ▼ ▲

Figure 3.7 Analyze Product Cost Collector Selection Screen

Follow these steps to run the product cost collector analysis report:

1. Complete the **Material** and **Plant** fields
2. Select the **Limited Time Frame** radio button
3. Complete the **Period** fields
4. Click on the execute (clock) icon

The screen shown in Figure 3.8 is displayed. You can double-click on any line to display actual posting line item details. Double-clicking on actual **Goods Issues** and **Goods Receipts** displays material documents generated during the goods movements. Double-clicking on actual

activity **Confirmations** displays a list of confirmations. You can continue drilling down (double-clicking) on any line in the screen shown in Figure 3.8 to the original source document generated during the original transaction.

BusTran.	Origin	Σ	Total tgt	Σ	Ttl actual	Σ	Variance
Goods Issues	0021/MB...		12,057.49		11,940.48		117.01-
	0021/MB...		12,022.64		11,904.04		118.60-
Confirmations	1400/RUN		2.36		180.00		177.64
	1610/RUN		745.48		1,243.79		498.31
	1660/RUN		0.00		131.33		131.33
	1680/RUN		286.03		134.58		151.45-
	1700/RUN		0.00		0.00		0.00
	1610/SET		0.00		23.85		23.85
Debit		∎	25,114.00	∎	25,558.07	∎	444.07
Goods Receipt	0021/MB...		25,114.01-		25,114.18-		0.17-
Delivery		∎	25,114.01-	∎	25,114.18-	∎	0.17-
Settlement			0.00		443.89-		443.89-
Settlement		∎	0.00	∎	443.89-	∎	443.89-
		∎ ∎	0.01-	∎ ∎	0.00	∎ ∎	0.01

Figure 3.8 Analyze Product Cost Collector Results Screen

3.6 Summary

In this chapter, I discussed the relationship between postings in Controlling and Financial Accounting and how postings to general ledger expense accounts result in parallel postings to cost centers, product cost collectors, or manufacturing orders in Controlling. I also discussed how activity confirmations result in secondary postings within Controlling, with no effect on general ledger accounts. I demonstrated a production order activity confirmation and ran a report to display the actual postings.

In previous chapters, we carried out initial planning and created cost estimates. Now that actual cost postings are created, we are ready to analyze variance postings by comparing actual and target costs in Chapter 4.

4 Period-End Processing

We prepared for variance analysis by doing the initial planning (explained in Chapter 1), creating cost estimates (explained in Chapter 2), and posting actual costs (explained in Chapter 3). We are now ready to calculate and analyze variances during period-end processing. In this chapter I'll cover in detail the different types of variance calculations, configuration, categories, period-end processing, cost center variances, purchase price variances, and material ledger. In Chapter 5 we'll analyze scrap variance in detail, and in Chapter 6 we'll look at standard reporting.

4.1 Types of Variance Calculation

The three common types of variance calculation are as follows:

▶ Total Variance
▶ Production Variance
▶ Planning Variance

First, let's gain an overview of each type of variance, which will be discussed in the following subsections.

Total Variance

Total variance is the difference between actual cost debited to the order and credits from deliveries to inventory. You calculate total variance with target cost version 0, which determines the basis for calculation of target costs. Target costs are the expected costs when a quantity is delivered to inventory. Total variance is the only variance relevant to settlement. The difference between debits and credits is settled to Financial Accounting, Profit Center Accounting, and Profitability Analysis.

Case Scenario

A product cost collector has a balance of $100 at period-end, and during variance analysis, with target cost version 0, $40 is assigned to input price variance, and $60 is assigned to lot size variance. During settlement, $100 is settled to Financial Accounting and Profit Center Accounting, while $40 is settled to an input price variance value field, and $60 is settled to a lot size variance value field in Profitability Analysis. You can report on the calculations and postings with standard reports, as described in Chapter 6.

Production Variance

Production variance is the difference between net actual costs debited to the order and target costs based on the preliminary cost estimate and quantity delivered to inventory. You calculate production variances with target cost version 1. Production variances are for information only and are not relevant for settlement.

Case Scenario

A product cost collector has a balance of $100 at period-end, and during variance analysis, with target cost version 1, $30 is assigned to input price variance, and $50 is assigned to lot size variance. During settlement, target cost version 1 calculations are not relevant. You can report on the calculations with standard reports, as described in Chapter 6.

Planning Variance

Planning variance is the difference between costs on the preliminary cost estimate for the order and target costs based on the standard cost estimate and planned order quantity. You calculate planning variances with target cost version 2. Planning variances are for information only and are not relevant for settlement.

Now that we've looked at the different types of variance calculations, let's examine the configuration required for variance analysis to help in understanding the calculations, which occur during variance analysis.

4.2 Variance Configuration

Variance configuration for Product Cost by Period and Product Cost by Order are similar. Let's look at variance configuration for Product Cost by Period, and I'll highlight the differences along the way.

Define Variance Keys

You define variance keys with transaction OKV1 or via menu path: **IMG • Controlling • Product Cost Controlling • Cost Object Controlling • Product Cost by Period • Period-End Closing • Variance Calculation • Variance Calculation for Product Cost Collectors • Define Variance Keys**. The screen shown in Figure 4.1 is displayed.

Figure 4.1 Define Variance Keys

The overview screen displays a list of available variance keys. Double-click on a variance key in the **Variance Key** column to display the details screen shown in Figure 4.2.

Select the **Scrap** indicator to ensure the value of scrap is calculated and subtracted from total variances during variance calculation. Any difference between plan and actual scrap is shown as scrap variance. If planned scrap

equals actual scrap, there is no scrap variance. Target costs for the valuation of scrap are calculated according to the valuation variant for work in process and scrap. If a valuation variant for work in process (WIP) and scrap is not defined, target costs are valuated on the basis of the standard cost estimate.

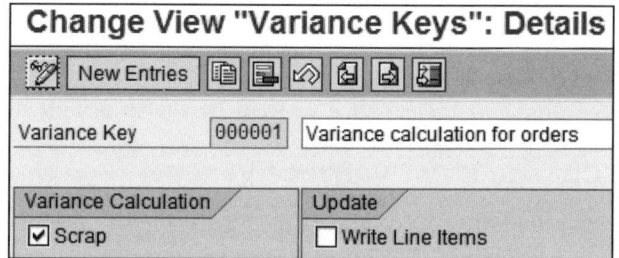

Figure 4.2 Edit Variance Keys

Select the **Write Line Items** indicator shown in Figure 4.2 to ensure a document is created when variances or target costs are calculated. The line items document records when the target costs or variances were calculated and who created them. It also displays which target costs or variances were changed. The **Write Line Items** indicator is not selected by default, since this level of detail is not generally needed and it increases system load requirements.

Define Default Variance Keys for Plants

You define default variance keys per plant with transaction OKVW or via menu path: **IMG • Controlling • Product Cost Controlling • Cost Object Controlling • Product Cost by Period • Period-End Closing • Variance Calculation • Variance Calculation for Product Cost Collectors • Define Default Variance Keys for Plants**. The screen shown in Figure 4.3 is displayed.

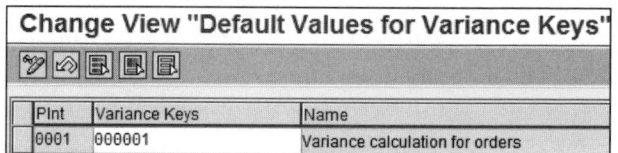

Figure 4.3 Default Variance Keys per Plant

When a material master is created, a default variance key is proposed for the Costing 1 view field, based on the **Variance Keys** entry in Figure 4.3. When a manufacturing order or product cost collector is created, a default variance key is proposed based on the variance key entered in the material master Costing 1 view.

Define Variance Variants

You define variance variants with transaction OKVG or via menu path: **IMG • Controlling • Product Cost Controlling • Cost Object Controlling • Product Cost by Period • Period-End Closing • Variance Calculation • Variance Calculation for Product Cost Collectors • Define Variance Variants**. The screen shown in Figure 4.4 is displayed.

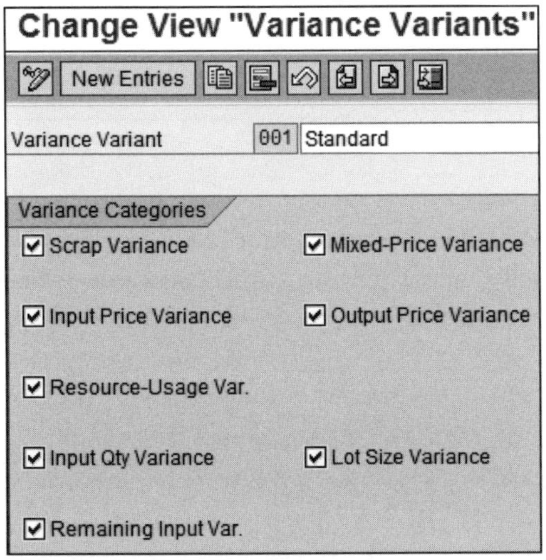

Figure 4.4 Define Variance Variants

Variance variants determine which variance categories are calculated. Variances are calculated for all variance categories that are selected in this view. If a variance category is not selected, variances of that category are assigned to remaining variances. Scrap variances are the only exception to this rule. If **Scrap Variance** is not selected, these variances enter all other variances on the input side.

You specify whether scrap variances are *calculated* by selecting the **Scrap** indicator, as discussed earlier in Section 4.2. You control whether scrap variances are *displayed* by selecting the **Scrap Variance** indicator in the variance variant. You can assign different variance variants to each target cost version. As long as you have specified that scrap variances are to be calculated in the variance key, you could, e.g., use a variance variant with the **Scrap Variance** indicator selected for target cost version 0 and deselected for target cost version 3. This would allow you one view of variances in target cost version 0 with scrap displayed separately, and another view of variances in target cost version 3 without scrap variances displayed separately.

Define Valuation Variant for Scrap and Work in Process (Target Costs)

The valuation variant allows a choice of cost estimates to valuate scrap and work in process (WIP). Prior to SAP R/3 Release 4.5, you could use only the standard cost estimate. If the structure of a routing was changed after a costing run, WIP could not be valuated, resulting in an error message. The system then posted all product cost collector costs as variances.

You can eliminate the error message only by creating and releasing another standard cost estimate. Since releasing a standard cost estimate can change inventory valuation, many companies prefer to only release standard cost estimates during main costing runs in a controlled and supervised environment. Costing runs are explained in detail in Chapter 2. WIP at target eliminates the need to create and release new standard cost estimates, since valuation is based on the preliminary cost estimate, which does not affect inventory valuation.

WIP at target allows the product cost collector preliminary cost estimate to valuate work in process, even if the routing structure is changed. If the valuation variant for scrap and WIP is not defined, scrap and WIP valuation are based on the current standard cost estimate.

You define the valuation variant for WIP and scrap (target costs) via menu path: **IMG • Controlling • Product Cost Controlling • Cost Object Controlling • Product Cost by Period • Period-End Closing • Variance Calculation • Variance Calculation for Product Cost Collectors • Define Valuation Variant for WIP and Scrap (Target Costs)**. The screen shown in Figure 4.5 is displayed.

WIP at target is used by product cost collectors in repetitive manufacturing. Repetitive manufacturing eliminates the need for production or process orders in manufacturing environments with production lines and long production runs. It reduces the work involved in production control and simplifies confirmations and goods receipt postings.

Production orders can also be assigned to product cost collectors starting with SAP R/3 Release 4.5. Assignment to a product cost collector occurs automatically when a

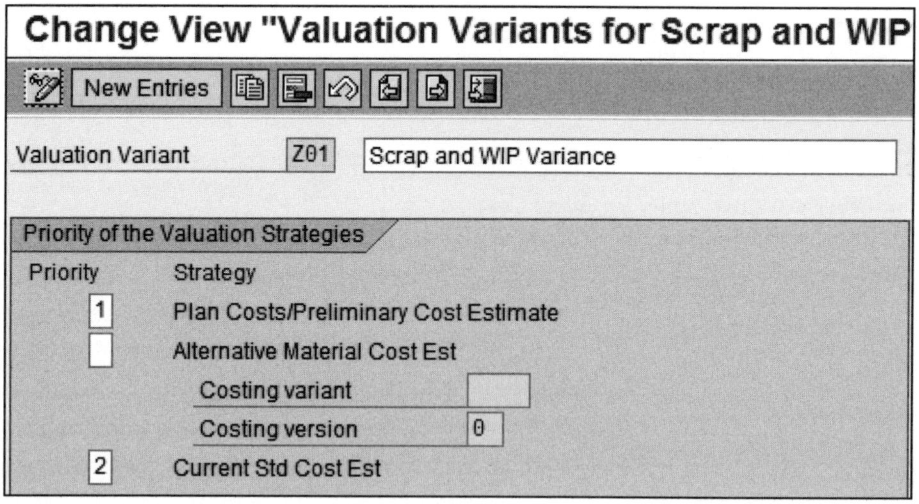

Figure 4.5 Define Valuation Variant for Scrap and WIP

production order is created in this scenario. At period-end, target costs (plan costs adjusted for confirmed yield not yet delivered to inventory) are temporarily moved from product cost collectors to WIP financial accounts. Variance is also calculated and posted at the same time.

> **Note**
> In Product Cost by Order, WIP and scrap are valuated at actual, so there is no need to calculate WIP and scrap. The valuation variant for WIP and scrap does not apply in that environment.

Define Target Cost Versions

You define target cost versions with transaction OKV6 or via menu path: **IMG • Controlling • Product Cost Controlling • Cost Object Controlling • Product Cost by Period • Period-End Closing • Variance Calculation • Variance Calculation for Product Cost Collectors • Define Target Cost Versions**. An overview screen is displayed, as shown in Figure 4.6.

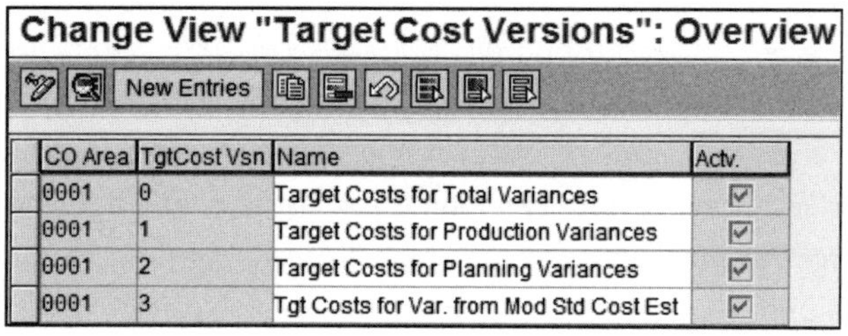

CO Area	TgtCost Vsn	Name	Actv.
0001	0	Target Costs for Total Variances	☑
0001	1	Target Costs for Production Variances	☑
0001	2	Target Costs for Planning Variances	☑
0001	3	Tgt Costs for Var. from Mod Std Cost Est	☑

Figure 4.6 Define Target Cost Versions

The overview screen presents a list of all available target cost versions. Double-click on target cost version **0** to display the details screen shown in Figure 4.7.

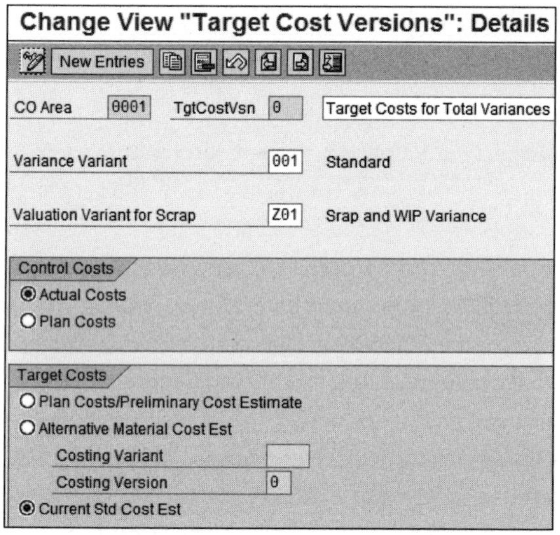

Figure 4.7 Target Cost Version 0 Details Screen

Control Costs are based on **Actual Costs**, or in other words, actual debits. **Target Costs** are based on the **Current Std Cost Est** (current standard cost estimate), or in other words, actual credits.

Target cost version 0 calculates *total variance* and is used to explain the difference between actual debits and credits on an order. It is the only target cost version that can be settled to Financial Accounting, Profit Center Accounting, and Profitability Analysis.

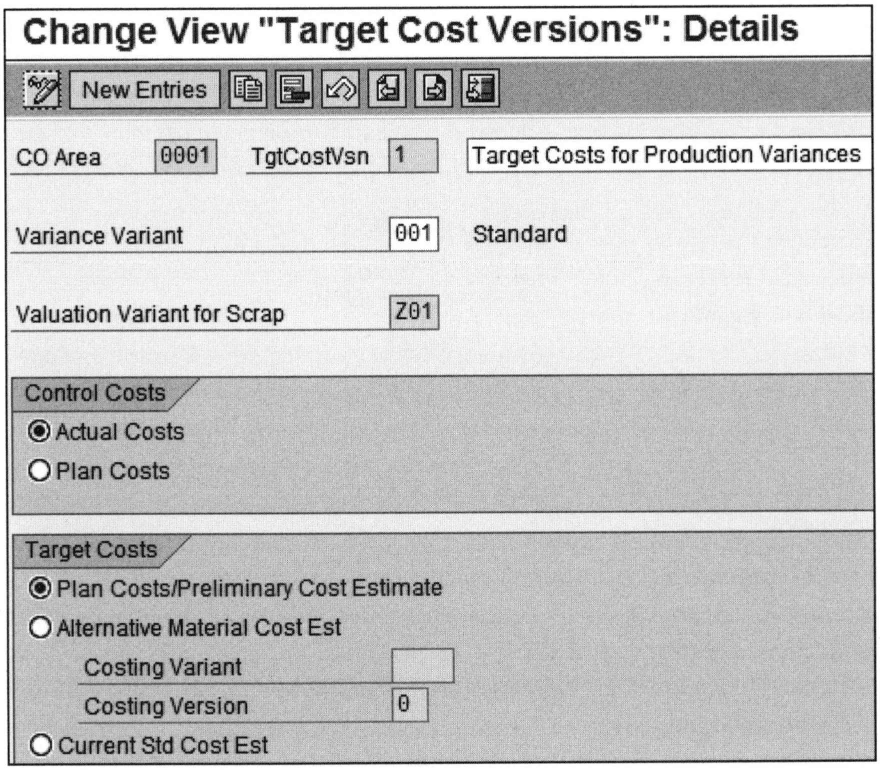

Change View "Target Cost Versions": Details

New Entries

CO Area	0001	TgtCostVsn 1	Target Costs for Production Variances

| Variance Variant | 001 | Standard |

| Valuation Variant for Scrap | Z01 |

Control Costs
- ● Actual Costs
- ○ Plan Costs

Target Costs
- ● Plan Costs/Preliminary Cost Estimate
- ○ Alternative Material Cost Est
  - Costing Variant
  - Costing Version   0
- ○ Current Std Cost Est

Figure 4.8 Target Cost Version 1 Details Screen

You can specify a **Valuation Variant for Scrap** (and WIP) with target cost version 0. This allows you to control which cost estimate is used to valuate scrap, as discussed in Section 4.2. The valuation variant for scrap is not changeable in other target cost versions.

Now that I've explained target cost version 0 configuration, let's examine other target cost versions. Double-click on target cost version **1** in the screen shown in Figure 4.6 to display the details screen shown in Figure 4.8.

Target cost version 1 calculates *production variance*, which is the difference between net **Actual Costs** and **Target Costs** based on the **Preliminary Cost Estimate**. This allows you to exclude variances that occurred because a different quantity structure was used during production compared to the standard cost estimate quantity structure.

While this target cost version is for information only and cannot be settled, it is useful for analyzing production performance and efficiency.

Next, double-click on target cost version **2** in the screen shown in Figure 4.6 to display the details screen shown in Figure 4.9.

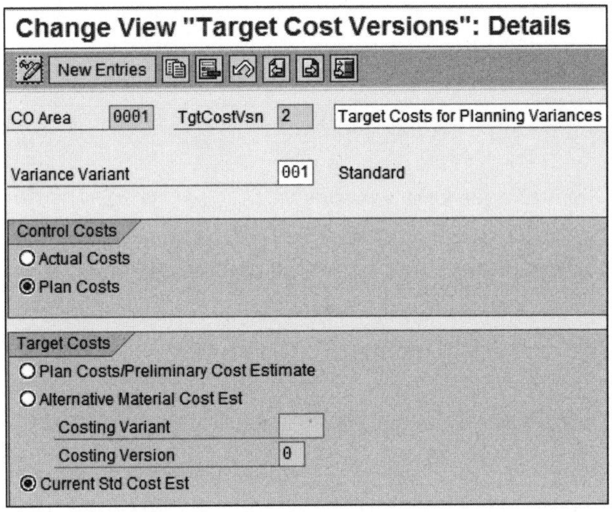

Change View "Target Cost Versions": Details

New Entries

CO Area	0001	TgtCostVsn 2	Target Costs for Planning Variances

| Variance Variant | 001 | Standard |

Control Costs
- ○ Actual Costs
- ● Plan Costs

Target Costs
- ○ Plan Costs/Preliminary Cost Estimate
- ○ Alternative Material Cost Est
  - Costing Variant
  - Costing Version   0
- ● Current Std Cost Est

Figure 4.9 Target Cost Version 2 Details Screen

Target cost version 2 calculates *planning variance*, which is the difference between **Plan Costs** based on the preliminary cost estimate of a manufacturing order and **Target Costs** based on the **Current Std Cost Est** (current standard cost estimate).

You can use target cost version 2 to decide whether to manufacture an order with a particular quantity structure. While this target cost version is for information only and cannot be settled, it is useful for analyzing production planning performance and efficiency.

The system does not allow calculation of a planning variance between a current standard cost estimate and a preliminary cost estimate for product cost collectors. Therefore, you cannot calculate variances with target cost version 2 for product cost collectors.

Next, double-click on target cost version **3** in the screen shown in Figure 4.6 to display the details screen shown in Figure 4.10.

Target cost version 3 calculates *production variance of the period*, which is the difference between net **Actual Costs** and **Target Costs** based on an **Alternative Material Cost Est** (alternative material cost estimate), which is based on costing variant **PPC2** in the example in shown in Figure 4.10.

You can use target cost version **3** to calculate production variances on the basis of monthly planning if a modified standard cost estimate is created every month. Target cost version 3 can also be used for the calculation of equivalences for the distribution of actual costs in cost object hierarchies. This target cost version is for information only and cannot be settled.

So far in this chapter we've analyzed types of variance calculation and configuration. Next we'll discuss variance categories and then follow a typical period-end processing scenario.

4.3 Variance Categories

During variance calculation, the order balance is divided into categories on the input and output sides. Variance categories provide reasons for the cause of the variance, which you can use when deciding what corrective action to take. There are no financial postings during variance calculation, and it can be run as often as necessary to control production processes. The frequency can be daily if variances are high and many corrective actions are necessary.

Continual improvements in master data and user knowledge and skills through frequent variance analysis usually results in reduced variances over time. First I'll discuss input variance categories, and then I'll discuss output variance categories. Scrap variances are discussed in detail in Chapter 5.

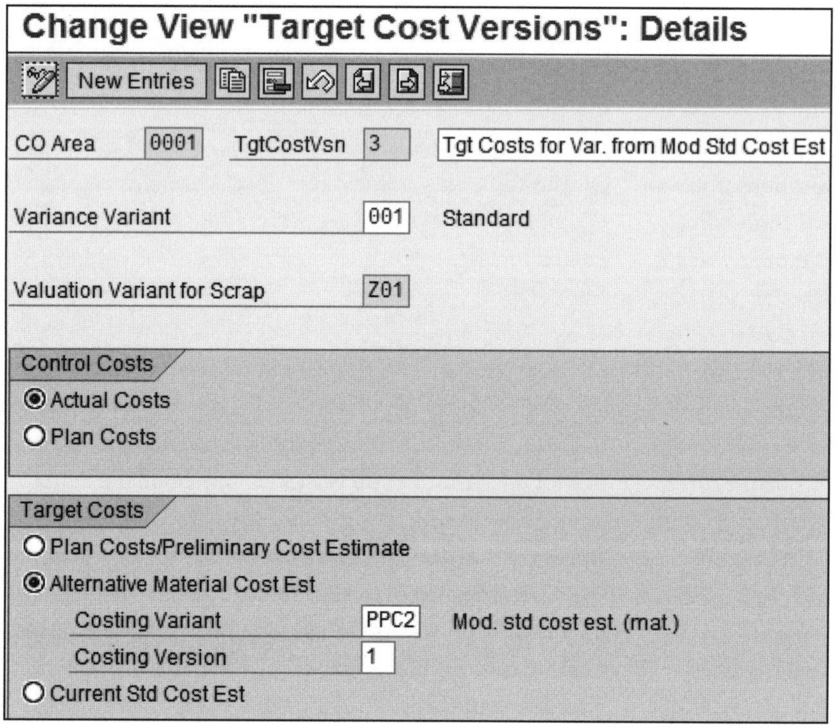

Figure 4.10 Target Cost Version 3 Details Screen

Input Variances

Variances on the input side are based on goods issues, internal activity allocations, overhead allocation, and general ledger account postings. Input variances are divided into the following categories during variance calculation, according to their source.

Input Price Variance

Input price variance occurs as a result of component price changes after the higher-level assembly cost estimate is released. This occurs in one of the two following ways:

▶ If the component valuation is based on standard price control, a standard cost estimate for the component could be released after the cost estimate for the assembly is released.

▶ If the component valuation is based on moving average price control, a goods receipt of the component could change the component price after the cost estimate for the assembly is released.

Case Scenario

A component is valued at $10 during the main costing run. Its price subsequently changes, and during goods issue to a production order it is valued at $11. Variance analysis will report an input price variance of $1.

Resource-Usage Variance

Resource-usage variance occurs as a result of substituting components. This could occur if a component is not available and another component with a different material number is used instead. The costs for both components are reported as resource-usage variances.

Case Scenario

The plan is to issue component **A**, valued at $10, to a production order. However, component **B**, valued at $15, is issued instead. The resource-usage variance is -$10 due to component **A** and $15 due to component **B**, resulting in a net resource-usage variance of $5.

Input Quantity Variance

Input quantity variance occurs as a result of a difference between plan and actual quantities of materials and activities consumed.

Case Scenario

An activity time of 10 minutes was planned and 12 minutes confirmed. If the activity price is $5 per minute, the result is an input quantity variance of $10.

Input quantity variance can also represent component scrap variance, as discussed in detail in Chapter 5.

Remaining Input Variance

Remaining input variance occurs when input variances cannot be assigned to any other variance category.

Case Scenario

A component is valued at $100, and associated material overhead is valued at $10 (10% of $100), during the main costing run. The component price subsequently changes, and during goods issue to a production order it is valued at $110. During period-end overhead calculation, actual overhead is posted as $11 (10% of $110). Variance analysis will report an input price variance of $10 due to the component price change and a remaining input variance of $1 due to the overhead change.

Output Variances

Variances on the output side result from too little or too much of planned order quantity being delivered, or because the delivered quantity was valuated differently. Output variances are broken down into the categories described in the following subsections during variance calculation.

Mixed-Price Variance

Mixed-price variance occurs when inventory is valuated using a mixed cost estimate for the material. If you want to perform mixed costing, create a procurement alternative for each production version and then define a mixing ratio. The mixed cost estimate calculates a mixed price. This price can be written to the material master as the standard price. The target credit is based on the confirmed quantity times the standard cost of the procurement alternative. The actual cost is based on the confirmed quantity times the standard price, where the standard price corresponds to the mixed price.

The mixed price variance is caused by a difference between target and actual costs. If you don't select the **Mixed-Price Variance** indicator in the variance variant, as discussed in Section 4.2, mixed-price variances are shown as output price variances.

Output Price Variance

Output price variance can occur in three situations. First, it occurs if the standard price is changed after delivery to inventory and before variance calculation.

Second, it occurs if the material is valuated at moving average price and it is not delivered to inventory at standard price during target value calculation. You control how the target value is calculated for delivery to stock when the price control indicator is set to **V** (moving average price) in customizing via menu path: **IMG • Controlling • Product Cost Controlling • Cost Object Controlling • Product Cost by Period • Simultaneous Costing • Define Goods Received Valuation for Order Delivery**.

Third, it can occur if you don't select the **Mixed-Price Variance** indicator in the variance variant, as discussed in Section 4.2.

Lot Size Variance

Lot size variance occurs if a manufacturing order lot size is different from the standard cost estimate costing lot size. Setup time does not usually change with lot size, so a different lot size will either increase or decrease the unit cost. Whenever a portion of manufacturing cost does not change with output quantity, such as setup or tear-down time, you can have lot size variance.

Note

Setup time is time needed to prepare equipment and machinery for production of assemblies, and is generally the same regardless of the quantity produced. Setup time allocated over a smaller production quantity increases the unit cost. The same concept applies to externally procured items, since vendors usually quote higher prices for smaller quantities.

Tear-down time is the time needed to disassemble equipment and machinery following production of assemblies, and it is generally the same regardless of quantity produced.

Like setup time, tear-down time allocated over a smaller production quantity increases the unit cost.

Remaining Variance

Remaining variance occurs if variances cannot be assigned to any other variance category. Rounding differences or overhead applied to costs that do not vary with lot size are reported as remaining variances.

Remaining variance is also reported when target costs cannot be calculated, such as when a standard cost estimate does not exist, or if a goods receipt for the order has not taken place. All variance is also reported as remaining variance when no variance categories have been selected in the variance variant. Scrap variances are an exception to this rule. If the **Scrap Variance** indicator is not selected in the variance variant, scrap variances can be reported against any other relevant variance on the input side.

Now that we've examined types of variance calculations, configuration, and variance categories, let's follow a typical period-end processing scenario.

4.4 Period-End

In this section I'll consider the period-end processes most relevant to variance analysis, which are: overhead, work in process, variance calculation, and settlement. If you use other period-end processes, you can apply the same principles you learn in this section to those processes as well.

Overhead

During a fiscal period, actual primary (external) costs, such as payroll and electricity, are debited to cost centers. Some of these costs may be included as part of the planned activity rate and allocated to products from cost centers during activity confirmations. Another commonly used method to allocate overhead costs to products is period-end overhead calculation. Overhead calculation offers flexible allocation across different products through costing sheet configuration, as discussed in Chapter 2. Allocating overhead with costing sheets requires an additional period-end activity, although this is a straightforward procedure.

You run period-end overhead calculation with transactions CO42 (individual) and CO43 (collective), or via menu path: **Accounting • Controlling • Product Cost Controlling • Cost Object Controlling • Product Cost by Period • Period-End Closing • Single Functions: Product Cost Collector • Overhead**. A selection screen is displayed, as shown in Figure 4.11.

> **Note**
> You carry out variance analysis for production and process orders with transactions KGI2 (individual) and CO43 (collective).

Actual Overhead Calculation: Production

Plant   0021   Production

☐ With Production Orders
☐ With Process Orders
☑ With Product Cost Collectors
☐ With QM Orders

☐ With Orders for Projects/Networks
☐ With Orders for Cost Objects

Parameters

| Period | 5 |
| Fiscal Year | 2007 |

Processing Options
☐ Background Processing
☐ Test Run
☑ Detail Lists
☐ Dialog display

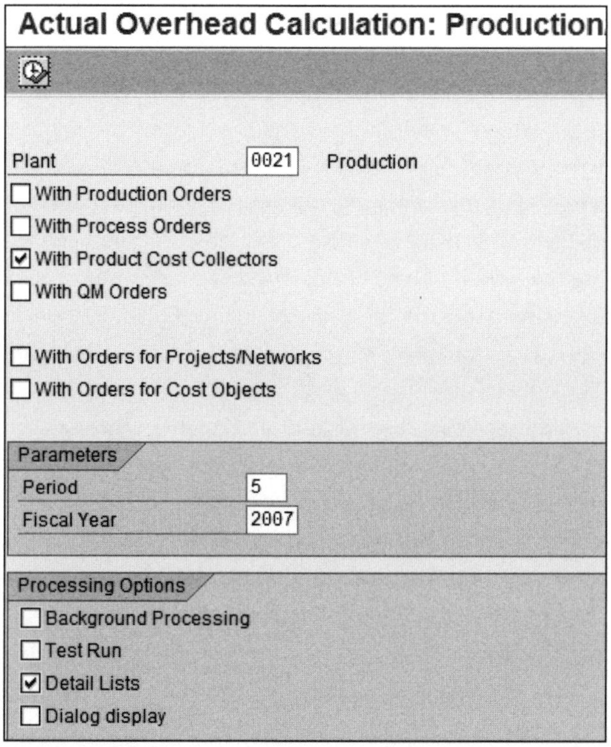

Figure 4.11 Actual Overhead Calculation Selection Screen

In this example, we will calculate overhead only for product cost collectors by selecting the **With Product Cost Collectors** indicator, as shown in Figure 4.11. You can include other objects in the calculation, without running another transaction, by selecting the relevant indicator shown in Figure 4.11.

If you select the **Dialog display** indicator, you are presented with more detailed information on how overhead was calculated after the transaction is run. This level of detail is normally only required if you are troubleshooting.

Complete the selection screen using the settings shown in Figure 4.11 as an example, and click on the execute (clock) icon to display the screen shown in Figure 4.12.

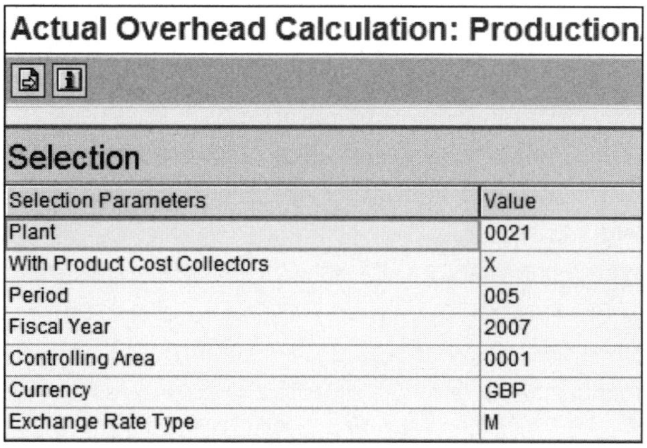

Actual Overhead Calculation: Production

Selection

Selection Parameters	Value
Plant	0021
With Product Cost Collectors	X
Period	005
Fiscal Year	2007
Controlling Area	0001
Currency	GBP
Exchange Rate Type	M

Figure 4.12 Actual Overhead Calculation Basic List

This screen provides you with basic information on the parameters you entered in the previous selection screen, such as **Period** and **Fiscal Year**. Click on the next list level (right pointing arrow) icon to proceed to a detailed list of overhead calculated, as shown in Figure 4.13.

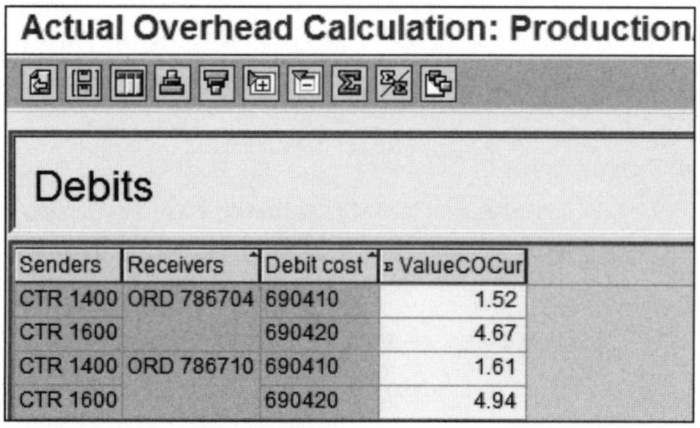

Actual Overhead Calculation: Production

Debits

Senders	Receivers	Debit cost	∑ ValueCOCur
CTR 1400	ORD 786704	690410	1.52
CTR 1600		690420	4.67
CTR 1400	ORD 786710	690410	1.61
CTR 1600		690420	4.94

Figure 4.13 Actual Overhead Calculation Details

In the screen shown in Figure 4.13, the **Senders** column shows the cost center credited, e.g., **CTR 1400** (cost center 1400), while the **Receivers** column shows the product cost collector or manufacturing order debited, e.g., **ORD 786704** (order 786704). The **Debit cost** column shows the secondary cost element identifying the type of overhead cost, e.g., **690410** (labor) or **690420** (material) in Figure 4.13. These cost elements also appear on cost center and product cost collector reports, which are discussed further in Chapter 6.

The **ValueCOCur** column shows the value of overhead allocated in controlling area currency. By following menu path: **Settings • Layout • Current** you can display additional columns, such as overhead value in object (company code) currency as well as controlling area currency.

Now that we've calculated overhead, the next period-end processing step is to calculate work in process. I'll discuss this process in detail in the next section.

Work in Process

Production costs associated with manufacturing orders are temporarily tracked on the profit and loss financial statement. Components removed from inventory to a manufacturing order are expensed and removed from the financial balance sheet. Production costs are returned to the balance sheet when assemblies and finished goods are delivered to inventory from the manufacturing order.

Work in process (WIP) represents production costs of incomplete assemblies at period-end. In order for balance sheet accounts to accurately reflect company assets at period-end, WIP costs are moved temporarily to WIP balance sheet and profit and loss accounts. Work in process postings are canceled during period-end processing following delivery of associated assemblies or finished products to inventory. There are two types of work in process valuations which are:

▶ **Target**
Work in process at target is valuated based on a cost estimate.

▶ **Actual**
Work in process at actual is valuated based on actual debits to a manufacturing order or product cost collector.

I'll now discuss WIP calculation for product cost collectors in detail. I'll then discuss only the differences for WIP calculation for manufacturing orders, since there are many similarities between the two processes.

Product Cost by Period

Work in process is valuated at target cost for Product Cost by Period. Operation quantities confirmed for manufacturing orders are valuated at the target cost of the operation, minus scrap and goods receipt quantities. Work in process at target value is not based on actual costs. Instead, it is based on what WIP value should be according to a cost estimate. You specify which cost estimate is used to calculate target costs in the valuation variant for scrap and WIP, as discussed in Section 4.2. For product cost collectors, SAP recommends calculating target costs based on the product cost collector preliminary cost estimate.

One of the main advantages of WIP at target is that variance and WIP can be posted at the same time. If production orders remain open for multiple periods, variance reconciliation is usually easier using WIP at target.

Say the price of natural gas used in drying kilns increases unexpectedly one month. If the production order is finally delivered three months later, the production order variances in Controlling (CO) are posted later than when the primary expenses occurred in Financial Accounting (FI). This makes reconciliation between CO and FI difficult during any one period. With product cost collectors, WIP and variance are posted together during the period in which they occur. Variance is posted in the same period as the primary financial postings, which caused the variance, simplifying reconciliation between CO and FI.

Another advantage of WIP at target is that variance analysis is based on material or product, usually a key reporting requirement. Variance comparison of different products allows analysis of which product is made more efficiently, improving product profitability. This analysis is usually more beneficial than analyzing variance per production order.

You run period-end work in process calculation with transactions KKAS (individual) and KKAO (collective), or via menu path: **Accounting • Controlling • Product Cost Controlling • Cost Object Controlling • Product Cost by Period • Period-End Closing • Single Functions: Product Cost Collector • Work in Process**. A selection screen is displayed, as shown in Figure 4.14.

> **Note**
> You carry out variance analysis for production and process orders with transactions KKAX (individual) and KKAO (collective).

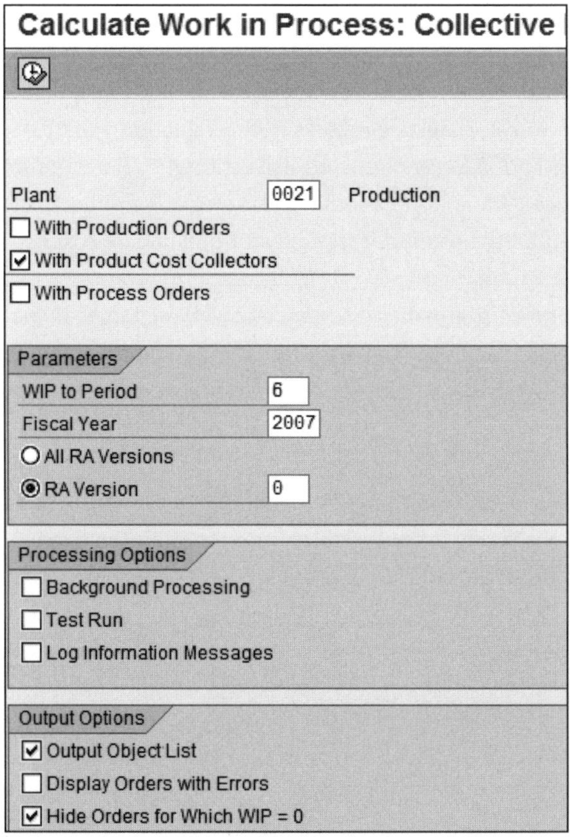

Calculate Work in Process: Collective

Plant: 0021 Production
- [ ] With Production Orders
- [x] With Product Cost Collectors
- [ ] With Process Orders

Parameters
- WIP to Period: 6
- Fiscal Year: 2007
- ( ) All RA Versions
- (•) RA Version: 0

Processing Options
- [ ] Background Processing
- [ ] Test Run
- [ ] Log Information Messages

Output Options
- [x] Output Object List
- [ ] Display Orders with Errors
- [x] Hide Orders for Which WIP = 0

Figure 4.14 Work in Process Selection Screen

In this example, we will calculate work in process only for product cost collectors by selecting the **With Product Cost Collectors** indicator, as shown in Figure 4.14. You can include other objects in the calculation, without running another transaction, by selecting the relevant indicator in Figure 4.14.

Complete the selection screen using the settings shown in Figure 4.14 as an example and click on the execute icon to display the screen shown in Figure 4.15.

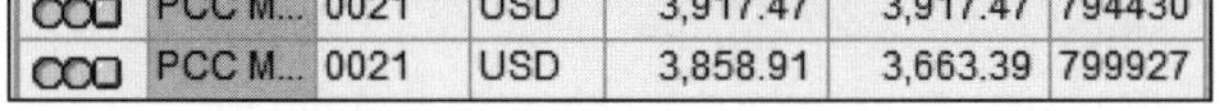

Calculate Work in Process: Object List

Basic List | WIP Explanation

Exce...	Cost o...	Plant	Crcy	Σ WIP (total)	Σ WIP (chg)	Order
⬤⬤⬤	PCC M...	0021	USD	8,825.78	8,825.78	799681
⬤⬤⬤	PCC M...	0021	USD	7,075.37	7,075.37	800146
⬤⬤⬤	PCC M...	0021	USD	7,932.15	4,780.64	786770
⬤⬤⬤	PCC M...	0021	USD	5,266.71	4,116.68	786781
⬤⬤⬤	PCC M...	0021	USD	3,917.47	3,917.47	794430
⬤⬤⬤	PCC M...	0021	USD	3,858.91	3,663.39	799927

Figure 4.15 Calculate Work in Process Results List

You can display messages by clicking on the red triangle icon. You should analyze all messages and take corrective action where necessary. If you identify specific materials with several messages, it is often easier to calculate work in process for the individual materials separately with transaction KKAS, and then analyze messages for the specific materials.

In Figure 4.15, the **WIP (chg)** column is sorted in descending order. This provides visibility to product cost collectors with the largest work in process accumulated during the period of WIP calculation. As a rule of thumb, I recommend analyzing product cost collectors with the six largest positive and negative values of change in WIP during the period. You can also use the same technique on the **WIP (total)** column if necessary.

To analyze WIP calculated for a product cost collector in more detail, click on the corresponding line and then click on the **WIP Explanation** button. The screen shown in Figure 4.16 is displayed.

Numbers shown in the **Activity** column correspond to operations in the routing. Work in process at target is based on quantities confirmed at each operation. The first four rows shown in Figure 4.16 correspond with overhead allocated to the product cost collector due to WIP quantities, and do not correspond to operations.

A quantity in the **Ref. qty** column indicates this is a reference quantity for calculating WIP. If you look to the left of the first quantity of **50** in the **Ref. qty** column, you see a quantity of **50** in the **Yield** column. This indicates there has been a confirmed yield of **50** for a partial assembly from operation 10, which has not yet been consumed in operation 20. Looking further to the left and one row down, in the **WIP (total)** column, you can see the value of the partial assemblies is **62.25**. This corresponds to the value of WIP at target residing on operation 10 during the period. The same process is used to determine WIP at each operation. The WIP value at each operation is added to the corresponding overhead value to determine the total WIP value for the period of **558.81**.

Values in the **GR qty** column in Figure 4.16 correspond to goods receipt quantity of finished assemblies. In the first line of operation 10, you can see there has been a goods receipt quantity of 90 for the finished assembly and a corresponding yield of 90 for operation 10. All subsequent operations show a corresponding first line and

Calculate WIP: Explanation

Activity	Cost Ele...	Name	Origin	Σ WIP (total)	Input qty	Unit	GR qty	Yield	Rel. scrap	Σ	Ref. qty
	690420	Labour Overhead	1600	24.42							
	690410	Quality Overhead	1400	7.97							
	690420	Labour Overhead	1600	119.77							
	690410	Quality Overhead	1400	39.11							
				■ 191.27							
0010						EA	90.000	90.000			
						EA	50.000	50.000			
	690020	Set-Up	1650/SET	8.89	0.250	HR					
	690010	Labour	1650/RUN	53.36	1.5	HR					
						EA		50.000			50.000
0010				■ 62.25		EA				■	50.000
						HR					
0020						EA	90.000	90.000			
						EA	50.000	50.000			
	690020	Set-Up	1650/SET	8.89	0.250	HR					
	690010	Labour	1650/RUN	296.40	8.333	HR					
						EA		50.000			50.000
0020				■ 305.29		EA				■	50.000
						HR					
0022						EA					
				■■ 558.81		EA				■■	100.000
						HR					

Figure 4.16 Calculate Work in Process Explanation Screen

no WIP. As long as the sum of the **Yield** and **Rel. scrap** columns equals the **GR qty** column, there will be no corresponding WIP for that row.

Case Scenario

A common problem during collective WIP at target calculation is that some work in process items re-occur every month, resulting in an ever increasing cumulative total work in process. How can WIP at target keep re-occurring? Say a manufacturing order is commenced with a plan quantity of 20. If 10 partial assemblies are discarded at an operation but not confirmed as scrap, the cost associated with the partial assemblies will remain as work in process until one of the following occurs: either the quantity of 10 is confirmed as scrap at the appropriate operation, or the production order deletion flag is set.

Note

The English spelling of the word labor (labour) is used in Figure 4.16, since a UK based company is used in this example.

A common misunderstanding is that work in process can be canceled by changing the status of underlying manufacturing orders to technically complete (TECO). This status prevents any further processing or costs posting to the product cost collector through the manufacturing order.

However, a status of TECO does not remove existing work in process, which remains associated with the product cost collector. Setting the manufacturing order deletion flag, corresponding with status DLFL, will cancel existing work in process. You can set the deletion flag while viewing a production order in change mode with menu path: **Functions • Deletion flag • Activate**.

52

The deletion flag can be revoked if necessary with menu path: **Functions • Deletion flag • Revoke**.

> **Tip**
>
> No financial postings occur during WIP calculation. You can run the WIP transaction as often as you like, and carry out analysis and fixes progressively during a fiscal period. Financial postings only occur during settlement, which is normally carried out at period-end.

Product Cost by Order

In this section I'll discuss work in process for Product Cost by Order, which means working with manufacturing orders. I'll focus on the differences between work in process calculation for manufacturing orders and product cost collectors.

Work in process is valuated at actual cost in Product Cost by Order. All order debit costs are considered WIP until valuated goods receipt into inventory occurs. At period-end, the actual balance of incomplete manufacturing orders not fully delivered to inventory is determined during WIP calculation.

During settlement, calculated WIP is posted to a WIP balance sheet account and an offsetting profit and loss account. The WIP calculation is based on the manufacturing order status, as seen below:

▸ **REL**

Released: Calculate work in process

▸ **DLV**

Fully Delivered: Cancel work in process

▸ **TECO**

Technically Complete: Cancel work in process

WIP is calculated each period until the status of the order is set to fully delivered or technically complete, and then the entire work in process is canceled and variance is calculated.

Now that we've calculated work in process, let's look at the next period-end process, which is variance calculation.

Variance Calculation

Variance calculation provides information to assist you during analysis of how the order balance occurred. In other words it helps you determine the reason for the difference between order debits and credits. It does this by analyzing causes of the variance and assigning categories, as we discussed in Section 4.3. The following is an overview of the three main types of variance calculation:

▸ **Total Variance Calculation (Target Cost Version 0)**

Based on the difference between actual debits and credits due to valuated goods receipts based on the standard cost estimate. Values assigned to variance categories assist when determining what caused the difference between actual production costs and planned production costs when the standard cost estimate was released.

▸ **Production Variance Calculation (Target Cost Version 1)**

Based on the difference between actual debits and credits based on the preliminary cost estimate. The results of this calculation are not settled to Financial Accounting, however, reports can be run to analyze the results. It allows analysis of production process efficiency, by excluding variances based on different types of manufacturing processes, such as different work centers or BOM alternatives and routings.

▸ **Planning Variance Calculation (Target Cost Version 2)**

Based on the difference between plan debits based on the preliminary cost estimate and credits based on the standard cost estimate. The results of this calculation are not settled to Financial Accounting, however, reports can be run to analyze the results. It allows analysis of variances due to different types of manufacturing processes, such as different work centers or BOM alternatives and routings.

There are differences in variance calculation for product cost collectors and manufacturing orders. Variance is calculated every period-end for product cost collectors, while the timing is dependent on order status for manufacturing orders. Work in process and scrap variances are subtracted from actual costs to determine control costs for product cost collectors. Only scrap variances are subtracted from actual costs to determine control costs for manufacturing orders.

I'll now discuss variance calculation for product cost collectors in detail. Then I'll discuss only the differences for variance calculation for manufacturing orders, since there are many similarities between the two processes.

Product Cost by Period

Variance calculation compares target and control costs. For total variance, target costs are based on the standard cost estimate. Control costs are determined by deducting work in process and scrap variances from actual costs.

Target costs are determined during variance calculation. There are at least seven prerequisites that must be met for target costs to appear in the target column. Let's look at each condition in turn:

► There must be a variance key in the product cost collector in order to calculate target costs. The variance key in the product cost collector defaults from the material master Costing 1 view when the product cost collector is created. To exclude a product cost collector from variance calculation, you can either delete the variance key from the product cost collector or activate the product cost collector deletion flag.

► There must be a goods receipt of the assembly or finished good for at least one of the manufacturing orders associated with the product cost collector during the period of variance analysis. Target costs are calculated on the basis of the quantity delivered to inventory. If there are no deliveries to inventory, target costs cannot be calculated, and an error message is issued.

► There must be a released standard cost estimate valid on the last day of the posting for product cost collectors. For manufacturing orders, the standard cost estimate must be valid at the time of the last delivery. The cost estimate must include an itemization.

► The Material Origin indicator in the material master Costing 1 view must be selected for all cost-critical components. This allows the system to allocate component variances to primary cost elements. If you have already created material master records without the Material Origin indicator selected, you can use report RKHKMAT0 to select the indicator.

► Variance configuration must be carried out, as discussed in Section 4.2 (Configuration).

► The product cost collector must have settlement type periodic (PER) in the settlement rule. This settlement type means that work in process and variance calculated for a period can only be settled in the same period. Settlement type PER also requires that that each period be settled sequentially.

► Variance calculation must be carried out. Target costs are calculated during execution of the variance calculation transaction. To see target costs, you must first carry out variance calculation.

You run period-end variance calculation with transactions KKS6 (individual) and KKS5 (collective), or via menu path: **Accounting • Controlling • Product Cost Controlling • Cost Object Controlling • Product Cost by Period • Period-End Closing • Single Functions: Product Cost Collector • Variances**. A selection screen is displayed, as shown in Figure 4.17.

> **Note**
> You can also carry out variance analysis for production and process orders with transactions KKS2 (individual) and KKS1 (collective).

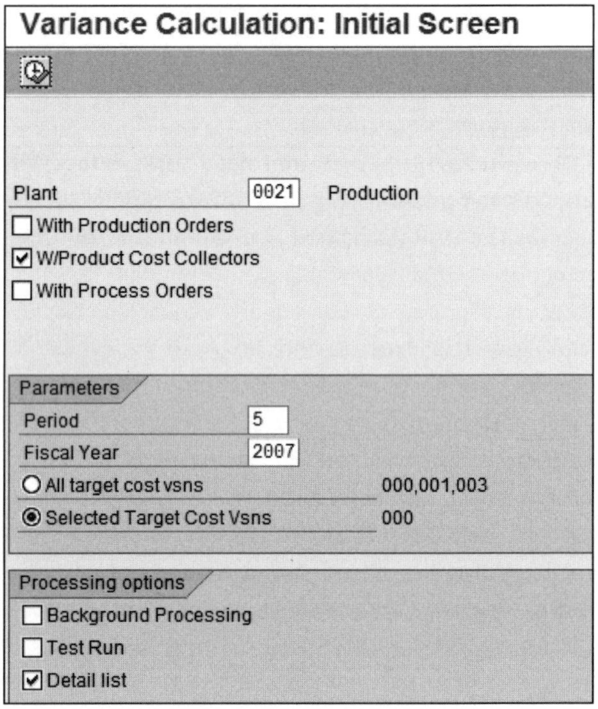

Figure 4.17 Variance Calculation Selection Screen

In this example, we will calculate variance only for product cost collectors by selecting the **W/Product Cost Collectors** indicator, as shown in Figure 4.17. You can include other objects in the calculation, without running another transaction, by selecting the relevant indicator in Figure 4.17.

Variance Calculation: List

| Basic List | Cost Elements | ℹ Scrap | ℹ Variance Categories |

| Period | 5 | Fiscal year | 2007 | Messages | 569 | ☼ | Currency | USD |
| Version | 0 Target Costs for Total Variances (0) | | | | | 10 Company code currency | | |

Plant	CO obj...	Σ Target cst	Σ Act. costs	Σ Act. alloc	Σ	WIP	Σ	Scrap	Σ Variance
0021	PCC M...	7,587.51	23,903.53	7,675.50		558.82		307.04	15,362.17
0021	PCC M...	23.33	8,652.95	0.00		341.88		0.00	8,311.07
0021	PCC M...	3,650.05	5,217.36	3,649.50		3,650.05-		0.00	5,217.91
0021	PCC M...	11,256.06	5,110.73	11,256.00		9,810.20-		0.00	3,664.93
0021	PCC M...	11,256.06	5,014.19	11,256.00		9,810.20-		0.00	3,568.39
0021	PCC M...	42.25	4,612.36	0.00		1,802.30		0.00	2,810.06
0021	PCC M...	2,244.78	6,817.29	2,247.60		1,664.07		128.71	2,776.91

Figure 4.18 Variance Calculation Results Screen

Target cost versions selected in this screen determine whether only total variances (target cost version 0) or all selected variances are calculated. You can adjust the target cost version selection with menu path: **Extras • Set Target Cost Versions**.

Collective processing time can be reduced by deselecting the **Detail list** indicator. Although variances are calculated, you do not see any variance calculation details in the following screens. You can then use summarized reporting (discussed in Chapter 6) to analyze the aggregated data. Orders that caused high variances can be identified by sorting on variance columns or by using exception rules. To find detailed information for an order that caused high variances, recalculate variance for the individual order with the **Test Run** and **Detail List** indicators selected.

Complete the selection screen using the settings in Figure 4.17 as an example and click on the execute icon to display the screen shown in Figure 4.18.

You should analyze all messages and take corrective action where necessary. You can display messages by clicking on the red traffic light icon in Figure 4.18. If you identify specific materials with several messages, it may be easier to calculate variance for the individual materials separately with transaction KKS6 and analyze the messages for the specific materials.

The formula for calculating variance in Figure 4.18 is:

Variance = Actual Costs—Actual Costs Allocated (credits)—WIP—Scrap

In Figure 4.18, the **Variance** column is sorted in descending order. This is indicated by the small red inverted triangle just to the left of the **Variance** column header. Sorting provides visibility to product cost collectors with large variances during the period. Let's follow an example that demonstrates how to analyze the causes of the largest variances. I'll analyze the product cost collector corresponding to the first line in Figure 4.18, since it has the largest unfavorable variance.

To display more details of the product cost collector variance calculation, click on the first row shown in Figure 4.18 and then click on the **Cost Elements** button. The screen shown in Figure 4.19 is displayed. If you don't see variance category columns as shown in Figure 4.19, click on the select layout (grid) icon and choose **Variance Categories** layout.

The sum of input and output variances in the **Variance** column shown in Figure 4.19 is equal to the total variance shown in the **Variance** column of the first row of Figure 4.18. Most of the variance is due to an input quantity variance in the **Qty var.** column of the third row in Figure 4.19. More actual labor time was confirmed than planned in the cost estimate. This could be due to

Cost ...	Cost Elem.	Origin	Σ	Variance	Σ Price Var.	Σ ResU...	Σ	Qty var.	Σ RemInputVa	Σ MxdPrcVar	Σ OutPricVar	Σ OtptQtyVar	Σ LotSizeVar	Σ Rem. var.
500100	Comp Mts - ...	0021/M...		0.24	0.24	0.00		0.00	0.00	0.00	0.00	0.00	0.00	0.00
500100	Comp Mts - ...	0021/P3...		3.98-	0.00	0.00		3.98-	0.00	0.00	0.00	0.00	0.00	0.00
690010	Labour	1650/R...		10,059.09	0.05	0.00		10,059.04	0.00	0.00	0.00	0.00	0.00	0.00
690010	Labour	1660/R...		47.86-	0.00	47.86-		0.00	0.00	0.00	0.00	0.00	0.00	0.00
690020	Set-Up	1650/SET		155.81	0.03	0.00		155.78	0.00	0.00	0.00	0.00	0.00	0.00
690020	Set-Up	1660/SET		16.52-	0.01-	16.51-		0.00	0.00	0.00	0.00	0.00	0.00	0.00
690030	Rework	1650/R...		14.41	0.00	14.41		0.00	0.00	0.00	0.00	0.00	0.00	0.00
690400	Material Over...			0.36-	0.00	0.00		0.00	0.36-	0.00	0.00	0.00	0.00	0.00
690410	Quality Overh...			1,301.63	0.00	0.00		0.00	1,301.63	0.00	0.00	0.00	0.00	0.00
690420	Labour Overh...			3,987.70	0.00	0.00		0.00	3,987.70	0.00	0.00	0.00	0.00	0.00
Debit			■	15,450.16 ■	0.31 ■	49.96- ■		10,210.84 ■	5,288.97 ■	0.00 ■	0.00 ■	0.00 ■	0.00 ■	0.00
500600	Fin Goods - I...	0021/M...		32.68	0.00	0.00		0.00	0.00	0.00	0.08	0.00	0.00	32.60
690020	Set-Up	1650/SET		91.17-	0.00	0.00		0.00	0.00	0.00	0.00	0.00	91.17-	0.00
690020	Set-Up	1660/SET		29.50-	0.00	0.00		0.00	0.00	0.00	0.00	0.00	29.50-	0.00
Delivery			■	87.99- ■	0.00 ■	0.00 ■		0.00 ■	0.00 ■	0.00 ■	0.08 ■	0.00 ■	120.67- ■	32.60

Figure 4.19 Cost Elements Breakdown of Variance Calculation

an incorrect confirmation entry or because it took longer than planned. You can display a more detailed view of variances and target costs by clicking on the **Variances** and **Target Costs** buttons shown in Figure 4.19.

You can analyze input quantity variance further by displaying a detailed analysis of the product cost collector for the period with transaction KKBC_PKO or via menu path: **Accounting • Controlling • Product Cost Controlling • Cost Object Controlling • Product Cost by Period • Information System • Reports for Product Cost by Period • Detailed Reports • For Product Cost Collectors**. A selection screen is displayed, as shown in Figure 4.20.

> **Note**
>
> Use transaction KKBC_ORD for production/process orders.

Analyze Product Cost Collector: Cost trend

Report Object

Material	
Plant	0021
Production proc.	

Time Frame
- ○ Cumulated
- ● Limited
  - Period frm 5 2007
  -        to   5 2007

Figure 4.20 Analyze Product Cost Collector Selection Screen

Run the product cost collector analysis report with the following steps:

1. Complete the **Material** and **Plant** fields
2. Select the **Limited Time Frame** radio button
3. Complete the **Period** fields
4. Click on the execute icon

Next the screen shown in Figure 4.21 is displayed.

BusTran.	Origin	Origin (Text)	Σ Total tgt	Σ Ttl actual
Confirmations	1650/RUN	Sewing / Run Time	4,706.44	15,127.19
	1650/SET	Sewing / Set Time	47.41	218.71
	1650/REW...	Sewing / Rework	0.00	14.41
	1660/RUN	Painting / Run Time	46.02	0.00
	1660/SET	Painting / Set Time	15.34	0.00

Figure 4.21 Analyze Product Cost Collector Results Screen

Double-click on the first row shown in Figure 4.21 to display the line item details of the confirmations, which caused the large input quantity variance in the third row in Figure 4.19. The screen shown in Figure 4.22 is displayed.

Cost Elem.	CElem.name	Σ Val.in RC	Quantity	PUM	Off.acct	Offst.acct
690010	Labour	266.60	449.717	MIN		
690010	Labour	266.31	449.233	MIN		
690010	Labour	266.21	449.050	MIN		
690010	Labour	265.49	447.833	MIN		
690010	Labour	264.85	446.750	MIN		
690010	Labour	264.75	446.600	MIN		

Figure 4.22 Confirmation Line Items

In Figure 4.22, the **Quantity** column is sorted in descending order. This provides visibility to confirmations with the largest time bookings. By double-clicking on any line shown in Figure 4.22, you can drill down to individual activity confirmations. From the detailed confirmation screens, you can determine the original cause of the large input quantity variance.

In this example, I examined the cause of an input quantity variance due to labor confirmations. You can use the same technique to analyze any variance category, by sorting line items and drilling down to original transactions.

I've discussed variance calculation for product cost collectors in detail. I'll now discuss the differences for variance calculation for manufacturing orders, since there are many similarities between the two processes.

Product Cost by Order

In this section I'll examine variance calculation for Product Cost by Order, which means working with manufacturing orders. I'll analyze the differences between variance calculation for manufacturing orders and product cost collectors.

Variance calculation for manufacturing orders is also known as cumulative variance. Cumulative variance compares target costs and cumulative control costs. As shown in the configuration for target cost version 0 in Section 4.2, target costs for total variance are based on the standard cost estimate, or in other words, the valuated goods receipt. Control costs are equal to actual costs less scrap variances. The manufacturing order must meet the following two conditions to calculate variance:

▶ Settlement type FUL (full settlement) in settlement rule

▶ Status DLV (delivered) or TECO (technically complete)

Settlement type FUL allows all unsettled work in process and variance from the current and previous periods to be settled in the current settlement period. Work in process and variances are calculated based on order status, not period. You normally settle manufacturing orders every period.

Status DLV is determined automatically when posting valuated goods receipts during manufacturing order confirmation. Status TECO is determined manually and indi-

cates processing is complete even though the order is not fully delivered. When either status is detected during period-end processing, work in process in canceled, and variance is calculated.

During variance calculation, target and control costs are compared, and variance categories are assigned. Variance categories are assigned in the following sequence:

▶ Input price variance
▶ Resource-usage variance
▶ Input quantity variance
▶ Remaining input variance
▶ Mixed-price variance
▶ Output price variance
▶ Lot size variance
▶ Remaining variance

Variance categories are discussed in detail in Section 4.3. Now that we've run overhead and work in process calculations, it's time to settle the results.

Settlement

Work in process and variances are transferred to Financial Accounting, Profit Center Accounting, and Profitability Analysis during settlement. Variance categories can also be transferred to value fields in Profitability Analysis.

You run period-end settlement with transactions KK87 (individual) and CO88 (collective), or via menu path: **Accounting • Controlling • Product Cost Controlling • Cost Object Controlling • Product Cost by Period • Period-End Closing • Single Functions: Product Cost Collector • Settlement**. A selection screen is displayed, as shown in Figure 4.23.

> **Note**
> You carry out settlement for production and process orders with transactions KO88 (individual) and CO88 (collective).

In this example, we will carry out settlement only for product cost collectors by selecting the **With Product Cost Collectors** indicator, as shown in Figure 4.23. You can include other objects in the settlement, without the running another transaction, by selecting the relevant indicator in Figure 4.23.

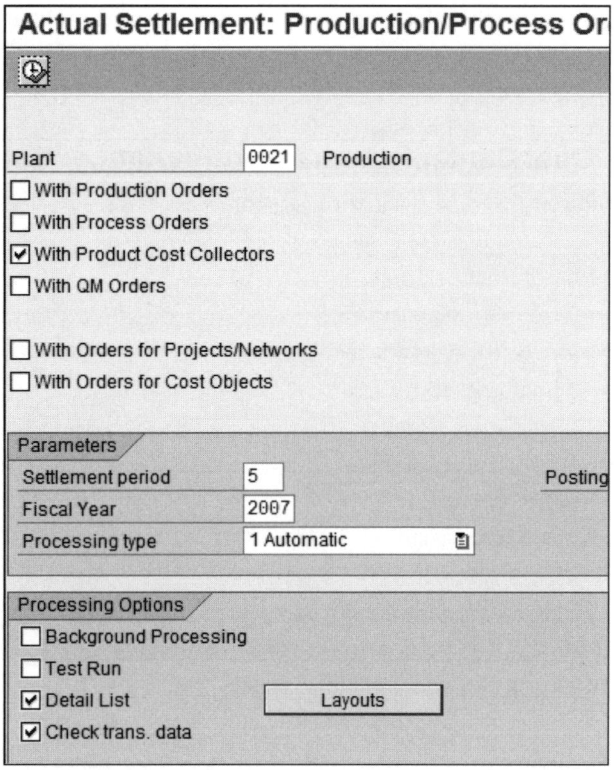

Actual Settlement: Production/Process Or

Plant   0021   Production
☐ With Production Orders
☐ With Process Orders
☑ With Product Cost Collectors
☐ With QM Orders

☐ With Orders for Projects/Networks
☐ With Orders for Cost Objects

Parameters
Settlement period   5   Posting
Fiscal Year   2007
Processing type   1 Automatic

Processing Options
☐ Background Processing
☐ Test Run
☑ Detail List   Layouts
☑ Check trans. data

Figure 4.23 Actual Settlement Selection Screen

Product Cost by Period requires each period to be settled sequentially, which can lead to difficulties if a prior period needs to be reversed. Using the Posting period field shown on the right in Figure 4.23, you can make reversals, corrections, and resettlements in prior periods by posting to the present or previous period.

When you select the **Detail List** indicator, a detail list becomes available for analysis following settlement (shown later, in Figure 4.25). If you do not select the indicator, only the **Basic List** is available following settlement, as shown in Figure 4.24. You can also analyze settlement postings by viewing and sorting the settlement account line item report in Financial Accounting with transaction FBL3N.

If you select the **Check trans. data** indicator, the system checks whether any transaction data was posted to the product cost collector or manufacturing order since last settlement. If no transaction data was posted, sender processing is stopped. This improves processing time. Error messages that could have been issued during settlement are not issued. This improves message analysis by reducing the number of redundant messages.

Complete the selection screen using the settings shown in Figure 4.23 as an example and click on the execute icon to display the screen shown in Figure 4.24.

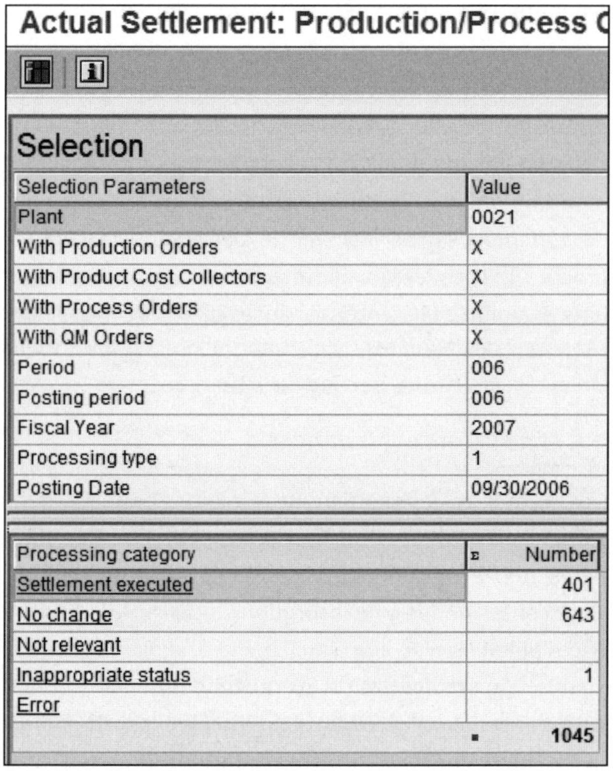

Actual Settlement: Production/Process (

Selection

Selection Parameters	Value
Plant	0021
With Production Orders	X
With Product Cost Collectors	X
With Process Orders	X
With QM Orders	X
Period	006
Posting period	006
Fiscal Year	2007
Processing type	1
Posting Date	09/30/2006

Processing category	Σ	Number
Settlement executed		401
No change		643
Not relevant		
Inappropriate status		1
Error		
▪		1045

Figure 4.24 Actual Settlement Basic List

This screen provides you with basic information on the parameters you entered in the previous selection screen, such as **Period** and **Fiscal Year**. Click on the detail lists (grid) icon to proceed to a detailed list of settlement values, as shown in Figure 4.25.

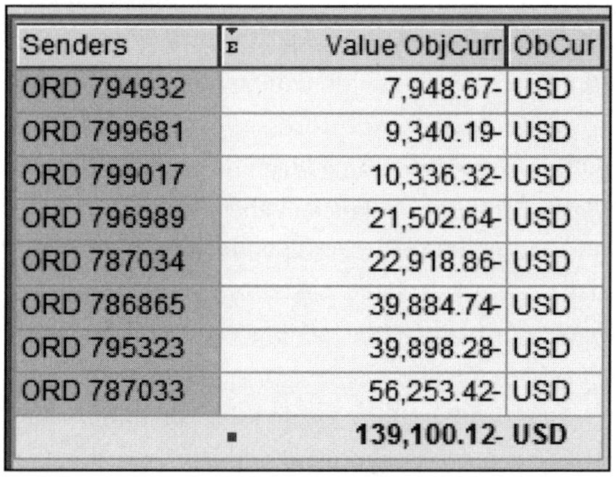

Senders	Σ	Value ObjCurr	ObCur
ORD 794932		7,948.67-	USD
ORD 799681		9,340.19-	USD
ORD 799017		10,336.32-	USD
ORD 796989		21,502.64-	USD
ORD 787034		22,918.86-	USD
ORD 786865		39,884.74-	USD
ORD 795323		39,898.28-	USD
ORD 787033		56,253.42-	USD
▪		139,100.12-	USD

Figure 4.25 Actual Settlement Detail List

In Figure 4.25, the **Value ObjCurr** (value in object currency) column is sorted in descending order. This provides visibility to product cost collectors with the largest settlement amounts. You can reconcile the sum of values settled at the bottom of Figure 4.25 with the sum of the collective variance calculation, by scrolling to the bottom of the screen shown in Figure 4.18. You can also reconcile Figure 4.25 with postings to settlement financial accounts, by sorting the settlement account line item report in Financial Accounting (transaction FBL3N).

Settlement is the last step in period-end closing for product cost collectors and manufacturing orders. We'll now examine cost center variances and how they relate to production variances.

4.5 Cost Center Variances

Cost center balance, otherwise known as under/overabsorption, represents the difference between cost center debits and credits during a period or range of periods. Cost center under/overabsorption occurs due to differences between plan and actual debits and plan and actual credits. You can analyze cost center under/overabsorption with the standard actual/plan cost center report, and for most companies, this provides sufficient information to manage overhead costs. More advanced functionality is available to analyze cost center balance if required, such as cost center target cost and variance analysis. I'll first discuss cost center analysis using the standard cost center report, and then look at more advanced functionality.

Information System

Standard cost center actual/plan reports provide excellent analysis capabilities in a single report. You can use them to monitor cost center debits and credits during a period. After period-end processing is complete, you can use them to analyze under/overabsorption. Let's first look at the cost center balance in the cost center report and then analyze debit and credit variances.

Cost Center Balance

You can view the standard cost center actual/plan report with transaction S_ALR_87013611 or via menu path: **Accounting • Controlling • Cost Center Accounting • Information System • Reports for Cost Center Account-** ing • **Plan/Actual Comparisons • Cost Centers: Actual/ Plan/Variance**. A selection screen is displayed, as shown in Figure 4.26.

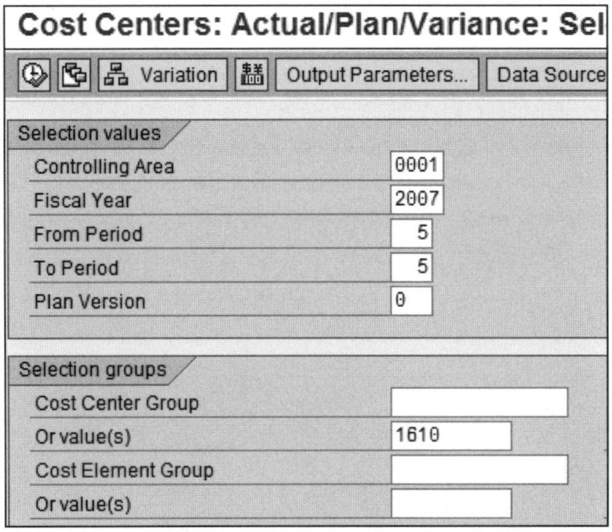

Figure 4.26 Actual/Plan Cost Center Report Selection Screen

Complete the selection fields with data relevant to your company, using Figure 4.26 as an example. Click on the execute icon to display a report similar to the screen shown in Figure 4.27.

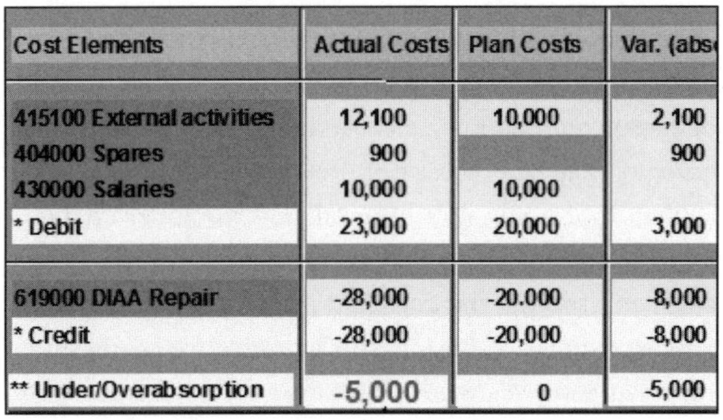

Cost Elements	Actual Costs	Plan Costs	Var. (abs
415100 External activities	12,100	10,000	2,100
404000 Spares	900		900
430000 Salaries	10,000	10,000	
* Debit	23,000	20,000	3,000
619000 DIAA Repair	-28,000	-20.000	-8,000
* Credit	-28,000	-20,000	-8,000
** Under/Overabsorption	-5,000	0	-5,000

Figure 4.27 Actual/Plan Cost Center Report Balance

The resulting report, shown in Figure 4.27, displays cost center debits and how much has been allocated to products resulting in cost center credits. The highlighted **Under/Overabsorption** in the last row in Figure 4.27 is negative, indicating actual cost center costs incurred were less than the activity costs debited to product cost collectors and manufacturing orders.

Now let's analyze the cost center balance by examining the debit and credit sections of the report in detail.

Cost Center Debits

Cost center plan debits appear in the cost center report as you carry out primary cost element planning with transaction KP06, as discussed in Chapter 1.

Prior to a costing run, cost center debits are planned by primary cost elements. For example, external activities and salaries costs are planned for the cost center by the primary cost elements corresponding to the financial accounts for external activities and salaries. Following the costing run, if actual external activities and salaries costs are different from planned costs, a debit variance will result as highlighted in the **Debit** summary row shown in Figure 4.28.

Cost Elements	Actual Costs	Plan Costs	Var. (abs(
415100 External activities	12,100	10,000	2,100
404000 Spares	900		900
430000 Salaries	10,000	10,000	
* Debit	23,000	20,000	3,000
619000 DIAA Repair	-28,000	-20,000	-8,000
* Credit	-28,000	-20,000	-8,000
** Under/Overabsorption	-5,000	0	-5,000

Figure 4.28 Actual/Plan Cost Center Report Debit Variance

Since actual debits are greater than planned, the **Debit** variance is unfavorable. The external activities variance of **2,100** could be due to increased vendor prices, or the quantity may have increased. To investigate the variance further, drill down (double-click) on the **External activities** row in the **Actual Costs** column shown in Figure 4.28, and analyze the cost center line item postings. The **Spares** debit variance of **900** occurred because spares costs were not planned. Drill down on the **Actual Costs** column in the **Spares** row to analyze the cost center line item postings. This may indicate that it is a nonrecurring expense or that spares costs should be planned in future fiscal years.

Cost Center Credits

Cost center plan credits appear in the cost center report as you carry out activity quantity and price planning with transaction KP26, as discussed in Chapter 1. You need to populate both the plan activity field and at least one of the activity price fields for the system to calculate and display plan credits.

Activity rates are planned by dividing cost center plan debits by plan activity quantity. For example, if plan debits are $100,000 and plan activity quantity is 10,000 minutes, the plan activity rate is $10 per minute. If actual debits equal $100,000, there will be no variances due to primary cost planning. However, if only 9,000 minutes are confirmed, the cost center only receives a credit of $90,000, leaving $10,000 underabsorbed.

This represents $10,000 of production costs not allocated to cost of sales. While this may not affect relative profitability between products receiving allocations from the cost center, it should be taken into account when determining overall profitability of the profit center or company. For production cost centers, the balance is usually transferred to Profitability Analysis using assessment. If actual and plan activity debits allocated are different, a credit variance will result as highlighted in the **Credit** summary row in Figure 4.29.

Cost Elements	Actual Costs	Plan Costs	Var. (abs(
415100 External activities	12,100	10,000	2,100
404000 Spares	900		900
430000 Salaries	10,000	10,000	
* Debit	23,000	20,000	3,000
619000 DIAA Repair	-28,000	-20,000	-8,000
* Credit	-28,000	-20,000	-8,000
** Under/Overabsorption	-5,000	0	-5,000

Figure 4.29 Actual/Plan Cost Center Report Credit Variance

Since actual credits are greater than planned, the highlighted **Credit** variance is favorable. The receivers of the activities are burdened with higher debits than planned. The additional credits could be due to an increase in production output or an increase in plan activity price. By scrolling further down the cost center report shown in Figure 4.29, you can compare actual and plan activity quantities. This will help you determine if the credit variance is due to a change in activity quantity or price.

Standard actual/plan cost center reports are commonly used to analyze cost center under/overabsorption. Now let's examine some advanced functionality for analyzing cost center variance.

Target Cost Analysis

Cost center target costs are based on plan costs adjusted by activity quantity consumed. Let's follow a short example to help explain how target costs are calculated. If plan costs are $1,000 and no activities are consumed, target cost is zero. If 100% of plan activities are consumed, target cost is $1,000. If 200% of plan activities are consumed, target cost is $2,000.

Target cost allows a more detailed analysis of cost center balance, since an increase in actual costs may be due to an increase in activities consumed. Target costs are higher than plan costs in this example due to an increase in activity quantity. Target costs differ from plan costs when the following two conditions are met:

▶ **Activity-Dependent Planning**

You carry out activity-dependent planning by entering an activity type in the selection screen of transaction KP06 and entering fixed and variable costs in the following screen, when carrying out cost element planning, as discussed in Chapter 1 (Initial Planning). Let's follow an example in parallel to help illustrate how target costs work. Enter $10,000 fixed and $10,000 variable costs, and 100 hours variable quantity during activity-dependent primary cost planning.

▶ **Plan Activity Quantity and Prices**

You need to enter plan activity quantity and prices (with transaction KP26), as discussed in Chapter 1. For this example, enter 100 hours plan activity, and $100 fixed and $100 variable during activity price planning.

Before any activities are consumed, target costs equal only the fixed portion of plan costs. In the example, plan costs are $20,000, the sum of fixed and variable costs. Target costs, however, are only $10,000, calculated by adding fixed costs to the result of variable costs times the operating rate. The operating rate, as a percentage, is defined as (actual activity / plan activity) x 100. Since actual activity quantity is zero, the operating rate is zero, and no variable costs are added to the target costs.

When 50 hours of activity are consumed, target costs equal the fixed portion of plan costs, plus 0.5 (50 actual hours/100 plan hours) times the variable costs. In the example, plan costs remain at $20,000. Meanwhile, tar-

get costs are $15,000, calculated by adding fixed costs of $10,000 to variable costs times the operating rate, or $5,000.

If 140 hours of activity are consumed, target costs equal the fixed portion of plan costs, plus 1.4 (140 actual hours/100 plan hours) times variable costs. In the example, plan costs remain at $20,000. Meanwhile, target costs are $24,000, calculated by adding fixed costs of $10,000 to variable costs times the operating rate, or $14,000. This is the scenario presented in the actual/target report in Figure 4.31.

Target costs are continuously calculated, so they can be reported on in real time during a period. No additional transactions need to be run to display target costs.

You can view the standard cost center actual/target report with transaction S_ALR_87013625, or via menu path: **Accounting • Controlling • Cost Center Accounting • Information System • Reports for Cost Center Accounting • Target/Actual Comparisons • Cost Centers: Actual/Target/Variance**. A selection screen is displayed, as shown in Figure 4.30.

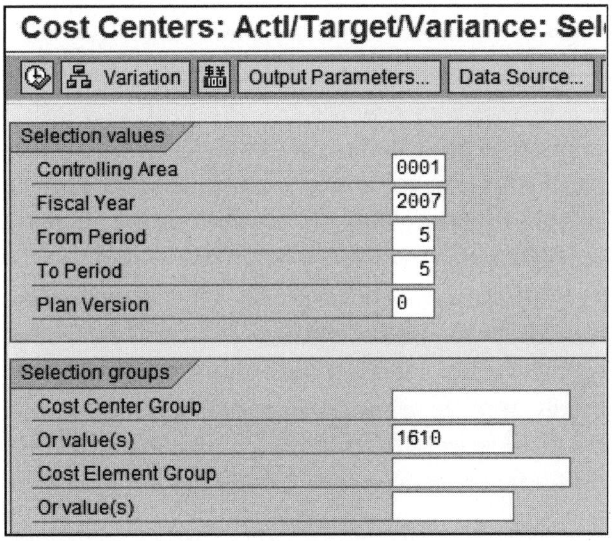

Figure 4.30 Actual/Target Cost Center Report Selection Screen

Complete the selection fields with data relevant to your company, using Figure 4.30 as an example. Click on the execute icon to display a report similar to the screen shown in Figure 4.31.

Cost Elements	Actual Costs	Target Costs	Plan Costs
415100 External acty.	12,100	14,000	10,000
404000 Replacement	900		
430000 Salaries	10,000	10,000	10,000
* Debit	**23,000**	**24,000**	20,000
619000 DILV Production	-28,000	-28,000	-20,000
* Credit	-28,000	-28,000	-20,000
** Under/Overabsorption	-5,000	-4,000	0

Figure 4.31 Actual/Target Cost Center Report Debit Variance

Actual Costs and **Target Costs** both increase with resource consumption, while **Plan Costs** remain constant. The **Plan Costs** shown in Figure 4.31 are based on activity consumption resulting in a credit of **20,000**. Actual activity consumption is greater than planned, resulting in actual credit of **28,000**. The target debit is more realistic than the plan debit, since it is increased by rising variable costs due to increased activity consumption. There is only a 1,000 variance between actual and target in the **Under/Overabsorption** row in Figure 4.31, compared with a 5,000 variance between actual and plan in the **Under/Overabsorption** row in Figure 4.27.

While a detailed analysis of cost center variance is possible with target cost analysis, more work is involved in initial planning of primary cost element costs and activity prices. Primary cost element costs must be divided into fixed and variable components and entered during activity-dependent planning. Also, you need to enter plan activity quantity and prices during activity price planning. If your costs can be divided into fixed and variable components and you're not presently using activity-dependent planning, you could test it out on one production cost center first to examine the benefits.

The cost center balance is normally transferred to Profitability Analysis for use in margin analysis, as is the case with actual/plan analyses.

Variance Analysis

If you need to analyze the cause of variances in target cost analysis in more detail, automatic variance calculation divides the variance into categories. You may need to carry out variance analysis if target cost analysis does not

provide enough information on the source of the variance or the responsible person. The two steps involved during variance analysis are examined in the following subsections.

Actual Cost Splitting

Actual costs are posted to a cost center, while variance calculation requires that activity-independent actual costs be distributed to a cost center/activity type combination. During variance calculation, the actual cost of each activity is determined with *actual cost splitting*. Two steps are involved during actual cost splitting per cost element, which are listed below:

1. The cost center actual costs are allocated to activity types based on target costs per activity type for each cost element. If target costs do not exist for a cost element, costs are split according to target costs of the cost element group assigned in customizing of the target version. If no target costs exist for the cost element group, the costs are split in the second step.

2. This step is necessary if there are no target costs for the cost element or cost element group, or if activity-independent costs exist. In this step, actual costs are allocated to activity types according to splitting rules. If no splitting rules exist, costs are allocated based on equivalence numbers.

At the end of the actual cost splitting process, all actual costs per cost element are distributed to activity types. Actual cost splitting happens automatically during variance calculation.

Variance Calculation

Variance calculation provides information on the reasons for variances when analyzing the difference between actual and target costs. The cost center balance is assigned to input and output variance categories based on the source of the variance.

Configuration required for cost center variance calculation includes creating a target cost version and creating a variance variant and assigning it to the target cost version. You calculate cost center variance with transaction KSS1 or via menu path: **Accounting • Controlling • Cost Center Accounting • Period-End Closing • Single Functions • Variances**.

Variances are saved automatically if you deselect the test run indicator in the selection screen.

You report on variance calculation in the information system with transaction S_ALR_87013627 or via menu path: **Accounting • Controlling • Cost Center Accounting • Information System • Reports for Cost Center Accounting • Target/Actual Comparisons • Variance Analysis • Cost Centers: Variances**. You can view variance categories on the third page of the report.

Variance calculation assigns the cost center balance to variance categories on the input and output side. Variances on the input side are based on actual costs minus target costs. Variances on the output side are based on target costs minus allocated actual costs. The sum of the variances represents the total variance, or the cost center balance.

Input Variances

Input variances are based on the sum of cost center debits minus target debits. The four input variances are described below:

▶ **Input Price Variances**
These indicate changes in costs due to prices. These variances represent differences between target and actual costs due to differences in planned and actual prices of materials or services. The formula is: Input price variance = (Actual price – Plan price) x Actual input quantity. For example, if you plan 100 hours at $100 per hour and post 110 actual hours at $110 per hour, input price variance is ($110 – $100) x 110 h = $1,100.

▶ **Input Quantity Variances**
These result from under/overconsumption for cost elements. These variances represent differences between target and actual costs caused by different quantities being consumed than planned. Input price variances include variances caused by both price and quantity differences. The formula is: Input quantity variance = (Actual input quantity – Target input quantity) x Plan price. For example, 100 hours are planned as a variable quantity for external services during activity-dependant cost planning with transaction KP06, and 100 hours are entered as plan activity consumption with transaction KP26. Actual activity consumption was 140 hours, so the target quantity for

external services is 140 hours. Only 110 hours were actually consumed by entering the quantity with transaction FB50 and by choosing a screen variant with cost center and quantity. Input quantity variance is: (110 h – 140 h) x $100 = -$3,000.

▶ **Resource-Usage Variance**
This indicates changes in the plan consumption of cost elements. It occurs if you post an actual cost against an unplanned cost element, or if no actual data exists for a plan cost element. The formula is: Resource-usage variance = Actual costs — Target costs — Input price variance. For example, if there is $900 of unplanned consumption of replacement parts, as shown in Figure 4.31, resource-usage variance is $900.

▶ **Remaining Input Variance**
This includes all input variances that cannot be assigned to any other input variance category. This variance can occur if you planned cost elements and made actual postings but did not record consumption quantities. It can also occur if you deactivate one of the other input variance categories in the variance variant, as discussed in Section 4.2.

Output Variances

Output variances are based on target minus the sum of cost center credits due to activity allocation. The four output variances are described below:

▶ **Output Price Variance**
This occurs if you use a price that differs from the plan price that is calculated iteratively each month based on planned activity. The target credit posting (Plan price x Actual activity) varies from the actual credit posting (Allocation price x Actual activity) on the cost center. Output price variance can result if you use average prices instead of period-based prices, if the capacity of the activity type is used as the basis of the price calculation, or if you set a price manually. The formula is: Output price variance = Actual activity x (Plan price - Actual price).

▶ **Output Quantity Variance**
This is the difference between manually entered actual costs and allocated actual quantities. The formula is: Output quantity variance = (Actual quantity – Manual actual quantity) x Plan price. Variances aris-

ing from both price and quantity differences appear as output price variances.

▶ **Fixed Cost Variances**
These occur when the actual operating rate varies from the plan operating rate and some of the planned fixed costs are either underabsorbed or overabsorbed due to credit postings. The system only reports a fixed cost variance if the operating rate is not 100%.

▶ **Remaining Variance**
This includes all output variances that cannot be assigned to any other output variance category. This variance can occur if you deactivated calculation of variance categories on the output side, or if you deactivated all variance categories in the variance variant.

Actual Price Calculation

Cost center under/overabsorption can be allocated to products, if necessary, with an additional period-end process called *Revaluation at Actual Prices*. This process calculates the incremental planned activity price needed to allocate all cost center debits. Orders are then revalued with the incremental debits, and the cost center receives corresponding credits. Following revaluation, the cost center actual balance is zero, as shown in the last row of the target/actual cost center report in Figure 4.32.

Cost Elements	Actual Costs	Target Costs	Plan Costs	T/A-Var.(abs
415100 External activities	12,100	14,000	10,000	-1,900
404000 Spares	900			900
430000 Salaries	10,000	10,000	10,000	
* Debit	23,000	24,000	20,000	-1,000
619000 DIAA Production	-23,000	-28,000	-20,000	
* Credit	-23,000	-28,000	-20,000	
** Under/Overabsorption	0	-4,000	0	-1,000

Figure 4.32 Actual/Target Cost Center Report Revaluation

The actual credits to the cost center, which were **28,000** before revaluation, are reduced to **23,000**. The original product cost collectors and manufacturing orders receive a credit calculated with the formula: *Consumed quantity x (Original price – Actual price)*. Product cost collectors need to be resettled following revaluation due to the incremental debit received during revaluation.

There are two requirements for carrying out revaluation: a version configuration setting and an activity type setting. I'll discuss each in turn.

Version Configuration Setting

You maintain version configuration with transaction OKEQ or via menu path: **IMG • Controlling • General Controlling • Organization • Maintain Versions**.

You are presented with a screen similar to the one displayed in Figure 4.33. Use the following steps to navigate to the version configuration setting displayed:

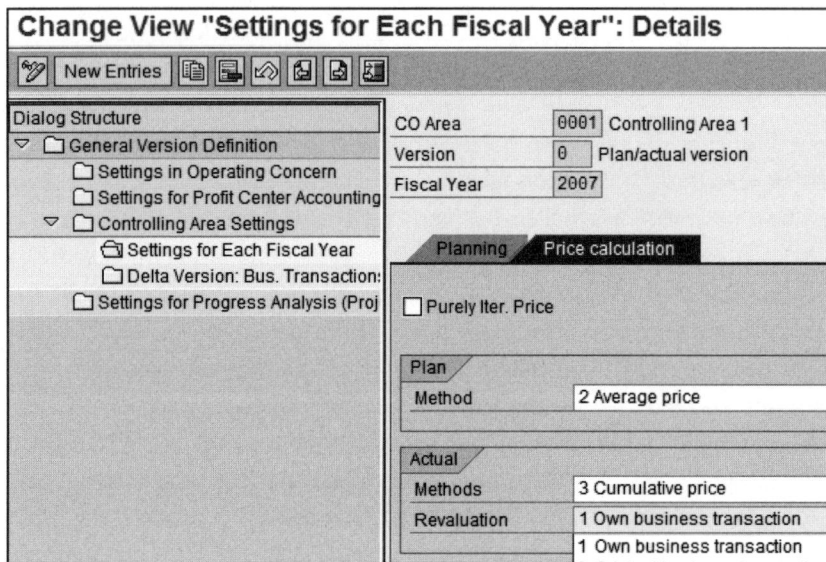

Figure 4.33 Revaluation Setting in Version Configuration

1. Select **Version 0**
2. Double-click on **Settings for Each Fiscal Year**
3. Double-click on the current **Fiscal Year**
4. Click on the **Price calculation** tab

The screen shown in Figure 4.33 is displayed. Now that we've navigated to the correct tab, you make the configuration setting with the following steps:

1. Right-click in the **Revaluation** field
2. Choose **Own business transaction**
3. Save your work

Activity Type Setting

The second requirement for carrying out revaluation is setting the **Actual price indicator** for activity types to be revalued. You set the actual price indicator with transaction KL02 or via menu path: **Accounting • Controlling • Cost Center Accounting • Master Data • Activity Type • Individual Processing • Change**. Complete the **Activity Type** field and press Enter to display screen shown in Figure 4.34.

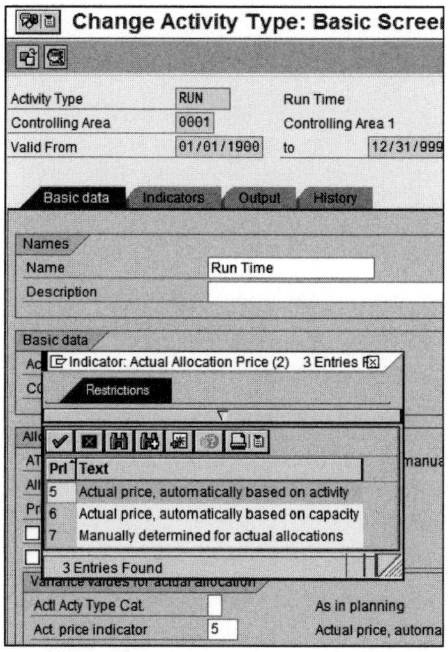

Figure 4.34 Actual Price Indicator in Activity Type

You make the activity type setting with the following steps:

1. Right-click in the **Act. price indicator** field and choose **Possible Entries**

2. Choose **Actual price, automatically based on activity**
3. Save your work

Now that we've ensured that the configuration and activity type settings are correct, I'll explain how to carry out actual price calculation. Revaluation occurs automatically during actual price calculation.

Actual Price Calculation

You carry out actual price calculation with transaction KSII or via menu path: **Accounting • Controlling • Cost Center Accounting • Period-End Closing • Single Functions • Price Calculation**. The screen shown in Figure 4.35 is displayed.

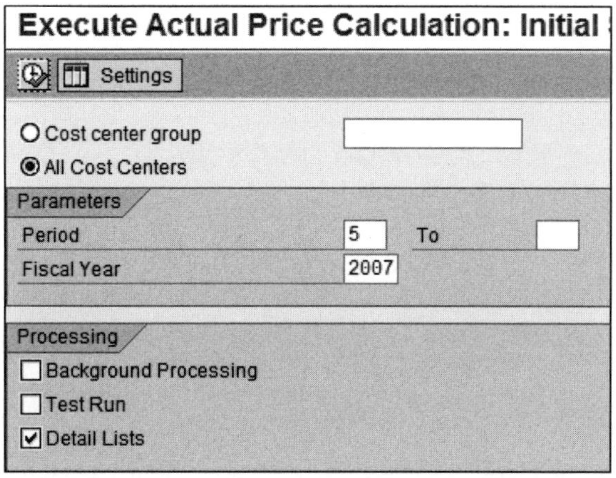

Figure 4.35 Actual Price Calculation Selection Screen

Complete the selection screen fields and click on the execute icon to run the transaction.

You can analyze the results of actual price calculation in the information system with transaction KSBT or via menu path: **Accounting • Controlling • Cost Center Accounting • Information System • Reports for Cost Center Accounting • Prices • Cost Centers: Activity Prices**. You can compare plan and actual activity prices with the resulting report.

As long as you have set the revaluation indicator in the version as shown in Figure 4.33 and set the actual activity indicator in the activity type as shown in Figure 4.34, revaluation automatically occurs during actual price calculation. You can confirm the cost center balance is zero following revaluation with the standard actual/target cost center report (shown in Figure 4.32).

Actual price calculation and revaluation allow you to post cost center variances to product cost collectors and manufacturing orders. If you need to allocate all purchasing and manufacturing differences to finished products as well, you should consider actual costing with material ledger, as discussed in Section 4.7.

In addition to production and cost center variances, purchase price variances should be analyzed at period-end, as well as frequently during each period. The following section explains how this works.

4.6 Purchase Price Variance

When raw materials are valued at standard price, there will be a purchase price variance posting during goods receipt if the purchase price is different from the material standard price. Figure 4.36 shows typical purchase price variance postings during goods receipt when the purchase price and standard price are different.

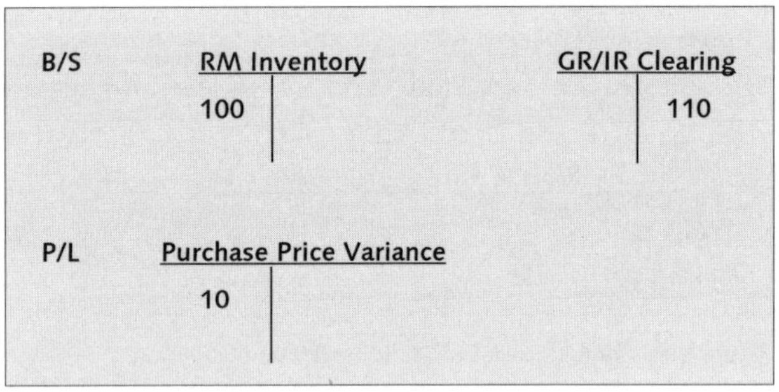

Figure 4.36 Purchase Price Variance at Goods Receipt

The raw material (RM) inventory balance sheet (B/S) account posting occurs during goods receipt, based on the standard price. The offsetting posting to the goods receipt/invoice receipt (GR/IR) clearing account is based on purchase order price. If the purchase order price is different from the standard price, the difference is posted to a **Purchase Price Variance** profit and loss (P/L) expense account.

Prior to a costing run, purchasing info records are updated with current vendor quotations. During a costing run, purchasing info records provide standard cost estimates with current component standard prices. Immediately following a costing run, purchase price variance postings are usually minimal, since component standard price is based on current vendor quotations.

Purchase price variance (PPV) postings can be used as a measure of purchasing department performance. An increase in unfavorable PPV postings may need to be explained by purchasing. This will be highlighted if you nominate the purchasing cost center as the receiving cost object in Controlling for PPV expense account postings.

There are two methods for assigning the purchasing cost center. One method involves a master data change, and the other involves a configuration change. I'll now discuss each method in more detail.

Master Data
You can assign the purchasing cost center automatically by entering it in the default account assignment tab of the PPV cost element with transaction KA02 or via menu path: **Accounting • Controlling • Cost Center Accounting • Master Data • Cost Element • Individual Processing • Change**. A selection screen is displayed, as shown in Figure 4.37.

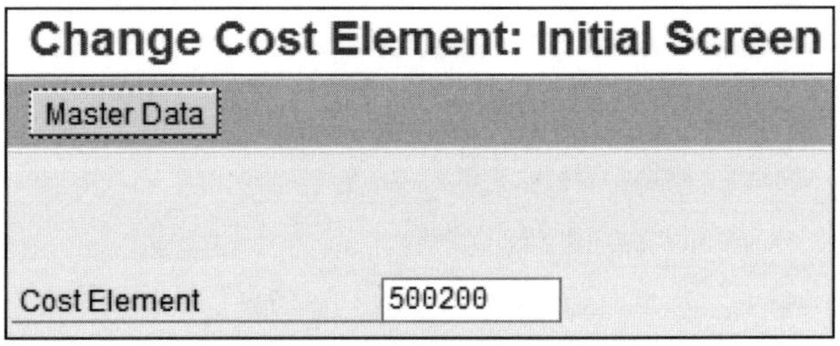

Figure 4.37 Change Cost Element Selection Screen

Proceed to the change cost element detail screen by completing the **Cost Element** field shown in Figure 4.37 and clicking on the **Master Data** button. The screen shown in Figure 4.38 is displayed.

In the **Default Acct Assgnmt** (default account assignment) tab, complete the **Cost Center** field and save your work. This procedure assigns a default cost center for postings to the PPV account per controlling area. This is the easiest method, but it may not be suitable if two plants within the same controlling area need different cost centers assigned to the same cost element. In this case, you'll need to assign the cost centers with configuration, as described in the next section.

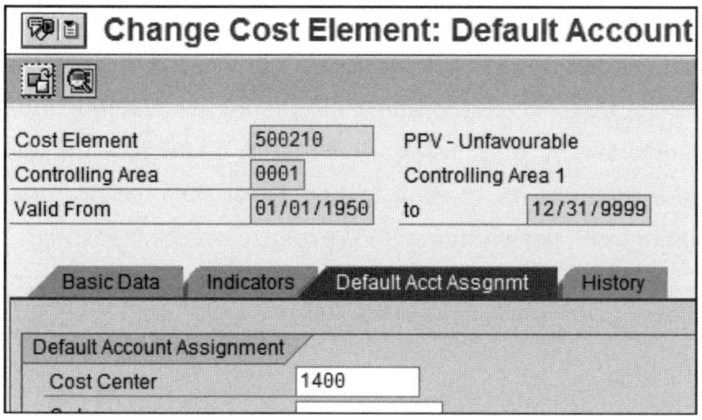

Figure 4.38 Default Account Assignment Tab

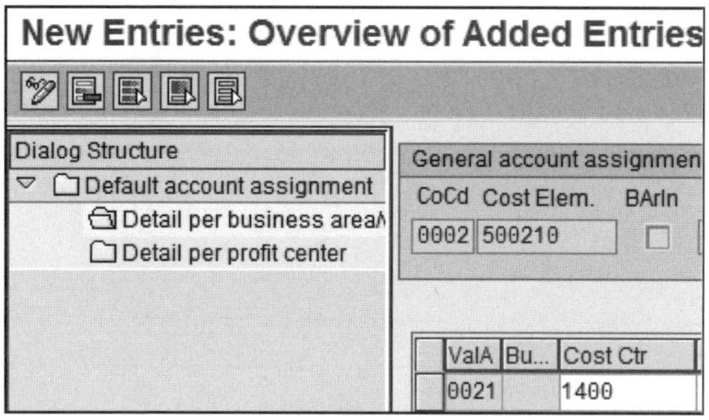

Figure 4.40 Default Cost Center per Plant Configuration

Configuration

Alternatively, you can enter default account assignment in configuration, which gives you more flexibility, e.g., if you need to assign a default cost center per plant. You can assign the purchasing cost center as the default cost center in configuration with transaction OKB9 or via menu path: **IMG • Controlling • Cost Center Accounting • Actual Postings • Manual Actual Postings • Edit Automatic Account Assignment**. The screen shown in Figure 4.39 is displayed.

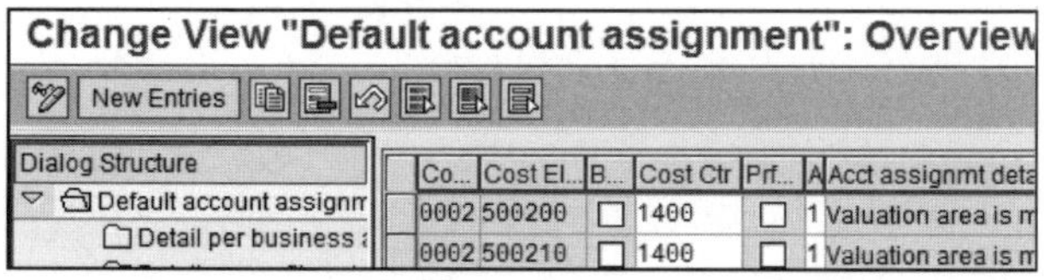

Figure 4.39 Default Account Assignment Configuration

Complete the following steps to proceed to a screen where you can assign a cost center per plant:

1. Type "1" in the **A** (account assignment detail) column
2. Select the required PPV cost element
3. Double-click on **Detail per business** (detail per business area/valuation area)
4. Click on the **New Entries** button

The screen shown in Figure 4.40 is displayed.

Complete the **ValA** (valuation area) and **Cost Center** fields and save your work to make the cost center assignment.

Now that we've examined how PPV postings occur and how to assign the purchasing cost center to a PPV cost element, let's look at the standard reports available for analyzing PPV.

Reporting

Since PPV is treated as an expense, it posts to a cost center. You can analyze PPV by sorting line item postings against the PPV primary cost element in the standard actual/plan cost center report. You can view the standard actual/plan cost center report with transaction S_ALR_87013611 or via menu path: **Accounting • Controlling • Cost Center Accounting • Information System • Reports for Cost Center Accounting • Plan/Actual Comparisons • Cost Centers: Actual/Plan/Variance**. A selection screen is displayed, as shown in Figure 4.41.

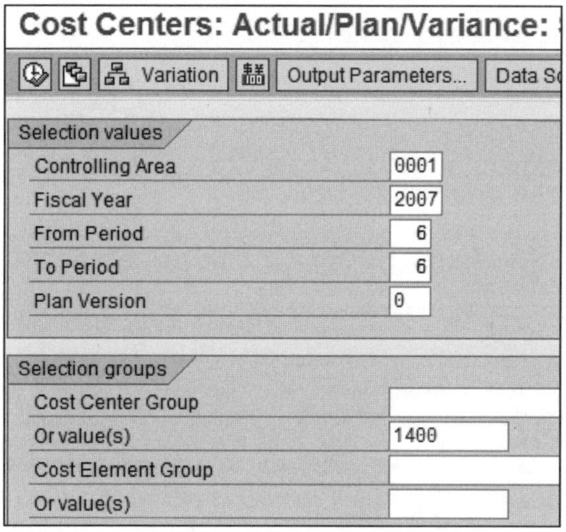

Figure 4.41 Actual/Plan Cost Center Report Selection Screen

Complete the selection screen fields and click on the execute icon to display the screen shown in Figure 4.42.

Double-click on PPV cost element **500210** to display the dialog box shown in Figure 4.43.

Cost Centers: Actual/Plan/Variance

```
Cost Centers: Actual/Plan/Variance     Date:

Cost Center/Group        1400
Person responsible:      John Jordan
Reporting period:        6   to   6   2007

Cost Elements                  Act. Costs

  500200   PPV - Favourable        9,092.47-
  500210   PPV - Unfavourable     11,671.34
  500300   Stock Reval Gains       9,768.56-
  500310   Stock Reval Losses     18,225.10
```

Figure 4.42 Cost Center Report Results Screen

```
Select Report                              ☒

Cost Centers: Actual Line Items
Cost Centers: Planning Overview
Cost Centers: Plan Line Items
CCtrs: Period Breakdown Actual/Plan
Activity Types: Period Breakdown
Stat. Key Figs: Period breakdown
Cost Centers: Breakdown by Partner
Cost Centers: Breakdown by BusTrans
Area: Actual/plan 2 currencies
Display Planning Long Texts

  ✓  Technical names on/off   ☒
```

Figure 4.43 Cost Center Line Items Dialog Box

Double-click on **Cost Centers: Actual Line Items** to display the screen shown in Figure 4.44.

Display Actual Cost Line Items for Cost

```
 Document   Master Record

Layout                /US PPV        PPV A
Cost Center           1400           Purcha
Report currency       *              Object

Cost Ele...  Cost element name  Val.in RC  OffAct
500210       PPV - Unfavourable  3,600.00   S
500210       PPV - Unfavourable  1,829.88   S
500210       PPV - Unfavourable  1,829.88   S
```

Figure 4.44 Cost Center Actual Line Items Report

The **Val.in RC** (value in reporting currency) column is sorted in descending order. This provides visibility to the largest PPV postings. By double-clicking on any line

shown in Figure 4.44, you can drill down to the transaction document that caused the PPV posting. In many cases, this will be the material document created during the goods receipt. Double-click on the first row (largest variance) shown in Figure 4.44 to display the material document shown in Figure 4.45.

```
    Material   Quantity   Where   Purchase Order Data

Purchase order         4500048049   2
Reference document     5000141830   1
```

Figure 4.45 Material Document Details Area

You can analyze the cause of the PPV posting by examining different areas within the material document details area to determine the standard price and the purchase price. Since differences between standard and purchase prices result in PPV postings, the source documents can provide insight into the original cause.

To determine the *standard price*, price unit, and costing lot size of the component, click on the **Material** tab, double-click on the material number, and then navigate to the Costing 2 view of the material master. The screen shown in Figure 4.46 is displayed.

Standard Cost Estimate		
Cost Estimate	Future	Current
Period / Fiscal Year	0	4 2007
Planned price	0.00	49.50
Standard price		49.50

Planned prices		
Planned price 1	0.00	Planned price date 1
Planned price 2	0.00	Planned price date 2
Planned price 3	0.00	Planned price date 3

Valuation Data		
Valuation Class	7900	Valuation Categor
VC: Sales order stk		Proj. stk val. class
Price control	S	Current Period
Price unit	1	Currency

Figure 4.46 Material Master Costing 2 View

In this example, the standard price is **49.50**, and the **Price unit** is **1**. Click on the **Current** cost estimate button to display the cost estimate, and note the costing lot size the standard cost estimate is based on.

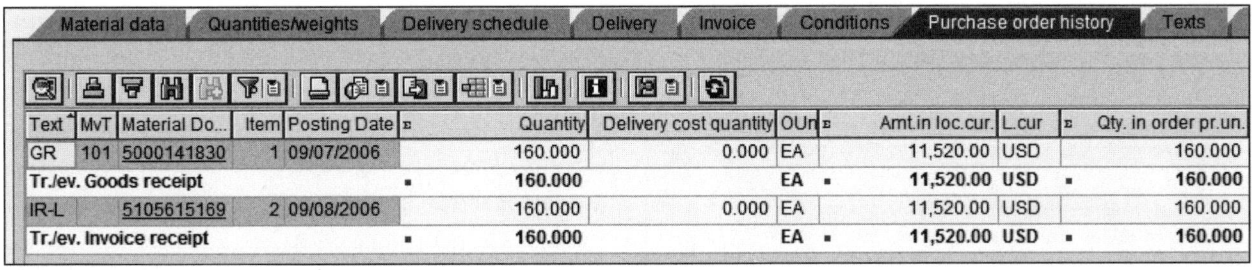

Text	MvT	Material Do...	Item	Posting Date	▣	Quantity	Delivery cost quantity	OUn	▣	Amt.in loc.cur.	L.cur	▣	Qty. in order pr.un.
GR	101	5000141830	1	09/07/2006		160.000	0.000	EA		11,520.00	USD		160.000
Tr./ev. Goods receipt					▪	160.000		EA	▪	11,520.00	USD	▪	160.000
IR-L		5105615169	2	09/08/2006		160.000	0.000	EA		11,520.00	USD		160.000
Tr./ev. Invoice receipt					▪	160.000		EA	▪	11,520.00	USD	▪	160.000

Figure 4.47 Purchase Order Line Item Details

In this example, the costing lot size in the cost estimate is 200 (not displayed in Figure 4.46).

To determine the *purchase price* of the component, in the material document shown in Figure 4.45, double-click on the underlined purchase order number to display the purchase order. Then click on the **Purchase order history** tab to display the line item quantity and value, as shown in Figure 4.47.

If you multiply the purchase order quantity of **160.000**, determined from the **Quantity** column in Figure 4.47, by the standard price of **49.50**, determined from the material master Costing 2 view in Figure 4.46, the expected goods receipt value is 7,920. The expected goods receipt value, subtracted from the purchase order line item value of **11,520**, determined from the **Amt.in loc.cur.** column in Figure 4.47, equals the PPV posting of **3,600** (shown in the first row of the cost center line item report in Figure 4.44).

Analyzing the purchasing info record often helps explain why the purchase price is different from the standard price. Let's look at two common scenarios leading to differences between standard and purchase prices.

First, the component standard price is usually based on the purchasing info record. It's possible that a new vendor quotation was received, and the purchasing info record was updated based on the new quotation, since the standard cost estimate was created. You can display the purchasing info record from the purchase order screen shown in Figure 4.47 by following the menu path: **Environment • Info record**. While displaying the purchasing info record initial screen, click on the **Conditions** button to display the screen shown in Figure 4.48.

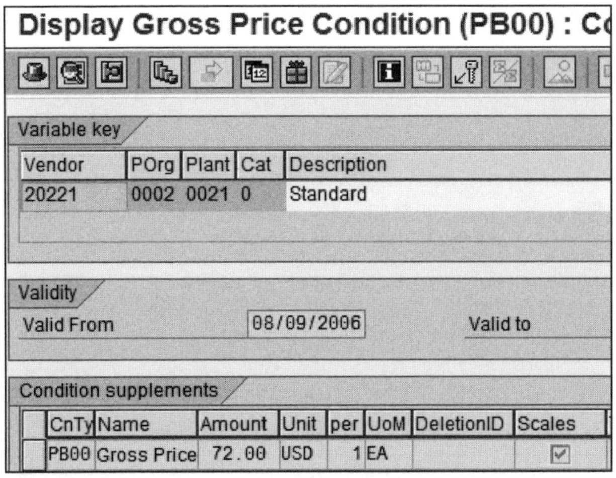

Figure 4.48 Purchasing info record Condition Screen

Click on the validity periods (calendar) icon to show details of changes to the purchasing info record price due to new vendor quotations. In this example, there is one validity period, so the difference between standard and purchase prices cannot be explained by a new vendor quotation.

Another possible reason for the PPV posting is purchasing info record scales. Scales represent vendor quotations that contain reduced prices for greater purchase quantities. In Figure 4.48, the indicator in the **Scales** column is selected. This means that more than one vendor price has been entered based on quantity ordered. To see details of the scales, double-click on the selected indicator in the **Scales** column. The screen shown in Figure 4.49 is displayed.

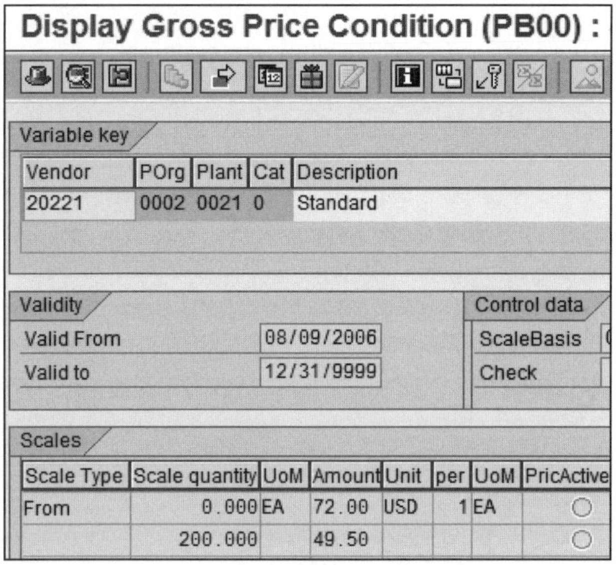

Display Gross Price Condition (PB00) :

Variable key

Vendor	POrg	Plant	Cat	Description
20221	0002	0021	0	Standard

Validity		Control data	
Valid From	08/09/2006	ScaleBasis	
Valid to	12/31/9999	Check	

Scales

Scale Type	Scale quantity	UoM	Amount	Unit	per	UoM	PricActive
From	0.000	EA	72.00	USD	1	EA	○
	200.000		49.50				○

Figure 4.49 Purchasing info record Scales

The scale in Figure 4.49 indicates that the purchase price for a quantity between 1 and 199 is **72.00 USD**, which is discounted to **49.50** for a quantity of **200.000** or more. Since the purchase order quantity is 160, as we saw in Figure 4.47, the purchase price is based on the first line of the scale, and is **72.00 USD**. Since the costing lot size of the standard cost estimate is **200.000**, the cost estimate accessed the second line of the scale, with a price of **49.50**. The reason for the difference between the standard and purchase price resulting in the PPV posting is that the purchase quantity is fewer than the standard cost estimate costing lot size.

During a costing run, the cost estimate costing lot size is determined from the material master Costing 1 view

costing lot size field. This should be set as close as possible to normal purchase order quantities of components to minimize PPV postings.

When a purchase order is created, if a lower price is available by ordering a larger quantity due to a scale, a warning message is generated before the purchase order is saved, as shown in Figure 4.50.

This allows purchasing to investigate the possibility of ordering a larger quantity in order to receive a price break. During the investigation, the costing lot size in the material master Costing 1 view should also be compared with the scale to determine if there will be a PPV posting.

4.7 Actual Costing/Material Ledger

Just as it's possible to allocate cost center variances to orders at period-end, as we discussed in Section 4.5, it's also possible to allocate all purchasing and manufacturing difference postings upward through the BOM to assemblies and finished goods. Actual costing determines what portion of the variance is debited to the next highest level using material consumption. Variances can be rolled up over multiple production levels to the finished product.

While actual costing and material ledger are beyond the scope of this guide, it could be worthwhile to investigate possible benefits through a test scenario in a test system. Actual costing can provide advantages, however it does introduce additional configuration, period-end processes, and analysis. As always, benefits need to be weighed against additional processing and complexity.

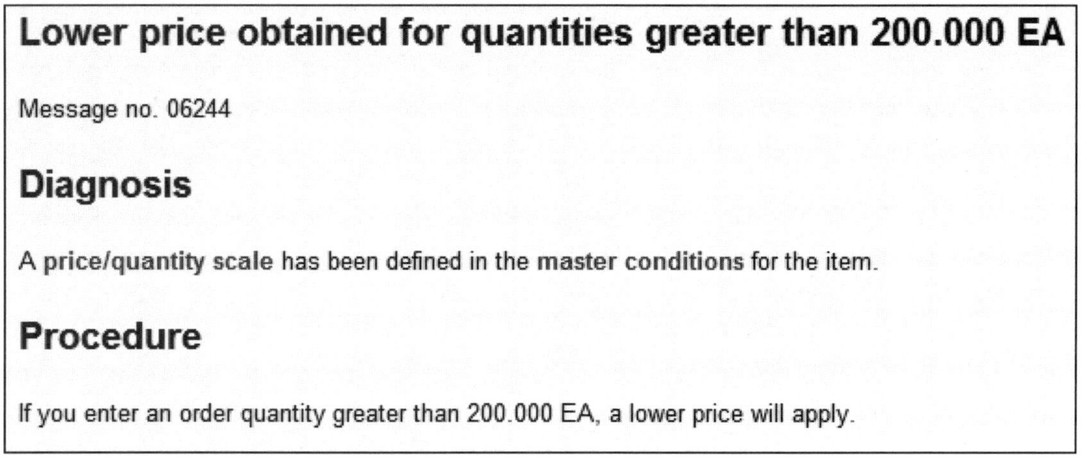

Lower price obtained for quantities greater than 200.000 EA

Message no. 06244

Diagnosis

A price/quantity scale has been defined in the master conditions for the item.

Procedure

If you enter an order quantity greater than 200.000 EA, a lower price will apply.

Figure 4.50 Message Indicating Lower Available Price

4.8 Summary

In this chapter, I initially discussed the items needed in preparation for period-end processing. The three common types of variance calculation, which are total, production, and planning were discussed, and case scenarios were presented. Then I examined variance configuration settings, to help in understanding the basis of the variance calculation. In the final step in preparation for period-end processing, I described variance categories in detail. I presented case scenarios for all four input variance categories and described all four output variance categories.

We walked through the four period-end processes most relevant to variance analysis, which are overhead, work in process, variance calculation, and settlement. I presented many examples and provided step-by-step procedures for analyzing variances by sorting line item reports and drilling down to original transactions.

We then examined cost center variances and how they relate to production variances. I demonstrated how to analyze cost centetr variance with standard cost center actual/plan reports, which have sufficient analysis capabilities for most companies. We also explored more advanced analysis functionality, including target cost analysis, variance analysis, and revaluation.

Purchase price variance (PPV) analysis was examined by drilling down from a standard cost center actual/plan report to material documents and purchase orders. I walked through an example PPV investigation involving purchasing info record price validity periods and scales. You can follow this same technique to analyze most PPV postings. I also presented an overview of actual costing and material ledger functionality.

In Chapter 5 we will examine scrap variances in detail, again following many example scenarios and reports. I'll demonstrate procedures for examining scrap variances that you can use in nearly any scenario to understand the cause of the posting.

In Chapter 6 I'll provide a general overview of the many excellent standard reports available for Controlling reporting, and a detailed overview of variance reporting.

5 Scrap Variance Analysis

In Chapter 4 we analyzed all scrap categories in detail, except for scrap variance. Scrap processing and analyzing scrap variances has its own chapter, since there is more involved in master data settings and cost estimate analysis than any of the other variance categories.

In this chapter I will analyze scrap processing and scrap variance analysis in detail. I discuss scrap basics, types of scrap, and master data settings, carry out plan and actual scrap postings, and then analyze scrap postings in detailed reports. The method of analyzing scrap variance in this chapter can be used as a model in analyzing variances in general.

5.1 Scrap Basics

Since no production process is perfect, there is always some percentage of scrap produced. Assemblies or components that do not meet quality standards may either become scrap or require rework. Depending on the problem, cheaper items may become scrap, while more costly assemblies may justify rework.

Case Scenario
The mounting holes for a metal plate are accidentally drilled larger than they were supposed to be. Filling the holes with weld and re-drilling correctly sized holes would cost more than the plate is worth. The plate is scrapped, and a new plate is drilled correctly and delivered to inventory. Statistics show that one in every 10 plates is drilled incorrectly, so you plan 10% assembly scrap for the drilled metal plate.

A drilled metal plate is issued from inventory as a component in a higher-level assembly, and during inspection, before production use, it is found that the mounting holes are oversize. The plate is discarded, and another plate is issued from inventory. Statistics show that one in every 50 drilled plates issued from inventory is drilled incorrectly and discarded, so you plan 2% component scrap for the drilled metal plate. You enter both 10% assembly scrap and 2% component scrap in the material master Material Requirements Planning (MRP) views of the drilled plate.

If the plates were made of an expensive metal alloy that is not readily available, it may be cost effective to rework the oversize holes by welding and re-drilling. In this case, you do not plan scrap.

Scrap is different from other losses during the manufacturing of a product, since it can be analyzed and predicted. SAP R/3 allows known scrap amounts to be entered and stored in master data as planned scrap percentages. Scrap percentages increase the planned manufacturing costs of a product, via the released cost estimate and standard price. If actual scrap equals planned scrap, no variance occurs, since postings are as planned. Benefits of planning for scrap include the following:

▶ Margin analysis is more accurate
▶ Variances highlight processes that need analysis
▶ Production resources can be more accurately planned
▶ Cost of sales more accurately reflect manufacturing costs

Target and actual scrap costs are calculated from plan scrap quantity, and actual scrap quantity posted during activity confirmation. Scrap variance is calculated and subtracted from total variances. Scrap variance is displayed in a scrap variance column in cost reports. A requirement to display the scrap variance column is to activate scrap calculation and reporting in the variance key and variance variant as was described in Chapter 4.

The three different types of scrap that can be planned for are described below:

▶ **Assembly Scrap**
This includes the entire cost of faulty or lost assemblies in the cost of sales. The plan quantity of the assembly is increased.

▶ **Component Scrap**
This includes the cost of faulty or lost individual components in the cost of sales. The plan quantity of components is increased.

▶ **Operation Scrap**
This optimizes the use of valuable components. The plan quantity of components in subsequent operations is decreased.

Now that we've covered scrap basics, I'll discuss each of the three different types of scrap in detail.

5.2 Assembly Scrap

Assembly scrap includes the entire cost of faulty or lost assemblies in the cost of sales. If assembly scrap is not planned, all scrap costs post as a variance. Although variance can be included at a higher level in profitability reporting, planned assembly scrap is included at the material level. This results in more accurate analysis of profitability at the product level.

Assembly Scrap Definition
Assembly scrap can be defined as the percentage of assembly quantity that does not meet required production quality standards. For example, planned assembly scrap of 25% means that in order to deliver 100 pieces of an assembly, you plan to produce 125. Planned assembly scrap also improves the Material Requirements Planning (MRP) process by ensuring you start with an increased quantity in order to achieve the required product yield. Assembly scrap is an *output* scrap, since it affects the planned output quantity of items in the production process.

Effect of Assembly Scrap on Quantities
Scrap quantities are important, since they cause scrap values. Let's follow a simple example of how assembly scrap applied at the assembly level affects lower-level component and activity quantities.

You plan to produce 100 finished printed circuit boards (PCBs). If planned assembly scrap is entered for the finished PCBs, all component and activity quantities are increased by 10%, as highlighted in the **Quantity costed** column in Figure 5.1.

	Quantity no scrap	Quantity costed	Assembly scrap
Finished PCBs	**100 PC**	**100 PC**	**0 PC**
▲— Blank PCBs	100 PC	110 PC	10 PC
┃— BIOS	100 PC	110 PC	10 PC
┃—*Operation 1*	*100 h*	*110 h*	*10 h*
┃— Processor	100 PC	110 PC	10 PC
┗—*Operation 1*	*100 h*	*110 h*	*10 h*

Figure 5.1 Effect of Assembly Scrap on Component and Activity Quantities

By increasing the quantity of components and activities, assembly scrap increases the plan cost of producing the finished PCBs. MRP will propose a production quantity of **110** assemblies, with the expectation that **100** will be delivered to inventory and 10 will be confirmed as scrap.

Now that we know what assembly scrap is and how it affects scrap quantities, we'll investigate how to plan assembly scrap in the next section.

Assembly Scrap Master Data
You can plan assembly scrap in two different master data fields. The most commonly used field is located in the MRP 1 view of the material master, which you access with transaction MM02 or via menu path: **Logistics • Materials Management • Material Master • Material • Change • Immediately**. Click on the MRP 1 tab to display the screen shown in Figure 5.2.

Lot size data		
Lot size	Z4	20 day Lot (4 Working Weeks)
Minimum lot size		Maximum lot
Fixed lot size		Maximum sto
Ordering costs		Storage costs
Assembly scrap (%)	10.00	Takt time

Figure 5.2 Assembly Scrap Field in MRP 1 View

Complete the **Assembly scrap (%)** field with a flat rate percentage determined by your production statistics of scrap rates. You should update this field prior to the next costing run if the statistics change during the current year. Later in Section 5.2 I'll explain how assembly scrap affects standard cost estimates.

Another master data field used to affect assembly scrap is located in the **Basic Data** tab of a BOM item. You can view or change BOM item details with transaction CS02 or via menu path: **Logistics • Production • Master Data • Bills of Material • Bill of Material • Material BOM • Change**. Double-click on a BOM item to display BOM item details, as shown in Figure 5.3.

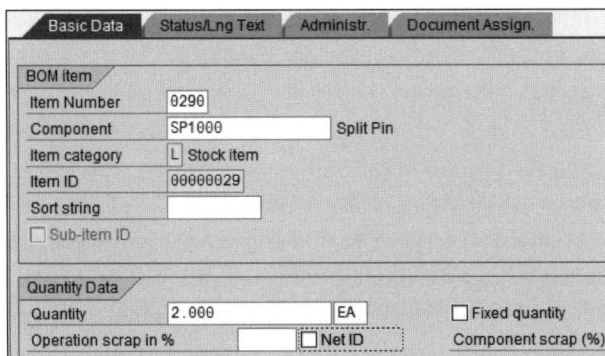

Figure 5.3 Inspect Net ID Indicator of BOM Component

You can select the **Net ID** indicator to ignore assembly scrap for this component. This is useful if you need to enter a scrap percentage for a particular component that is different than the assembly scrap percentage of the assembly. In this case, select the **Net ID** indicator and enter the percentage scrap for the component in either the **Operation scrap in %** or **Component scrap (%)** field.

If you make an entry in the **Component scrap (%)** field without selecting the **Net ID** indicator, assembly is calculated first, and then component scrap is calculated in addition, as discussed in detail in Section 5.3.

Planned Assembly Scrap Costs

Planned assembly scrap costs are included in the standard cost estimate. Let's compare two cost estimates, one without assembly scrap, and one with assembly scrap, to highlight the difference. To display the screen shown in Figure 5.4, use transaction CK13N or menu path: **Accounting • Controlling • Product Cost Controlling • Product Cost Planning • Material Costing • Cost Estimate with Quantity Structure**.

The **Total value** of the **STANDARD FG** cost estimate *without* assembly scrap is **46,254.68**. The figures in the **Scrap** and **Scrap quantity** columns indicate there is no planned output scrap. Now let's display a cost estimate for material **STANDARD FG** with 10% assembly scrap planned, as shown in Figure 5.5.

The **Total value** of the **STANDARD FG** cost estimate *with* assembly scrap is **50,880.14**, which is 10% higher than the cost estimate *without* assembly scrap. This is because the quantity of all components has increased by 10%, illustrated by comparing the **Quantity** columns in both cost estimates. The increase in component quantities is shown in the **Scrap quantity** column, while the corresponding increase in value is shown in the **Scrap** column. While only material cost estimates are displayed in Fig-

Costing structure	E...	Total value	Scrap	Currency	Quantity	Scrap quantity	U...	Resource
▽ 📇 STANDARD FG	◉	46,254.68	0.00	USD	1,000.000	0.000	EA	1303 100010682
📇 PRIMER	◉	227.44	0.00	USD	7.000	0.000	GAL	1303 400000691
▷ 📇 SFG	◉	23,271.40	0.00	USD	1,000.000	0.000	EA	1303 300002252
📇 URETHANE A 16	◉	6,155.17	0.00	USD	6,034.483	0.000	LB	1303 400000693
📇 MDI ISO B MATERIAL	◉	1,525.52	0.00	USD	965.517	0.000	LB	1303 400000694

Figure 5.4 Cost Estimate without Assembly Scrap

Costing structure		Total value	Scrap	Currency	Quantity	Scrap quantity	U...	Resource
▽ 📇 STANDARD FG	◉	50,880.14	0.00	USD	1,000.000	0.000	EA	1303 100010682
📇 PRIMER	◉	250.19	22.74	USD	7.700	0.700	GAL	1303 400000691
▷ 📇 SFG	◉	25,598.54	2,327.14	USD	1,100.000	100.000	EA	1303 300002252
📇 URETHANE A 16	◉	6,770.69	615.52	USD	6,637.932	603.448	LB	1303 400000693
📇 MDI ISO B MATERIAL	◉	1,678.07	152.55	USD	1,062.069	96.552	LB	1303 400000694

Figure 5.5 Cost Estimate with Assembly Scrap

ure 5.5, the quantity and value of all other cost estimate items, such as activities, are also increased by 10%.

To quickly determine if assembly scrap is included in a cost estimate, click on the cost estimate **Qty Struct.** (quantity structure) tab, which displays the screen shown in Figure 5.6.

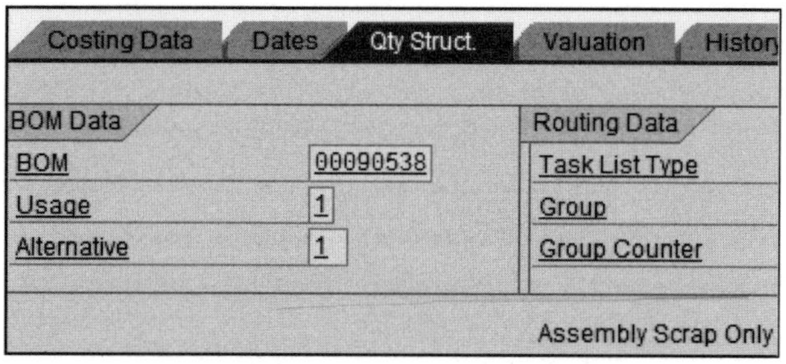

Figure 5.6 "Assembly Scrap Only" Text in Cost Estimate

The **Assembly Scrap Only** text indicates assembly scrap is included in the cost estimate, without the need to refer to the MRP 1 view of the material master. Information text also appears in the same tab if operation scrap is included in the cost estimate, as discussed in Section 5.4.

Now that we've looked at planning for assembly scrap with master data entries and the effect on cost estimates, let's examine how actual scrap postings occur.

Actual Assembly Scrap Costs

Actual scrap costs usually occur during production order confirmation. This is when activities are confirmed and goods movements occur during backflushing and auto goods receipt, as discussed in detail in Chapter 3. I'll now create a production order and carry out a confirmation to demonstrate how actual assembly scrap costs occur.

You create a production order with transaction CO01 or via menu path: **Logistics • Production • Production Control • Order • Create • With Material**. The screen shown in Figure 5.7 is displayed.

The production order quantity is automatically increased by 10% due to assembly scrap in the material master MRP 1 view, as discussed in Section 5.2. MRP proposes a total quantity of **1,100.000**, as shown in the **Total quant.** field, even though only 1,000 are required. This is because a confirmed scrap assembly quantity of **100.000** is expected, as shown in the **Scrap portion** field.

Actual assembly scrap is posted during production order confirmation. In Chapter 3 I demonstrated a confirmation per operation. In this example, I'll demonstrate a confirmation at the order header level with transaction CO15 or via menu path: **Logistics • Production • Production Control • Confirmation • Enter • For Order**. The screen shown in Figure 5.8 is displayed.

A quantity of **100.000**, due to planned assembly scrap, defaults in the **Confirmed scrap** field in the **Current confirm.** column. If the default **Confirmed scrap** quantity is manually changed, a scrap variance will result. The expected scrap quantity of **100.000** is displayed in the **Total to confirm** column of the **Confirmed scrap** row.

After scrap is confirmed, you carry out variance calculation, as discussed in the next section.

Variance Calculation

Variance calculation is done via transactions KKS6 (individual) and KKS5 (collective) or menu path: **Accounting • Controlling • Product Cost Controlling • Cost Object Controlling • Product Cost by Period • Period-End Closing • Single Functions: Product Cost Collector • Variances**. The screen shown in Figure 5.9 is displayed following variance calculation.

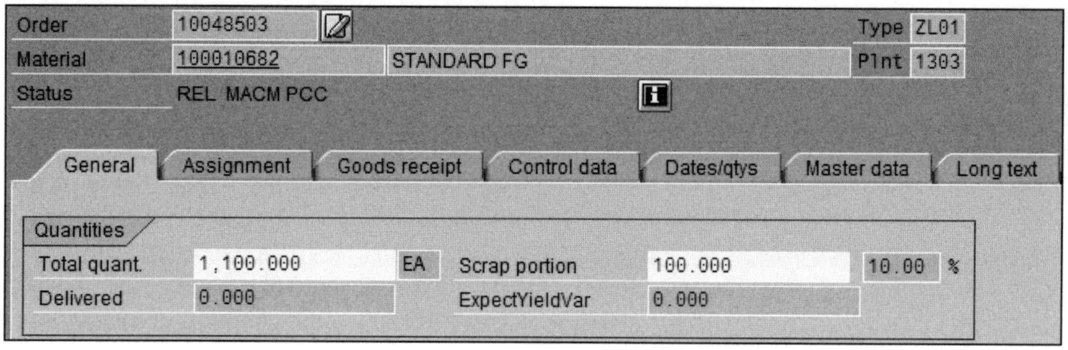

Figure 5.7 Production Order Quantity Increased by Planned Assembly Scrap

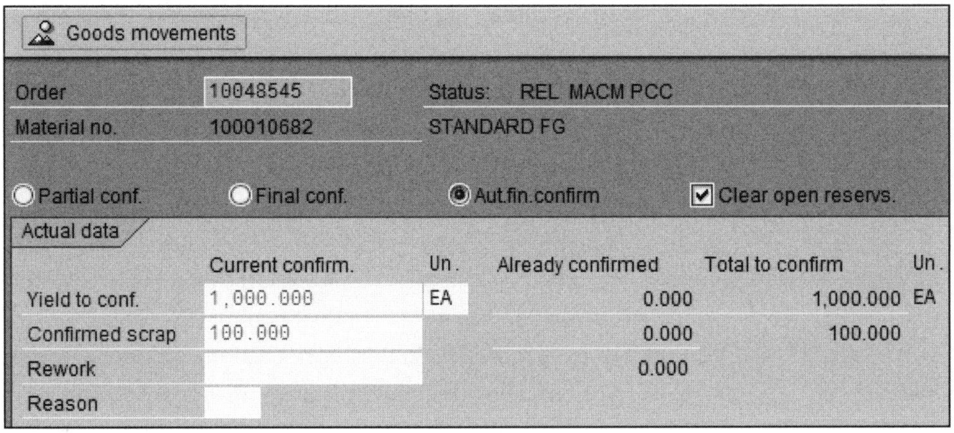

Figure 5.8 Confirmation Screen Includes Confirmed Scrap Field

Target cst	Σ	Act. costs	Σ	Ctrl costs	Σ	Variance	Σ	Scrap	Σ	Rem. var.	Actual qty
46,254.68		50,880.14		46,254.66		0.02-		4,625.48		0.00	1,000.000
46,254.68	■	50,880.14	■	46,254.66	■	0.02-	■	4,625.48	■	0.00	

Figure 5.9 Variance Calculation Scrap Output Screen

You carry out variance analysis for production and process orders with transaction codes KKS2 (individual) and KKS1 (collective).

Assembly scrap maintains the expected **Actual qty** delivered to inventory at **1,000.000** by increasing the manufactured quantity. After the planned assembly scrap quantity is actually confirmed as scrap, the output quantity is the quantity required.

The unfavorable scrap variance of **4,625.48** indicates that assembly scrap was posted but not planned in this example. Scrap variance is subtracted from total variance during variance calculation, which simplifies the task of analyzing total variance. Click on the **Scrap** button (not shown) in the variance calculation output screen to display details of the scrap variance by cost element and operation. Now that I've demonstrated how to plan and post actual scrap and calculate variance, let's look at how to report and analyze scrap postings.

Assembly Scrap Target/Actual Analysis

During a period, or at period-end, you may need to carry out further detailed analysis of scrap variance. Before doing so, you should first run variance calculation to determine the target costs. You can display and analyze target vs. actual costs in detailed product cost collector

reports with transaction PKBC_PKO or via menu path: **Accounting • Controlling • Product Cost Controlling • Product Cost by Period • Information System • Reports for Product Cost by Period • Detailed Reports**. A similar report is available for production and process orders with transaction PKBC_ORD.

Let's compare a series of three detailed reports to demonstrate how assembly scrap affects variance.

Assembly Scrap Not Planned and Actual Scrap Posted
The first detailed report contains an unfavorable scrap variance, since assembly scrap is not planned, while actual scrap is posted, as shown in Figure 5.10.

Since assembly scrap is not planned, actual assembly scrap posts as an unfavorable scrap variance with a value of **4,625.48**, as shown in the **Scrap** column.

Activity and component quantities to make **1,100.000 STANDARD FG** are issued from inventory, as shown in the **Total act.qty** column. This corresponds to the value of **50,880.14** in the **Debit** row and **Ttl actual** (total actual costs) column.

A quantity of **1,000.000 STANDARD FG** is delivered to inventory, as shown in the **Total act.qty** column. This corresponds to the credit value of **46,254.68** in the **Delivery** row and **Ttl actual** column.

Transact.	Origin	Origin (Text)	Σ	Total tgt	Σ	Ttl actual	Σ	Variance	Σ	Scrap	Total act.qty
Confirmations	1303B-5420/LABOR	Production / Labor Hours		4,578.48		5,036.32		457.84		457.85	255.521
	1303B-5420/OVHD	Production / Overhead Hours		6,027.98		6,630.77		602.79		602.80	255.521
	1303B-5420/MNT	Production / Maintenance Hours		3,349.65		3,684.61		334.96		334.97	255.521
	1303B-5420/ELEC	Production / Electricity		770.99		848.09		77.10		77.10	5,848.910
	1303B-5420/NATGAS	Production / Natural Gas		348.05		382.86		34.81		34.81	957.151
Goods issues	1303/400000691	PRIMER		227.44		250.19		22.75		22.74	7.700
	1303/400000693	URETHANE A 16		6,155.17		6,770.69		615.52		615.52	6,637.931
	1303/400000694	MDI ISO B MATERIAL		1,525.52		1,678.07		152.55		152.55	1,062.069
	1303/300002252	SFG		23,271.40		25,598.54		2,327.14		2,327.14	1,100.000
Debit			■	46,254.68	■	50,880.14	■	4,625.46	■	4,625.48	
Goods receipt	1303/100010682	STANDARD FG		46,254.68-		46,254.68-		0.00		0.00	1,000.000-
Delivery			■	46,254.68-	■	46,254.68-	■	0.00	■	0.00	
			■ ■	0.00	■ ■	4,625.46	■ ■	4,625.46	■ ■	4,625.48	

Figure 5.10 Assembly Scrap Not Planned and Actual Scrap Posted

Since the total actual debits of **50,880.14** are greater than the total actual credits of **46,254.68**, an unfavorable variance of **4,625.46** results, as shown in the summary (last) row of the **Total actual** column.

Now that we've looked at how posting assembly scrap without planning for it results in an unfavorable variance, let's see the effect of planning but not posting assembly scrap.

Assembly Scrap Planned and Actual Scrap Not Posted
Compare the report in the previous section with an *unfavorable* scrap variance to a report in this section with a *favorable* scrap variance, since assembly scrap is planned and not posted, as shown in Figure 5.11.

Since assembly scrap is planned, all planned scrap that is not actually posted results in a favorable scrap variance, with a value of **4,625.50-** as seen in the **Scrap** column in Figure 5.11.

Activity and component quantities needed to make **1,000.000 STANDARD FG** are issued from inventory, as shown in the **Total act.qty** column. This corresponds to the value of **46,254.68** in the **Debit** row and **Ttl actual** (total actual costs) column.

A quantity of **1,000.000 STANDARD FG** is delivered to inventory, as shown in the **Total act.qty** column. This corresponds to the credit value of **50,880.14-** in the **Delivery** row and **Ttl actual** column. The credit value is based on the standard cost estimate which contains the costs for making 1,100 assemblies, since assembly scrap is planned.

Since total actual debits of **46,254.68** are less than the total actual credits of **50,880.14**, a favorable variance of **4,625.46-** is shown in the summary (last) row of the **Total actual** column.

Now that we've looked at how posting assembly scrap without planning for it results in an unfavorable variance,

Transact.	Origin	Origin (Text)	Σ	Total tgt	Σ	Ttl actual	Σ	Variance	Σ	Scrap	Total act.qty
Confirmations	1303B-5420/LABOR	Production / Labor Hours		5,036.32		4,578.48		457.84-		457.85-	232.292
	1303B-5420/OVHD	Production / Overhead Hours		6,630.77		6,027.98		602.79-		602.80-	232.292
	1303B-5420/MNT	Production / Maintenance Hours		3,684.61		3,349.65		334.96-		334.97-	232.292
	1303B-5420/ELEC	Production / Electricity		848.09		770.99		77.10-		77.10-	5,317.191
	1303B-5420/NATGAS	Production / Natural Gas		382.86		348.05		34.81-		34.81-	870.137
Goods issues	1303/400000691	PRIMER		250.19		227.44		22.75-		22.74-	7.000
	1303/400000693	URETHANE A 16		6,770.69		6,155.17		615.52-		615.52-	6,034.483
	1303/400000694	MDI ISO B MATERIAL		1,678.07		1,525.52		152.55-		152.55-	965.517
	1303/300002252	SFG		25,598.54		23,271.40		2,327.14-		2,327.16-	1,000.000
Debit			■	50,880.14	■	46,254.68	■	4,625.46-	■	4,625.50-	
Goods receipt	1303/100010682	STANDARD FG		50,880.14-		50,880.14-		0.00		0.00	1,000.000-
Delivery			■	50,880.14-	■	50,880.14-	■	0.00	■	0.00	
			■ ■	0.00	■ ■	4,625.46-	■ ■	4,625.46-	■ ■	4,625.50-	

Figure 5.11 Assembly Scrap Planned and Actual Scrap Not Posted

and how planning assembly scrap and not actually posting it results in a favorable variance, let's see the effect of both planning and posting assembly scrap.

Assembly Scrap Planned and Actual Scrap Posted
Compare the reports in the previous two sections with unfavorable and favorable scrap variances to the report in this section with no scrap variance, since assembly scrap is planned and actual scrap is posted, as shown in Figure 5.12.

Since assembly scrap is planned and actual scrap is posted, only rounding differences of **0.04-** remain in the **Scrap** variance column.

Activity and component quantities needed to make **1,100.000 STANDARD FG** are issued from inventory, as shown in the **Total act.qty** column. This corresponds to the value of **50,880.13** in the **Debit** row and **Ttl actual** (total actual costs) column.

A quantity of **1,000.000 STANDARD FG** is delivered to inventory, as shown in the **Total act.qty** column. This corresponds to the credit value of **50,880.14-** in the **Delivery** row and **Ttl actual** column. The credit value is based on the standard cost estimate, which contains the costs for making 1,100 assemblies, since assembly scrap is planned.

Since total actual debits of **50,880.13** are nearly equal to total actual credits of **50,880.14**, variance is nearly eliminated, as shown by the **0.01-** in the summary (last) row of the **Total tgt** column.

Total variance ideally should only include unplanned production costs. If you don't plan scrap, all scrap costs will post as a scrap variance, as demonstrated in Figure 5.10. When you plan assembly scrap based on production statistics, scrap costs are separated from variance, and only the difference between plan and actual scrap costs posts as a variance, as shown in Figure 5.12.

Now that we've examined assembly scrap, let's look at the next type of scrap, which is component scrap.

5.3 Component Scrap

Component scrap includes the cost of faulty or lost components in the cost of sales. A case scenario involving component scrap was presented in Section 5.1. If component scrap is not planned, all scrap costs post as a variance. Although variance can be included at a higher level in profitability reporting, planned component scrap is included at the material level. This results in more accurate analysis of profitability at the product level.

Component Scrap Definition
Component scrap can be defined as the percentage of component quantity that does not meet required production quality standards, before being inserted in the production process. Planned component scrap is treated as additional consumption of the relevant component. Planned component scrap also improves the Material Requirements Planning (MRP) process by ensuring you start with an increased component quantity in order to achieve the required product yield. Component scrap is an *input* scrap, since it is detected before use in the production process.

Transact.	Origin	Origin (Text)	Σ	Total tgt	Σ	Ttl actual	Σ	Variance	Σ	Scrap	Total act.qty
Confirmations	1303B-5420/LABOR	Production / Labor Hours		5,036.32		5,036.32		0.00		0.00	255.521
	1303B-5420/OVHD	Production / Overhead Hours		6,630.77		6,630.77		0.00		0.01-	255.521
	1303B-5420/MNT	Production / Maintenance Hours		3,684.61		3,684.61		0.00		0.00	255.521
	1303B-5420/ELEC	Production / Electricity		848.09		848.09		0.00		0.00	5,848.910
	1303B-5420/NATGAS	Production / Natural Gas		382.86		382.86		0.00		0.00	957.151
Goods issues	1303/400000691	PRIMER		250.19		250.18		0.01-		0.00	7.700
	1303/400000693	URETHANE A 16		6,770.69		6,770.69		0.00		0.01-	6,637.931
	1303/400000694	MDI ISO B MATERIAL		1,678.07		1,678.07		0.00		0.00	1,062.069
	1303/300002252	SFG		25,598.54		25,598.54		0.00		0.02-	1,100.000
Debit			▪	50,880.14	▪	50,880.13	▪	0.01-	▪	0.04-	
Goods receipt	1303/100010682	STANDARD FG		50,880.14-		50,880.14-		0.00		0.00	1,000.000-
Delivery			▪	50,880.14-	▪	50,880.14-	▪	0.00	▪	0.00	
			▪▪	0.00	▪▪	0.01-	▪▪▪	0.01-	▪▪	0.04-	

Figure 5.12 Assembly Scrap Planned and Actual Scrap Posted

Effect of Component Scrap on Quantities

Scrap quantities are important, because they cause scrap values. Let's follow a simple example of how component scrap applied at the component level affects component quantities. We'll also examine the interaction between component and assembly scrap.

When planning to produce 100 finished printed circuit boards (PCBs), assembly scrap is calculated first, then component scrap. Assembly scrap applied to the finished PCBs increases all component and activity quantities by 10%, as shown in the highlighted **Quantity costed** column in Figure 5.13.

	Quantity no scrap	Quantity costed	Assembly scrap	Component scrap
Finished PCBs	100 PC	100 PC	0 PC	0 PC
⌐ Blank PCBs	100 PC	110 PC	10 PC	0 PC
BIOS	100 PC	110 PC	10 PC	0 PC
Operation 1	*100 h*	*110 h*	*10 h*	-
Processor	100 PC	116 PC	10 PC	6 PC
⌐ *Operation 1*	*100 h*	*110 h*	*10 h*	-

Figure 5.13 Component Scrap Increases Component Quantities

If 5% component scrap is also applied to the **Processor** component, the quantity is increased from **110** to **116**, as shown in the highlighted **Processor** row in Figure 5.13. Since component scrap is applied after assembly scrap, the component scrap quantity is 6 PC (pieces).

Assembly and component scrap increase the plan cost of producing finished PCBs by increasing the plan quantity of components and activities. MRP will propose a production quantity of 110 assemblies, with the expectation that 100 will be delivered to inventory, with 10 confirmed as scrap. MRP will also propose the consumption of a quantity of 116 pieces of the Processor component, even though only 100 would be needed without planned scrap.

Now that we know what component scrap is and how it affects quantities, we'll look at how to plan assembly scrap.

Component Scrap Master Data

You can plan component scrap in two different master data fields. The most commonly used field is located in the MRP 4 view of the material master, which you can access with transaction MM02 or via menu path: **Logistics • Materials Management • Material Master • Material • Change • Immediately**. Click on the MRP 4 tab to display the screen shown in Figure 5.14.

Complete the **Component scrap (%)** field with a flat rate percentage determined by your production statistics of scrap rates. You should update this field prior to the next costing run if the statistics change during the current year. Later in Section 5.3 I'll explain how component scrap affects standard cost estimates.

Another field used to plan component scrap is located in the **Basic Data** tab of the BOM item. You can view or change BOM item details with transaction CS02 or via menu path: **Logistics • Production • Master Data • Bills of Material • Bill of Material • Material BOM • Change**. Double-click on a BOM item to display BOM item details, as shown in Figure 5.15.

Case Scenario

A component is used in many assemblies, and generally the component scrap rate is 10%, which is entered in the material master MRP 4 view of the component. One assembly is manufactured close to the inventory store, and only 5% of components are lost or damaged on the way to production of this assembly. A component scrap rate of 5% is entered in the component BOM item for this particular assembly. The component scrap rate of 5% in the BOM item takes priority over the 10% component scrap rate entered in the material master MRP 4 view of the assembly.

An entry in the **Component scrap (%)** field in the BOM item takes priority over an entry in the material master, MRP 4 view. Complete the **Component scrap (%)** field

```
BOM explosion/dependent requirements
   Selection method        2          Component scrap (%)    10.00
   Individual/coll.         2          Requirements group
   ☑ Version Indicator      🗗 ProdVersions   MRP dep.requirements
```

Figure 5.14 Component Scrap Field in MRP 4 View of Component

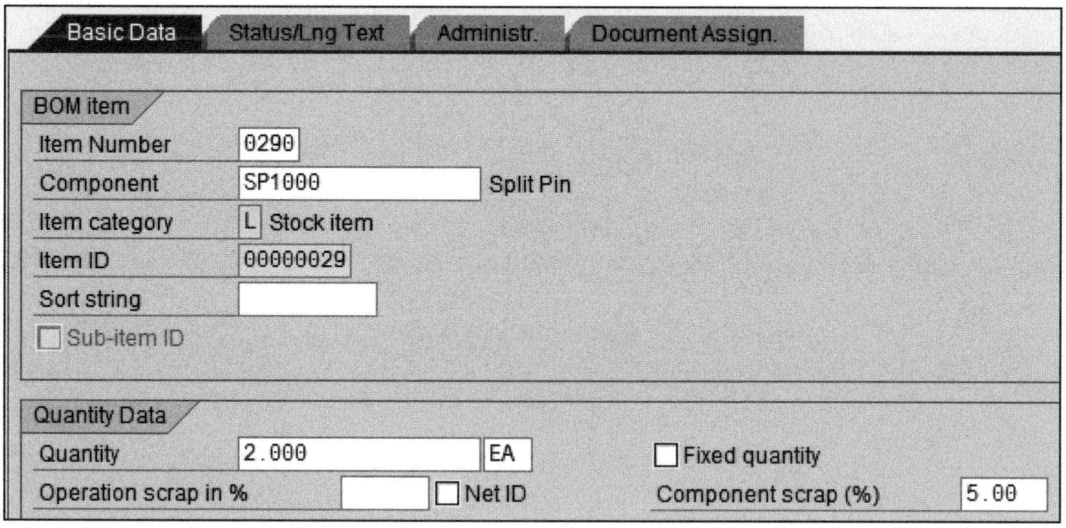

Figure 5.15 Component Scrap Field in BOM Item Details

with a flat rate percentage determined by your production statistics of scrap rates. You should update this field prior to the next costing run if the statistics change during the current year. In Section 5.3 I'll demonstrate how component scrap affects standard cost estimates.

Planned Component Scrap Costs

Planned component scrap costs are included in the standard cost estimate. Let's compare two cost estimates, one without component scrap, and one with component scrap, to highlight the difference. To display the screen shown in Figure 5.16, use transaction CK13N or menu

path: **Accounting • Controlling • Product Cost Controlling • Product Cost Planning • Material Costing • Cost Estimate with Quantity Structure**.

The **Total value** of the **STANDARD FG** cost estimate *without* component scrap is **46,254.68**. The figures in the **Scrap** and **Scrap quantity** columns indicate there is no planned output scrap. Now let's display a cost estimate for material **STANDARD FG** with 10% component scrap entered in the material master MRP 4 view, as shown in Figure 5.17.

The **Total value** of the **STANDARD FG** cost estimate *with* component scrap is **48,581.82**, which is higher than

Costing structure	E...	Total value	Scrap	Currency	Quantity	Scrap quantity	U...	Resource
▽ 🖩 STANDARD FG	◎	46,254.68	0.00	USD	1,000.000	0.000	EA	1303 100010682
🖩 PRIMER	◎	227.44	0.00	USD	7.000	0.000	GAL	1303 400000691
▷ 🖩 SFG	◎	23,271.40	0.00	USD	1,000.000	0.000	EA	1303 300002252
🖩 URETHANE A 16	◎	6,155.17	0.00	USD	6,034.483	0.000	LB	1303 400000693
🖩 MDI ISO B MATERIAL	◎	1,525.52	0.00	USD	965.517	0.000	LB	1303 400000694

Figure 5.16 Cost Estimate without Component Scrap

Costing structure		Total value	Scrap	Currency	Quantity	Scrap quantity	U...	Resource
▽ 🖩 STANDARD FG	◎	48,581.82	0.00	USD	1,000.000	0.000	EA	1303 100010682
🖩 PRIMER	◎	227.44	0.00	USD	7.000	0.000	GAL	1303 400000691
▷ 🖩 SFG	◎	25,598.54	0.00	USD	1,100.000	0.000	EA	1303 300002252
🖩 URETHANE A 16	◎	6,155.17	0.00	USD	6,034.483	0.000	LB	1303 400000693
🖩 MDI ISO B MATERIAL	◎	1,525.52	0.00	USD	965.517	0.000	LB	1303 400000694

Figure 5.17 Cost Estimate with Component Scrap

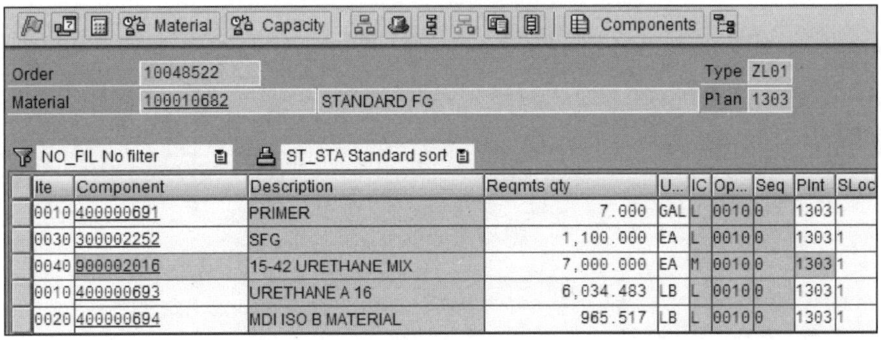

Ite	Component	Description	Reqmts qty	U...	IC	Op...	Seq	Plnt	SLoc
0010	400000691	PRIMER	7.000	GAL	L	0010	0	1303	1
0030	300002252	SFG	1,100.000	EA	L	0010	0	1303	1
0040	900002016	15-42 URETHANE MIX	7,000.000	EA	M	0010	0	1303	1
0010	400000693	URETHANE A 16	6,034.483	LB	L	0010	0	1303	1
0020	400000694	MDI ISO B MATERIAL	965.517	LB	L	0010	0	1303	1

Figure 5.18 Production Order Component Quantities Increased by Planned Component Scrap

the **Total value** of the cost estimate *without* component scrap. This is because the quantity of component **SFG** has increased by 10%, as shown by comparing the **Quantity** columns in both cost estimates. The **Total value** of component **SFG** has increased by 10% due to the increase in **Quantity**.

The increase in component quantity is *not* shown in the **Scrap quantity** column. Component scrap is an *input quantity* variance, not an output scrap variance. Later in Section 5.3 I'll explain how to analyze component scrap in detail.

Actual Component Scrap Costs

Actual scrap costs usually occur during production order confirmation. This is when activities are confirmed and goods movements occur during backflushing and auto goods receipt, as discussed in detail in Chapter 3. I'll now create a production order and carry out a confirmation to demonstrate how actual component scrap costs occur.

You create a production order with transaction CO01 or via menu path: **Logistics • Production • Production Control • Order • Create • With Material**. To display the component overview screen shown in Figure 5.18, from the initial production order header screen, follow menu path: **Goto • Overviews • Components**.

Component **SFG** quantity is automatically increased by 10% due to component scrap in the material master MRP 4 view, as we discussed earlier in Section 5.3. MRP proposes a total quantity of **1,100.000**, as shown in the **Reqmts qty** (requirements quantity) column in the **SFG** row, even though only 1,000 are required according to the BOM quantities. This is because it is expected that 100 of the components will be lost or damaged on the way to the production line, or will not pass inspection for some reason.

Actual component scrap is posted during production order confirmation. In Chapter 3 I demonstrated a confirmation per operation. In this example, I'll demonstrate a confirmation at the order header level with transaction CO15, or via menu path: **Logistics • Production • Production Control • Confirmation • Enter • For Order**. The screen shown in Figure 5.19 is displayed.

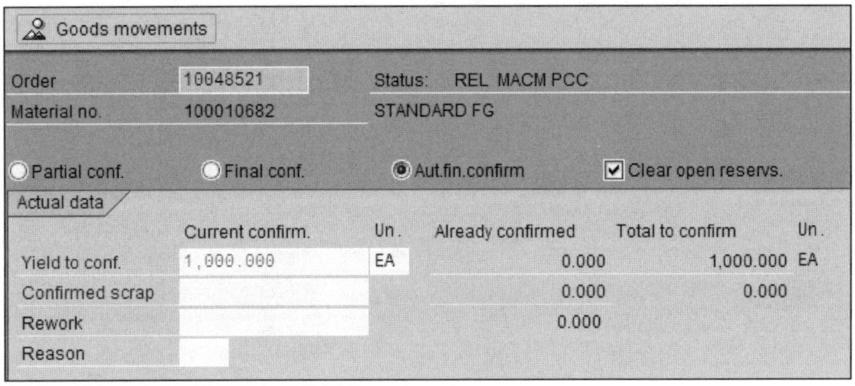

Figure 5.19 Confirmation Screen with Component Scrap Planned

Only *output* scrap, such as assembly or operation scrap, is entered in the **Confirmed scrap** field. There is no expected output scrap to confirm, as shown at the **Total to confirm** column of the **Confirmed scrap** row. Click on the **Goods movements** button to display the goods movements screen shown in Figure 5.20.

Batch determination

Order	10048540	Status:	REL MACM P
Material no.	100010682	STANDARD FG	

Material	Quantity	E...	Plant	Sto...	Batc
100010682	1,000.000	EA	1303	1	
400000691	7.000	GAL	1303	1	
300002252	1,100.000	EA	1303	1	
400000693	6,034.483	LB	1303	1	
400000694	965.517	LB	1303	1	

Figure 5.20 Confirmation Goods Movements Screen

A **Quantity** of **1,100.000** for **Material 300002252** (SFG) defaults from the production order. Production order quantity of component SFG was increased 10% due to component scrap entered in the material master MRP 4 view. If you manually adjust the default component quantity shown in Figure 5.20, you will introduce an unplanned input quantity variance.

After scrap is confirmed, you carry out variance calculation, as discussed in the next section.

Variance Calculation

Variance calculation is done using transactions KKS6 (individual) and KKS5 (collective) or via menu path: **Accounting • Controlling • Product Cost Controlling • Cost Object Controlling • Product Cost by Period • Period-End Closing • Single Functions: Product Cost Collector • Variances**. The screen shown in Figure 5.21 is displayed following variance calculation. You carry out variance analysis for production and process orders with transaction codes KKS2 (individual) and KKS1 (collective).

There is no **Scrap** variance, because component scrap is categorized as an input quantity variance, as shown by the **2,327.14** value in the **Input qty var.** (input quantity variance) column. Detailed variance analysis for component scrap occurs in product cost collector reports, as explained in the next section.

Component Scrap Target/Actual Analysis

During a period, or at period-end, you may need to carry out further detailed analysis of scrap variance. Before doing so, you should first run variance calculation to determine the target costs. You can display and analyze plan vs. actual costs in detailed product cost collector reports with transaction PKBC_PKO or via menu path: **Accounting • Controlling • Product Cost Controlling • Product Cost by Period • Information System • Reports for Product Cost by Period • Detailed Reports**. A similar report is available for production and process orders with transaction PKBC_ORD.

Let's compare three detailed reports to demonstrate how component scrap affects variance.

Component Scrap Not Planned and Actual Scrap Posted

The first product cost collector report contains an unfavorable scrap variance, since component scrap is not planned, while actual scrap is posted, as shown in Figure 5.22.

Since component scrap is not planned, actual component scrap posts as an unfavorable input quantity variance, with a value of **2,327.14** in the **Variance** (total variance) and **Qty variance** (input quantity variance) columns.

A component quantity needed to make **1,100.000 STANDARD FG** is issued from inventory, as shown in the **Total act.qty** column. This corresponds to the value of **25,598.54** in the **SFG** row and **Ttl actual** (total actual costs) column.

Since the standard cost estimate doesn't contain planned component scrap, the component target value of **23,271.40** in the **SFG** row in the **Total tgt** (total tar-

Target cst	Σ Act. costs	Σ Ctrl costs	Σ Variance	Σ Scrap	Σ Rem. var.	Input qty var.	Actual qty
46,254.68	48,581.82	48,581.82	2,327.14	0.00	0.00	2,327.14	1,000.000
46,254.68	**▪ 48,581.82**	**▪ 48,581.82**	**▪ 2,327.14**	**▪ 0.00**	**▪ 0.00**		

Figure 5.21 Component Scrap Displays as Input Quantity Variance

Transact.	Origin	Origin (Text)	Σ	Total tgt	Σ	Ttl actual	Σ	Variance	Σ	Scrap	Σ	Qty variance	Total act.qty
Confirmations	1303B-5420/LABOR	Production / Labor Hours		4,578.48		4,578.48		0.00		0.00		0.00	232.292
	1303B-5420/OVHD	Production / Overhead Hours		6,027.98		6,027.98		0.00		0.00		0.00	232.292
	1303B-5420/MNT	Production / Maintenance Hours		3,349.65		3,349.65		0.00		0.00		0.00	232.292
	1303B-5420/ELEC	Production / Electricity		770.99		770.99		0.00		0.00		0.00	5,317.191
	1303B-5420/NATGAS	Production / Natural Gas		348.05		348.05		0.00		0.00		0.00	870.137
Goods issues	1303/400000691	PRIMER		227.44		227.44		0.00		0.00		0.00	7.000
	1303/400000693	URETHANE A 16		6,155.17		6,155.17		0.00		0.00		0.00	6,034.483
	1303/400000694	MDI ISO B MATERIAL		1,525.52		1,525.52		0.00		0.00		0.00	965.517
	1303/300002252	SFG		23,271.40		25,598.54		2,327.14		0.00		2,327.14	1,100.000
Debit			■	46,254.68	■	48,581.82	■	2,327.14	■	0.00	■	2,327.14	
Goods receipt	1303/100010682	STANDARD FG		46,254.68-		46,254.68-		0.00		0.00		0.00	1,000.000-
Delivery			■	46,254.68-	■	46,254.68-	■	0.00	■	0.00	■	0.00	
			■■	0.00	■■	2,327.14	■■	2,327.14	■■	0.00	■■	2,327.14	

Figure 5.22 Component Scrap Not Planned and Actual Scrap Posted

get costs) column is 10% less than the component actual value of **25,598.54**. This results in an unfavorable variance of **2,327.14**, as shown in the **Debit** row of the **Qty variance** column.

Overall, since total actual debits of **48,581.82** are greater than total actual credits of **46,254.68**, the result is an unfavorable variance due to an input quantity of **2,327.14** in the summary (last) row of the **Total actual** column.

Now that we've looked at how posting component scrap without planning for it results in an unfavorable variance, let's see the effect of planning but not posting component scrap.

Component Scrap Planned and Actual Scrap Not Posted
Compare the report in the previous section with an *unfavorable* variance to a report in this section with a *favorable* variance, since component scrap is planned, but

no actual increase in component quantity is posted, as shown in Figure 5.23.

Since component scrap is planned, all planned scrap that's not actually posted results in a favorable variance with a value of **2,327.14-** in the **Qty variance** (input quantity variance) column.

A component quantity needed to make **1,000.000 STANDARD FG** is issued from inventory, as shown in the **Total act.qty** column, and there is no increase in component quantity. This corresponds to the component actual value of **23,271.40** in the **SFG** row and **Ttl actual** (total actual costs) column. This results in total actual debits of **46,254.68**, as shown in the **Debit** row and the **Ttl actual** column.

Since the standard cost estimate contains 10% planned component scrap, the component target value of **25,598.54** in the **SFG** row in the **Total tgt** (total target costs) column is 10% greater than the component actual

Transact.	Origin	Origin (Text)	Σ	Total tgt	Σ	Ttl actual	Σ	Variance	Σ	Scrap	Σ	Qty variance	Total act.qty
Confirmations	1303B-5420/LABOR	Production / Labor Hours		4,578.48		4,578.48		0.00		0.00		0.00	232.292
	1303B-5420/OVHD	Production / Overhead Hours		6,027.98		6,027.98		0.00		0.00		0.00	232.292
	1303B-5420/MNT	Production / Maintenance Hours		3,349.65		3,349.65		0.00		0.00		0.00	232.292
	1303B-5420/ELEC	Production / Electricity		770.99		770.99		0.00		0.00		0.00	5,317.191
	1303B-5420/NATGAS	Production / Natural Gas		348.05		348.05		0.00		0.00		0.00	870.137
Goods issues	1303/400000691	PRIMER		227.44		227.44		0.00		0.00		0.00	7.000
	1303/400000693	URETHANE A 16		6,155.17		6,155.17		0.00		0.00		0.00	6,034.483
	1303/400000694	MDI ISO B MATERIAL		1,525.52		1,525.52		0.00		0.00		0.00	965.517
	1303/300002252	SFG		25,598.54		23,271.40		2,327.14-		0.00		2,327.14-	1,000.000
Debit			■	48,581.82	■	46,254.68	■	2,327.14-	■	0.00	■	2,327.14-	
Goods receipt	1303/100010682	STANDARD FG		48,581.82-		48,581.82-		0.00		0.00		0.00	1,000.000-
Delivery			■	48,581.82-	■	48,581.82-	■	0.00	■	0.00	■	0.00	
			■■	0.00	■■	2,327.14-	■■	2,327.14-	■■	0.00	■■	2,327.14-	

Figure 5.23 Component Scrap Planned and Actual Scrap Not Posted

Transact.	Origin	Origin (Text)	Σ	Total tgt	Σ	Ttl actual	Σ Variance	Σ	Scrap	Σ Qty var.	Total act.qty
Confirmations	1303B-5420/LABOR	Production / Labor Hours		4,578.48		4,578.48	0.00		0.00	0.00	232.292
	1303B-5420/OVHD	Production / Overhead Hours		6,027.98		6,027.98	0.00		0.00	0.00	232.292
	1303B-5420/MNT	Production / Maintenance Hours		3,349.65		3,349.65	0.00		0.00	0.00	232.292
	1303B-5420/ELEC	Production / Electricity		770.99		770.99	0.00		0.00	0.00	5,317.191
	1303B-5420/NATGAS	Production / Natural Gas		348.05		348.05	0.00		0.00	0.00	870.137
Goods issues	1303/400000691	PRIMER		227.44		227.44	0.00		0.00	0.00	7.000
	1303/400000693	URETHANE A 16		6,155.17		6,155.17	0.00		0.00	0.00	6,034.483
	1303/400000694	MDI ISO B MATERIAL		1,525.52		1,525.52	0.00		0.00	0.00	965.517
	1303/300002252	SFG		25,598.54		25,598.54	0.00		0.00	0.00	1,100.000
Debit			▪	48,581.82	▪	48,581.82	▪ 0.00	▪	0.00	▪ 0.00	
Goods receipt	1303/100010682	STANDARD FG		48,581.82-		48,581.82-	0.00		0.00	0.00	1,000.000-
Delivery			▪	48,581.82-	▪	48,581.82-	▪ 0.00	▪	0.00	▪ 0.00	
			▪▪	0.00	▪▪	0.00	▪▪ 0.00	▪▪	0.00	▪▪ 0.00	

Figure 5.24 Component Scrap Planned and Actual Scrap Posted

value of **23,271.40**. This results in a favorable variance of **2,327.14-**, as shown in the **Debit** row and **Qty variance** column.

Overall, since total actual debits of **46,254.68** are less than total actual total credits of **48,581.82**, the result is a favorable variance due to an input quantity of **2,327.14-** in the summary row of the **Total actual** column.

Now that we've looked at how posting component scrap without planning for it results in an unfavorable variance, and how planning component scrap and not actually posting it results in a favorable variance, let's see the effect of both planning and posting component scrap.

Component Scrap Planned and Actual Scrap Posted
Compare the reports in the previous two sections with unfavorable and favorable variances to the report in this section with no variance, since component scrap is planned and actual component quantity is posted, as shown in Figure 5.24.

Since component scrap is planned and actual component quantities are posted as planned, no variances remain in the **Variance** or **Qty var.** columns.

A component quantity needed to make **1,100.000** of **STANDARD FG** is issued from inventory, as shown in the **Total act.qty** column of the **SFG** row. This corresponds to the value of **25,598.54** in the **Ttl actual** (total actual costs) column of the **SFG** row.

Since the standard cost estimate contains 10% planned component scrap, the component target value of **25,598.54** in the **SFG** row in the **Total tgt** (total target costs) column is the same as the component actual value of **25,598.54**. This results in a value of **0.00** in the **Qty variance** column of the **Debit** row.

Overall, since total actual debits of **48,581.82** are equal to total actual credits of **48,581.82**, the result is a value of **0.00** in the summary row of the T+1 column.

Total variance ideally should only include unplanned production costs. If you don't plan scrap, all scrap costs will post as a variance, as demonstrated in Figure 5.22. When you plan component scrap based on production statistics, scrap costs are included in the cost estimate, and only the difference between plan and actual component scrap costs post as an input quantity variance, as demonstrated in Figure 5.24.

Now that we've examined assembly and component scrap, let's look at the third type of scrap, which is operation scrap.

5.4 Operation Scrap

Planned operation scrap includes the entire cost of faulty or lost assemblies in the cost of sales. If operation scrap is not planned, all scrap costs post as a variance. Although variances can be included at a higher level in profitability reporting, planned operation scrap is included at the material level. This results in more accurate analysis of profitability at the product level.

Operation Scrap Definition

Operation scrap can be defined as the percentage of assembly quantity that does not meet required production quality standards. For example, planned operation scrap of 20% means that if you start an operation with 125 pieces, you will lose 20% (25 pieces) during the operation. One hundred pieces will be available for the subsequent operation. Operation scrap is an output scrap, since it reduces the planned output quantity in the production process.

Operation scrap has different effects on quantities, depending on whether it is entered in the routing, BOM item, or both. I'll now discuss the three possible options in the following sections.

Operation Scrap in Routing

Operation scrap entered in the *routing* ensures faulty assemblies are discarded before valuable components are inserted. The *output* quantity of assembly operations is reduced by the operation scrap amount before valuable components are inserted in a subsequent operation. This reduces wastage of valuable components discarded in assemblies.

Case scenario

A music CD packaging facility inspects a CD case for scratches in operation 010 and inserts a CD in the case in operation 020. Operation scrap of 20% is applied at operation 010. For every 100 CD cases inspected, 20 are discarded, and CDs are inserted in 80 CD cases in operation 020. Since CDs are more expensive than cases, damaged cases are discarded before inserting the CDs.

However, the manufacturer still has a requirement to assemble 100 CDs in cases. Planned assembly scrap of 25% is added to the assembly material master. MRP generates a requirement for inspection of 125 cases in operation 010, and 20%, or 25 cases, are discarded due to operation scrap. One hundred cases are available for operation 020.

Operation Scrap in BOM Item

Operation scrap entered in the *BOM item* ensures the input quantity of valuable components inserted in an assembly is reduced. Assembly scrap entered in the material master of the assembly can be ignored by selecting a net indicator. This allows close control over the planning and use of individual valuable components in an assembly. This may also be useful when a component can be salvaged and reused, even if the assembly does not pass quality inspection. If BOM operation scrap is not entered, assembly scrap from the material master is used.

Operation Scrap in Operation and BOM Item

Operation scrap entered in *both* the routing and BOM item reduces the *output* quantity of an assembly before valuable components are inserted in the next operation. It also controls the *input* quantity of individual valuable components in the assembly.

Routing operation scrap refers to the *activity* quantity used, while BOM operation scrap refers to the *material* quantity used.

Effect of Operation Scrap on Quantities

Scrap quantities are important, since they cause scrap values. Let's follow a simple example of how operation scrap applied at the operation level affects component and activity quantities.

You begin a process with 100 finished printed circuit boards (PCBs). If planned operation scrap of 10% is entered in the first operation and 20% is entered in the second operation in the routing of the finished PCB, a quantity of 72 finished PCBs will be available at the end of the second operation, as shown in Figure 5.25.

By decreasing the output quantity of operations, operation scrap increases the cost of producing the finished PCBs. MRP will propose a production quantity of 100 assemblies, with the expectation that 72 will be delivered to inventory and 28 partial assemblies will be confirmed as scrap. No operation scrap is entered in the BOM item.

Now that we know what operation scrap is and how it affects scrap quantities, we'll investigate how to plan operation scrap.

Operation Scrap Master Data

You can plan operation scrap in two master data fields. The most commonly used field is located in the routing operation details view. To enter operation scrap, as displayed in Figure 5.26, use transaction code CA02 or

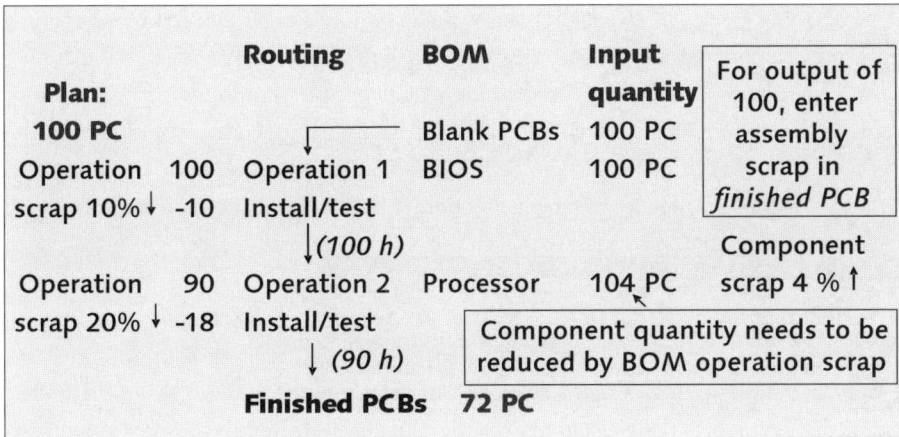

Figure 5.25 Operation Scrap Reduces Operation Output

menu path: **Logistics • Production • Master Data • Routings • Routings • Standard Routings.**

Figure 5.26 Operation Scrap Field in Operation Details

You enter operation scrap in the **Scrap in %** field of the **General data** section of the routing operation details screen.

Another field used to plan operation scrap is located in the **Bssic Data** tab of the BOM item. You can view or change BOM item details with transaction CS02 or via menu path: **Logistics • Production • Master Data • Bills of Material • Bill of Material • Material BOM • Change.** Double-click on a BOM item to display BOM item details, as shown in Figure 5.27.

You enter operation scrap in the **Operation scrap in %** field of the **Basic Data** tab of the BOM item. The **Net ID** indicator is selected to ignore assembly scrap, and it must be selected if you enter operation scrap. For a par-

ticular component, operation scrap allows you to enter a different scrap percentage, usually less than the assembly scrap percentage.

Figure 5.27 Operation Scrap Field in BOM Item

Planned Operation Scrap Costs

Planned operation scrap costs are included in the standard cost estimate. Let's compare two cost estimates, one without operation scrap, and one with operation scrap, to highlight the difference. To display the screen shown in Figure 5.28, use transaction CK13N or menu path: **Accounting • Controlling • Product Cost Controlling • Product Cost Planning • Material Costing • Cost Estimate with Quantity Structure.**

The **Total value** of the **STANDARD FG** cost estimate *without* operation scrap is **46,254.68**. The figures in the **Scrap** and **Scrap quantity** columns indicate there is no

Costing structure	E...	Total value	Scrap	Currency	Quantity	Scrap quantity	U...	Resource
▽ 🗎 STANDARD FG	●	46,254.68	0.00	USD	1,000.000	0.000	EA	1303 100010682
🗎 PRIMER	●	227.44	0.00	USD	7.000	0.000	GAL	1303 400000691
▷ 🗎 SFG	●	23,271.40	0.00	USD	1,000.000	0.000	EA	1303 300002252
🗎 URETHANE A 16	●	6,155.17	0.00	USD	6,034.483	0.000	LB	1303 400000693
🗎 MDI ISO B MATERIAL	●	1,525.52	0.00	USD	965.517	0.000	LB	1303 400000694

Figure 5.28 Cost Estimate without Operation Scrap

Costing structure	E...	Total value	Scrap	Currency	Quantity	Scrap quantity	U...	Resource
▽ 🗎 STANDARD FG	●	46,254.68	0.00	USD	900.000	0.000	EA	1303 100010682
🗎 PRIMER	●	227.44	22.74	USD	7.000	0.700	GAL	1303 400000691
▷ 🗎 SFG	●	23,271.40	2,327.14	USD	1,000.000	100.000	EA	1303 300002252
🗎 URETHANE A 16	●	6,155.17	615.52	USD	6,034.483	603.448	LB	1303 400000693
🗎 MDI ISO B MATERIAL	●	1,525.52	152.55	USD	965.517	96.552	LB	1303 400000694

Figure 5.29 Cost Estimate with Operation Scrap

planned output scrap. Now let's display a cost estimate for material **STANDARD FG** with 10% operation scrap entered in the first operation of the routing, as shown in Figure 5.29.

The **Total value** of the **STANDARD FG** cost estimate *with* operation scrap is **46,254.68**, the same as *without* operation scrap. However, the output **Quantity** of the cost estimate *with* operation scrap is reduced by 10%, from **1,000.000** *without* operation scrap, to **900.000** *with* operation scrap. It costs the same to produce **900.000** with operation scrap as it does to produce **1,000.000** without operation scrap, so per unit cost is increased by operation scrap.

To quickly determine if operation scrap is included in a cost estimate, click on the cost estimate **Quantity Struct.** (quantity structure) tab, which displays the screen shown in Figure 5.30.

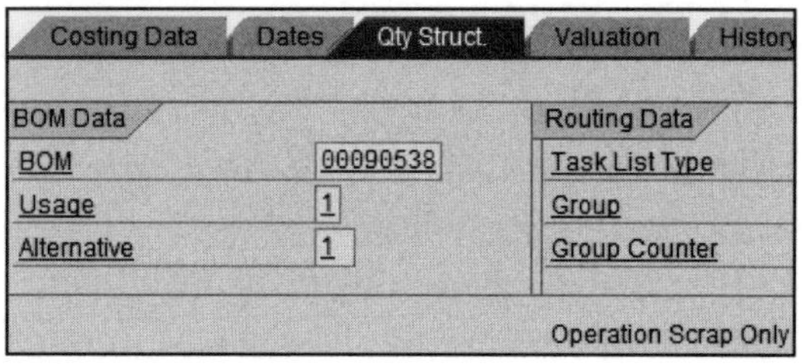

Figure 5.30 Operation Scrap Only Text in Cost Estimate

The **Operation Scrap Only** text indicates that operation scrap is included in the cost estimate, without the need to refer to operation details. Information text also appears in the same tab if assembly scrap is included in the cost estimate.

Now that we've looked at planning for operation scrap with master data entries and how it affects cost estimates, let's examine how actual scrap postings occur.

Actual Operation Scrap Costs

Actual scrap costs usually occur during production order confirmation. That is when operation output is either confirmed as yield or as scrap. I'll now create a production order and carry out a confirmation to demonstrate how actual operation scrap costs occur.

You create a production order with transaction CO01 or via menu path: **Logistics • Production • Production Control • Order • Create • With Material**. From the production order header screen, follow menu path: **Goto • Overviews • Operations** to display the operations overview screen. Then double-click on the operation in which you entered operation scrap in Section 5.4 to display the production order operation detail screen shown in Figure 5.31.

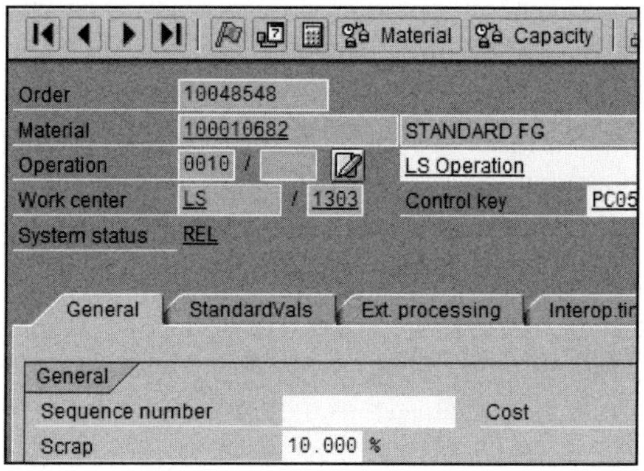

Figure 5.31 Production Order Operation Scrap Field

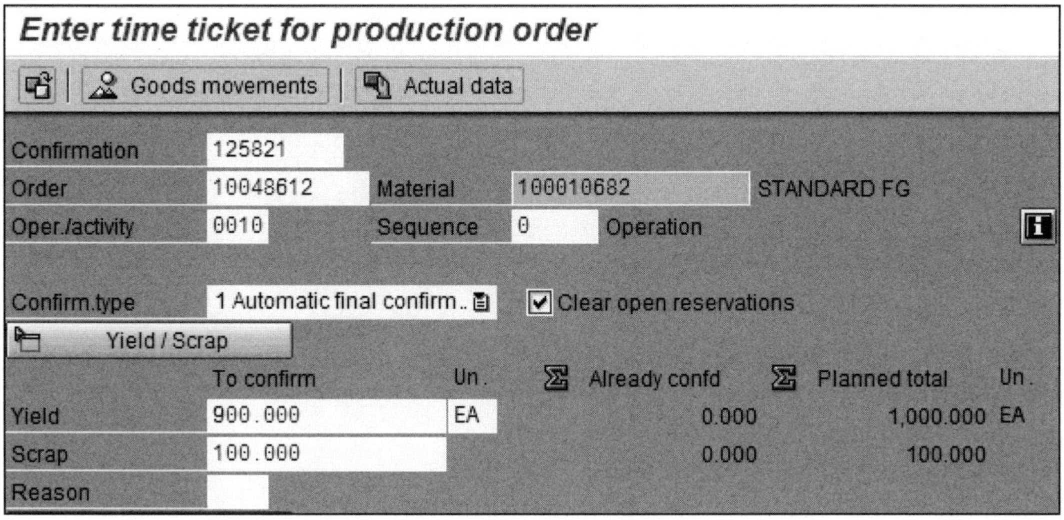

Figure 5.32 Production Order Confirmation Screen Includes Scrap Field

Operation **Scrap** defaults from the routing, as discussed in Section 5.4. Production order total quantity is unchanged by planned operation scrap. MRP proposes a quantity of 1,000, with plan yield of 900 and an operation scrap quantity of 100.

Actual operation scrap is posted during production order confirmation. A confirmed scrap field is available, and planned operation scrap defaults from the production order when using confirmation transaction CO11N or menu path: **Logistics • Production • Production Control • Confirmation • Enter • For Operation • Time Ticket**, as shown in Figure 5.32.

The **Planned total** yield quantity of **1,000.000** is reduced by default operation **Scrap** quantity of **100.000**, resulting in a default **Yield** quantity of **900.000**. If the default operation **Scrap** quantity is manually changed, a scrap variance will result.

After scrap is confirmed, you carry out variance calculation, as discussed next.

Variance Calculation

Variance calculation is done using transactions KKS6 (individual) and KKS5 (collective), or menu path: **Accounting •** **Controlling • Product Cost Controlling • Cost Object Controlling • Product Cost by Period • Period-End Closing • Single Functions: Product Cost Collector • Variances**. The screen shown in Figure 5.33 is displayed following variance analysis. You carry out variance analysis for production and process orders with transaction codes KKS2 (individual) and KKS1 (collective).

Operation scrap has reduced the expected **Actual qty** delivered to inventory to **900.000** from 1,000.000. Operation scrap doesn't increase the manufactured quantity, so after the planned operation scrap quantity is actually confirmed as scrap, the output quantity is less than the quantity required. You need to plan assembly scrap as well as operation scrap in order to output the required quantity, as described in the case scenario in Section 5.4.

The unfavorable scrap variance of **4,625.48** indicates that operation scrap was posted but not planned in this example. Scrap variance is subtracted from total variance, which simplifies the task of analyzing total variance.

Click on the **Scrap** button (not shown) in the variance calculation output screen to display details of the scrap variance by cost element and operation.

Target cst	Σ	Act. costs	Σ	Ctrl costs	Σ	Variance	Σ	Scrap	Σ	Rem. var.	Actual qty
41,629.21		46,254.68		41,629.20		0.01-		4,625.48		0.00	900.000
41,629.21	▪	46,254.68	▪	41,629.20	▪	0.01-	▪	4,625.48	▪	0.00	

Figure 5.33 Variance Calculation Output Screen

Now that I've demonstrated how to plan and post actual scrap and calculate variance, let's look at how to report and analyze scrap postings.

Operation Scrap Target/Actual Analysis

During a period or at period-end, you may need to do further detailed analysis of scrap variance. Before analysis during a period, you should first run variance calculation to determine the target costs. You can display and analyze target vs. actual costs in detailed product cost collector reports with transaction PKBC_PKO or via menu path: **Accounting • Controlling • Product Cost Controlling • Product Cost by Period • Information System • Reports for Product Cost by Period • Detailed Reports**. A similar report is available for production and process orders with transaction PKBC_ORD.

Let's compare a series of three detailed reports to demonstrate how operation scrap affects variance.

Operation Scrap Not Planned and Actual Scrap Posted
The first report contains an unfavorable scrap variance, since operation scrap is not planned, while actual scrap is posted, as shown in 5.34.

Since operation scrap is not planned, actual operation scrap posts as an unfavorable variance with a value of **4,625.48** in the **Scrap** variance column.

Activity and component quantities needed to make **1,000.000 STANDARD FG** are issued from inventory, as shown in the **Total act.qty** column. This corresponds to the value of **46,254.68** in the **Ttl actual** (total actual costs) column of the **Debit** row.

A quantity of **900.000 STANDARD FG** is delivered to inventory, as shown in the **Total act.qty** column. This corresponds to the credit value of **41,629.21-** in the **Ttl actual** column of the **Delivery** row.

Since total actual debits of **46,254.68** are greater than the total actual credits of **41,629.21**, an unfavorable variance of **4,625.47** results, as shown in the summary row of the **Total actual** column.

Now that we've looked at how posting operation scrap without planning for it results in an unfavorable variance, let's see the effect of planning but not posting operation scrap.

Operation Scrap Planned and Actual Scrap Not Posted
Compare the report in the previous section with an *unfavorable* scrap variance to a report in this section with a *favorable* scrap variance, since component scrap is planned but no actual scrap is posted, as shown in Figure 5.35.

Since operation scrap is planned, all planned scrap not actually posted results in a favorable scrap variance, with a value of **4,625.47-** in the **Scrap** column.

Activity and component quantities needed to make **900.000 STANDARD FG** are issued from inventory, as shown in the **Total act.qty** column. This corresponds to the value of **41,629.22** in the **Ttl actual** (total actual costs) column of the **Debit** row.

A quantity of **900.000 STANDARD FG** is delivered to inventory, as shown in the **Total act.qty** column. This corresponds to the credit value of **46,254.68** in the **Ttl actual** column of the **Delivery** row.

Transact.	Origin	Origin (Text)	Σ	Total tgt	Σ	Ttl actual	Σ	Variance	Σ	Scrap	Total act.qty
Confirmations	1303B-5420/LABOR	Production / Labor Hours		4,120.63		4,578.48		457.85		457.85	232.292
	1303B-5420/OVHD	Production / Overhead Hours		5,425.18		6,027.98		602.80		602.80	232.292
	1303B-5420/MNT	Production / Maintenance Hours		3,014.68		3,349.65		334.97		334.97	232.292
	1303B-5420/ELEC	Production / Electricity		693.89		770.99		77.10		77.10	5,317.191
	1303B-5420/NATGAS	Production / Natural Gas		313.25		348.05		34.80		34.81	870.137
Goods issues	1303/400000691	PRIMER		204.70		227.44		22.74		22.74	7.000
	1303/400000693	URETHANE A 16		5,539.65		6,155.17		615.52		615.52	6,034.483
	1303/400000694	MDI ISO B MATERIAL		1,372.97		1,525.52		152.55		152.55	965.517
	1303/300002252	SFG		20,944.26		23,271.40		2,327.14		2,327.14	1,000.000
Debit			■	41,629.21	■	46,254.68	■	4,625.47	■	4,625.48	
Goods receipt	1303/100010682	STANDARD FG		41,629.21-		41,629.21-		0.00		0.00	900.000-
Delivery			■	41,629.21-	■	41,629.21-	■	0.00	■	0.00	
			■ ■	0.00	■ ■	4,625.47	■ ■	4,625.47	■ ■	4,625.48	

Figure 5.34 Operation Scrap Not Planned and Actual Scrap Posted

Transact.	Origin	Origin (Text)	Σ	Total tgt	Σ	Ttl actual	Σ	Variance	Σ	Scrap	Total act.qty
Confirmations	1303B-5420/LABOR	Production / Labor Hours		4,578.48		4,120.63		457.85-		457.85-	209.063
	1303B-5420/OVHD	Production / Overhead Hours		6,027.98		5,425.18		602.80-		602.80-	209.063
	1303B-5420/MNT	Production / Maintenance Hours		3,349.65		3,014.69		334.96-		334.97-	209.063
	1303B-5420/ELEC	Production / Electricity		770.99		693.89		77.10-		77.10-	4,785.472
	1303B-5420/NATGAS	Production / Natural Gas		348.05		313.25		34.80-		34.80-	783.123
Goods issues	1303/400000691	PRIMER		227.44		204.70		22.74-		22.74-	6.300
	1303/400000693	URETHANE A 16		6,155.17		5,539.66		615.51-		615.52-	5,431.035
	1303/400000694	MDI ISO B MATERIAL		1,525.52		1,372.96		152.56-		152.55-	868.965
	1303/300002252	SFG		23,271.40		20,944.26		2,327.14-		2,327.14-	900.000
Debit			▪	46,254.68	▪	41,629.22	▪	4,625.46-	▪	4,625.47-	
Goods receipt	1303/100010682	STANDARD FG		46,254.68-		46,254.68-		0.00		0.00	900.000-
Delivery			▪	46,254.68-	▪	46,254.68-	▪	0.00	▪	0.00	
			▪ ▪	0.00	▪ ▪	4,625.46-	▪ ▪	4,625.46-	▪ ▪	4,625.47-	

Figure 5.35 Operation Scrap Planned and Actual Scrap Not Posted

The credit value is based on the standard cost estimate, which contains the costs for making 1,000 assemblies, because operation scrap is planned.

Since total actual debits of **41,629.22** are less than the total actual credits of **46,254.68**, a favorable variance of **4,625.46-** is shown in the summary row of the **Total actual** column.

Now that we've looked at how planning operation scrap and not actually posting it results in a favorable variance, let's see the effect of both planning and posting operation scrap.

Assembly Scrap Planned and Actual Scrap Posted

Compare the reports in the previous two sections with favorable and unfavorable scrap variances to the report in this section with no scrap variance, since operation scrap is planned and actual scrap is posted, as shown in Figure 5.36.

Since operation scrap is planned and actual scrap is posted, scrap variance is eliminated, as shown in the summary row of the **Scrap** variance column.

Activity and component quantities needed to make **1,000.000 STANDARD FG** are issued from inventory, as shown in the **Total act.qty** column. This corresponds to the value of **46,254.67** in the **Ttl actual** (total actual costs) column of the **Debit** row.

A quantity of **900.000 STANDARD FG** is delivered to inventory, as shown in the **Total act.qty** column. This corresponds to the credit value of **46,254.68-** in the **Ttl actual** column of the **Delivery** row. The credit value is based on the standard cost estimate, which contains the costs for making 1,000 assemblies, since operation scrap is planned.

Since the total actual debits of **46,254.67** are nearly equal to the total actual credits of **46,254.68**, variance is

Transact.	Origin	Origin (Text)	Σ	Total tgt	Σ	Ttl actual	Σ	Variance	Σ	Scrap	Total act.qty
Confirmations	1303B-5420/LABOR	Production / Labor Hours		4,578.48		4,578.47		0.01-		0.00	232.292
	1303B-5420/OVHD	Production / Overhead Hours		6,027.98		6,027.97		0.01-		0.00	232.292
	1303B-5420/MNT	Production / Maintenance Hours		3,349.65		3,349.65		0.00		0.00	232.292
	1303B-5420/ELEC	Production / Electricity		770.99		770.99		0.00		0.00	5,317.191
	1303B-5420/NATGAS	Production / Natural Gas		348.05		348.06		0.01		0.00	870.137
Goods issues	1303/400000691	PRIMER		227.44		227.44		0.00		0.00	7.000
	1303/400000693	URETHANE A 16		6,155.17		6,155.18		0.01		0.00	6,034.483
	1303/400000694	MDI ISO B MATERIAL		1,525.52		1,525.51		0.01-		0.00	965.517
	1303/300002252	SFG		23,271.40		23,271.40		0.00		0.00	1,000.000
Debit			▪	46,254.68	▪	46,254.67	▪	0.01-	▪	0.00	
Goods receipt	1303/100010682	STANDARD FG		46,254.68-		46,254.68-		0.00		0.00	900.000-
Delivery			▪	46,254.68-	▪	46,254.68-	▪	0.00	▪	0.00	
			▪ ▪	0.00	▪ ▪	0.01-	▪ ▪	0.01-	▪ ▪	0.00	

Figure 5.36 Operation Scrap Planned and Actual Scrap Posted

nearly eliminated, as shown by the **0.01-** in the summary row of the **Ttl actual** column.

Total variance ideally should only include unplanned production costs. If you don't plan scrap, all scrap costs will post as a scrap variance, as was demonstrated in Figure 5.34. When you plan operation scrap based on production statistics, scrap costs are separated from variance, and only the difference between plan and actual scrap costs post as a variance, as demonstrated in Figure 5.36.

5.5 Summary

In this chapter I discussed scrap basics, including the difference between scrap and rework, and presented a case scenario involving the interaction between assembly and component scrap, and the decision of whether to scrap or rework. I also briefly defined the three types of scrap, which are assembly, component and operation scrap.

I then analyzed each of the three types of scrap. I defined each at a detailed level and presented diagrams to help in understanding the effect of scrap on quantities and how costs are affected. I demonstrated how to plan scrap by making master data entries, and explained the priorities if two entries are made.

We analyzed the effect of plan scrap on cost estimates by analyzing cost estimates before and after the plan scrap entries. I also demonstrated a shortcut for determining if assembly and/or operation scrap influence a cost estimate: clicking on the cost estimate quantity structure tab.

We explained how actual scrap postings occur, by first creating a production order and then carrying out confirmations involving scrap. I then carried out variance calculation and analyzed the output results screen.

Finally, we examined three detailed reports for each type of scrap. First, I analyzed the effect of not planning scrap and then posting actual scrap, and the resulting unfavorable variance. Second, we saw the effect of planning for scrap but not actually posting scrap, and the resulting favorable variance. Finally, we examined the ideal scenario of planning for scrap and then posting the planned amounts of scrap. One of the main benefits of this scenario is the reduction in total variance, making it easier to analyze other variance categories, as described in Chapter 4.

Finally in Chapter 6, I'll walk through the many excellent standard reports available for Controlling reporting in general, and for variance reporting in particular.

6 Reporting

One of the most powerful features of standard reporting is the drill-down functionality. From high-level summarized reports, you can drill down through detailed and line item reports to source documents. This functionality is one of the key tools at your disposal during variance analysis.

The highest-level report you can drill down from is a summarized report, which allows you to display variances at a highly summarized level, e.g., plant manufacturing variances. A plant manager typically reviews plant manufacturing variances at period-end, while production personnel may review manufacturing variances weekly, or even daily if necessary. The only limit on how often you can run summarization reports is the data collection processing time. I'll discuss data collection in more detail in Section 6.1.

If you decide to investigate plant variances further, you can expand the plant summarization row to display the next level, e.g., material group. You can then expand individual material groups, which have a large variance, to display a list of materials within the material groups. You can set up exception rules and traffic light icons to highlight individual materials with high variances in this report.

When you have identified product cost collectors or manufacturing orders, which require further analysis, detailed reports provide analysis at a cost element level. Cost elements appear as rows in detailed reports and identify costs such as raw materials, activities, and overhead.

Tip

If you select the Material Origin indicator in the Costing 1 view of all material masters, you also see the material number displayed in detailed reports. This is one of the single most important indicators in providing greater visability to the cause of variances. If you have already created material master records without the Material Origin selected, you can use report RKH-KMATO to select the indicator.

You can drill down on a row in a detailed report to a line item report. The line item report displays a list of all line item postings, identified by the cost element, to the order. You can sort the Value or Quantity columns in a line item report to identify large line item postings that may need further investigation. To analyze a line item posting further, double-click on it to display the source document, such as Material Document in the case of a goods issue.

Production managers, production planners, and Material Requirements Planning (MRP) controllers typically run summarized reports and detailed and line item reports weekly or even daily. They look for, and analyze, large variances indicating problems such as incorrect activity confirmations or incorrect master data settings. Experienced plant personnel realize the importance of not leaving variance analysis until period-end, when it may be too late to correct some errors, or there may be too many errors to correct within the period-end closing time frame, and postings to the previous period are blocked.

Period-end processing and analysis is usually restricted to a time frame of just a couple of days, at the start of the following period. At the end of the time frame, postings to the previous period are blocked so the data underlying the previous period reports already supplied to managers does not change. If variances are not corrected within the narrow period-end time frame, they will remain in the previous period and need to be explained, even if they were due to mistakes, e.g., activity confirmations.

Now that I've introduced the standard reports most commonly used for variance analysis and explained who is likely to use them and the purpose for using them, let's examine summarized analysis and detailed and line item reports in more detail in the following sections.

6.1 Summarized Analysis Reports

Summarization analysis is based on *hierarchy structures* (like pyramids), with manufacturing orders or product cost collectors at the wide base, and progressively higher and narrower levels based on, e.g., material group and plant, on the way up to the Controlling area at the peak.

You regularly run a *data collection* program, which rolls up the order cost information from the base, through the nodes and levels, to the top of the hierarchy.

You then run a *summarization report*, which reads the information stored on the hierarchy nodes and presents the output either in a *product drilldown* report, which allows you to navigate between summarization levels, or in a *summarization hierarchy* report, with the hierarchy nodes presented as expandable and collapsible rows based on the hierarchy levels, and cost information presented in columns such as Target, Actual, and Variance.

Now that I've discussed summarization reports at a basic level and presented a case scenario demonstrating the benefits of regularly running and analyzing these reports, let's look more closely at the types of summarization reports available, and how they are set up and maintained.

There are two types of summarization reports available: *product drilldown* and *summarization hierarchy* reports. We'll examine each in detail in the following sections.

Product Drilldown Reports

Product drilldown reports allow you to slice and dice data based on characteristics such as product group, material, plant, cost component, and period. You can easily navigate between characteristics and drill down to lower-level characteristics. The navigation methods used for product drilldown reports are similar to those used with Profitability Analysis reports.

Case Scenario

A plant manager runs a summarization report at period-end to analyze plant manufacturing variances. Variances are higher than expected, and the manager examines the next hierarchy level down, which is order type, and notices that the unusually high variance is associated with the production order order type for manufacturing pumps. From the summarization report, the manager displays a list of all production orders of this order type, sorts the Variance column, and notices a production order with a particularly high variance. The plant manager notes the production order number and asks the production manager to explain the cause of the production order variance.

The production manager carries out variance analysis on the production order, and finds that most of the variance is identified as resource-usage variance. The production manager then clicks in the Cost Elements button in the variance calculation results screen and notices that a much more expensive component, sourced from overseas, was substituted for a less expensive component sourced locally. The production manager then reviews MRP-generated requirements and discovers that the sales order delivery date promised to the customer could not be met with locally sourced components that have a long delivery time. A more expensive component with a shorter delivery time was substituted to meet the sales order delivery date. The production manager then organizes a meeting with sales and the plant manager to review sales contract negotiation strategy for pumps.

By reviewing the Variance column and expanding the hierarchy in a summarization report, the plant manager has discovered a sales contract issue affecting company profitability. By regularly reviewing summarization reports and immediately investigating large and unusual variances, problems that otherwise may have gone unnoticed can be detected quickly, and corrective action can be taken. This assertive approach to variance analysis can provide companies with a competitive edge over others that allow (mainly communication-based) problems to continue until the effect on the bottom line is noticed, in a future period.

Product drilldown reports use predefined summarization levels, which means they are already set up for you. The predefined summarization levels are suitable for most scenarios. However, if they do not fully meet your requirements, you can create your own hierarchies.

Now that I've introduced product drilldown reports, I'll describe in detail, in the subsections that follow, the three steps necessary to display the reports.

Configuration

You can run production drilldown reports without this configuration step. Its only purpose is to add a group, such as material group, to drilldown reports. You can try running the reports first, to see if you have a requirement to add a group.

This configuration step is required only once. You should not need to change product drilldown configuration after making the initial settings with the following procedure.

You can change the configuration setting with transaction OKNO or via menu path: **IMG • Controlling • Product Cost Controlling • Information System • Control Parameters**. Click on the **Data Extraction/Product Drilldown** tab to display the screen shown in Figure 6.1.

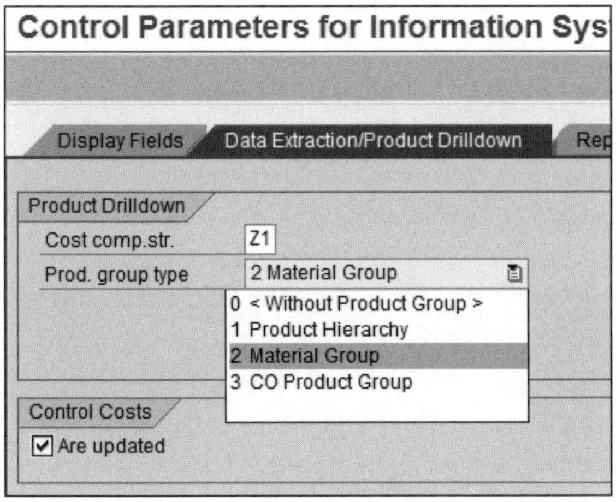

Figure 6.1 Product Drilldown Setting in Control Parameters

To display the list of possible groups, click in the **Prod. Group type** field, as shown in Figure 6.1. Click on your choice and save your work.

Product hierarchies and material groups may already be defined and assigned in your material masters. If so, making the selection in the screen shown in Figure 6.1

will cause the groups to appear in product drilldown reports with associated summarized data.

CO product groups allow you to define your own hierarchy and assign materials. You create CO product groups with transaction KKC7 or via menu path: **Accounting • Controlling • Product Cost Controlling • Cost Object Controlling • Product Cost by Period • Information System • Tools • Summarized Analysis: Preparation • Product Group • Create**. The screen shown in Figure 6.2 is displayed.

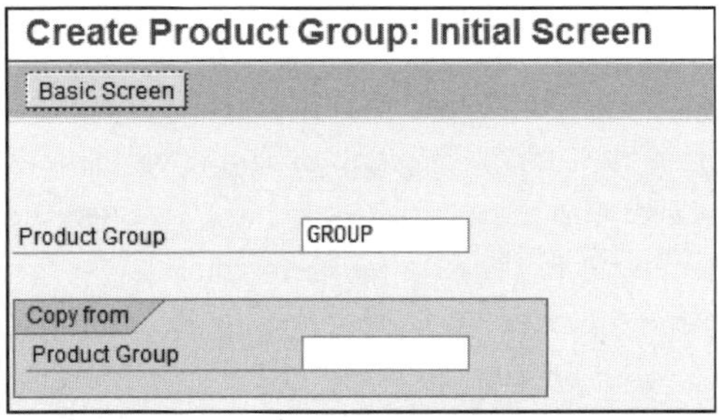

Figure 6.2 Create Product Group Initial Screen

This screen is where you enter the name of your new product group. Complete the **Product Group** field and click on the **Basic Screen** button to display the screen shown in Figure 6.3.

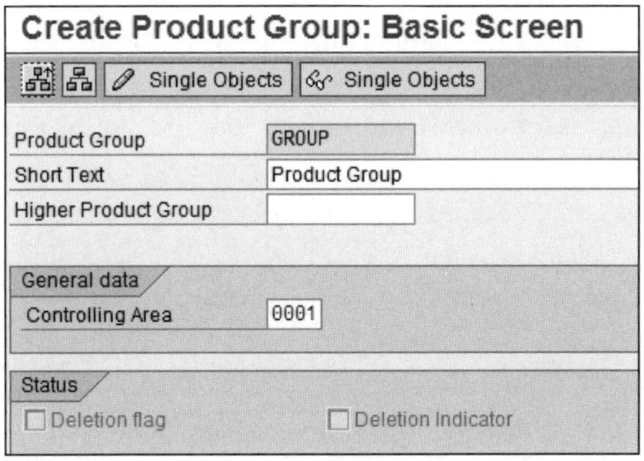

Figure 6.3 Create Product Group Basic Screen

In this screen you enter **Short Text** describing your new **Product Group**. You can also create a hierarchy by attaching this group to a higher-level group. You do this by making an entry in the **Higher Product Group** field. Complete the fields and save your work to create the new **Product Group**.

After you've created your new product groups, you'll need to assign materials to the lowest-level groups. You assign materials to the lowest-level CO product groups with transaction KKPN or via menu path: **Accounting • Controlling • Product Cost Controlling • Product Cost by Period • Information System • Tools • Summarized Analysis: Preparation • Product Group • Material Assignment**. The screen shown in Figure 6.4 is displayed.

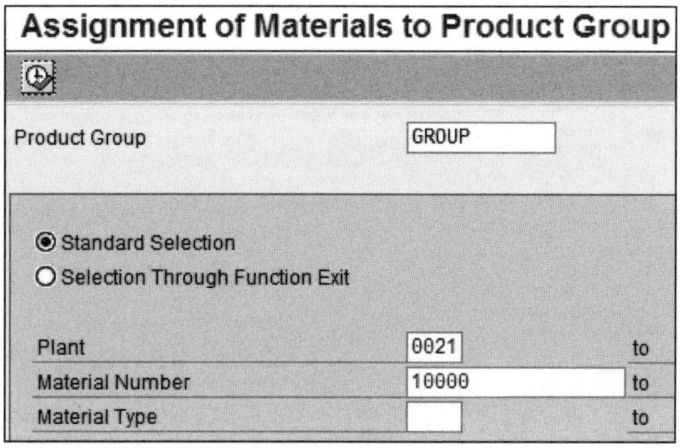

Assignment of Materials to Product Group

Product Group	GROUP

⦿ Standard Selection
○ Selection Through Function Exit

Plant	0021	to
Material Number	10000	to
Material Type		to

Figure 6.4 Assign Materials to Product Group

In this screen you enter a single lower-level **Product Group** and select materials to assign to the group. You can assign multiple materials by entering a **Material Number** range or list. You can also assign multiple materials by entering a **Material Type** range or list and/or a **Plant** range or list.

Complete the fields and click on the execute (clock) icon to display the screen shown in Figure 6.5.

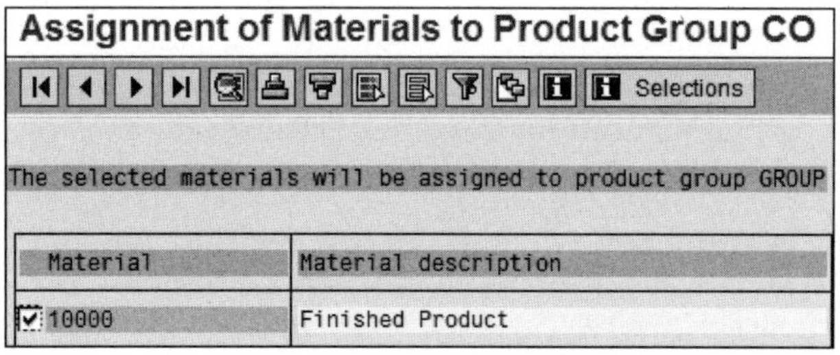

Assignment of Materials to Product Group CO

The selected materials will be assigned to product group GROUP

Material	Material description
☑ 10000	Finished Product

Figure 6.5 Assignment of Materials to Product Group

You are presented with a list of all the materials you selected in the screen shown in Figure 6.4. You have a chance to refine your selection by deselecting any **Material** in the list to be excluded from the product group. Or you may decide to return to the previous selection screen

before saving, so you can change the selection criteria. To assign the selected materials in the **Material** list to a product group save your work.

Now that we've assigned a group to the product drilldown report in configuration, the next step is to populate the predefined summarization hierarchy with data collection.

Data Collection
Product drilldown reports access a dataset, which must first be populated during a data collection run and saved. You run data collection for product drilldown reports with transaction KKRV or via menu path: **Accounting • Controlling • Product Cost Controlling • Cost Object Controlling • Product Cost by Period • Information System • Tools • Data Collection • For Product Drilldown**. The screen shown in Figure 6.6 is displayed.

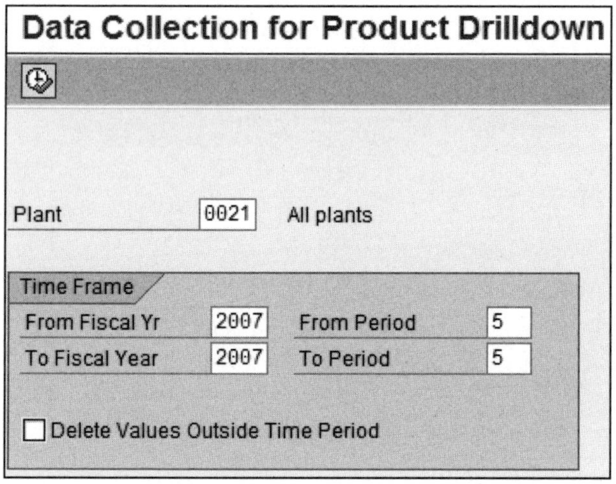

Data Collection for Product Drilldown

Plant	0021	All plants

Time Frame			
From Fiscal Yr	2007	From Period	5
To Fiscal Year	2007	To Period	5

☐ Delete Values Outside Time Period

Figure 6.6 Data Collection for Product Drilldown Reports

You normally run data collection following period-end closing for the current and previous period, since data on orders can change within open financial periods. If data collection has already been run, the system resets and recalculates all data within the summarization time frame of the new data collection run. Data outside the time frame is retained, unless you select the **Delete Values Outside Time Period** indicator.

Complete the fields seen in Figure 6.6 and save your work. A data collection results screen indicates the number of records read.

Now that we've populated the hierarchy, the next step is to run the report, as described in the next section.

Run Reports

Following data collection, you can run product drilldown reports, using transaction S_ALR_87013139 or menu path: **Accounting • Controlling • Product Cost Controlling • Cost Object Controlling • Product Cost by Period • Information System • Reports for Product Cost by Period • Summarized Analysis • With Product Drilldown • Variance Analysis • Target/Actual/Production Variances • Cumulative**. The screen shown in Figure 6.7 is displayed.

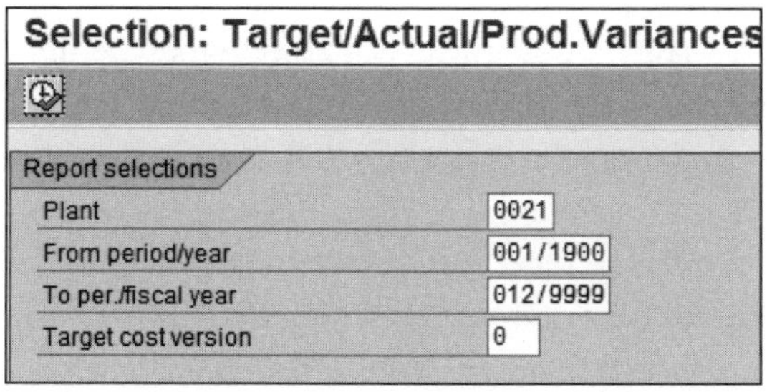

Figure 6.7 Product Drilldown Report Selection Screen

You can run the report with a wide period range, as shown in Figure 6.7, or you can restrict the period range to improve performance if you only need to report on one or two periods. Complete the fields and click on the execute icon to display the product drilldown report shown in Figure 6.8.

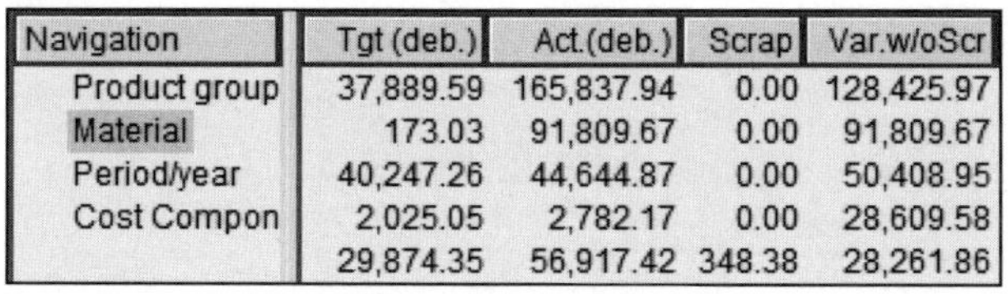

Navigation	Tgt (deb.)	Act.(deb.)	Scrap	Var.w/oScr
Product group	37,889.59	165,837.94	0.00	128,425.97
Material	173.03	91,809.67	0.00	91,809.67
Period/year	40,247.26	44,644.87	0.00	50,408.95
Cost Compon	2,025.05	2,782.17	0.00	28,609.58
	29,874.35	56,917.42	348.38	28,261.86

Figure 6.8 Product Drilldown Report Results Screen

In Figure 6.8, each line represents a **Material**, and the **Var.w/oScr** (variance) column is sorted in descending

order. This provides visibility to materials with the largest accumulated variance. You can drill down on any line to find out more details by **Period/year** and **Cost Compon** (cost component). You can analyze variance per **Material** further by displaying a detailed report of the product cost collector with transaction KKBC_PKO, or transaction KKBC_ORD for manufacturing orders, as described in Section 6.2.

In addition to the *cumulative* drilldown report discussed above, a *periodic* drilldown report is available in the same menu path. In periodic drilldown reports, results are shown by period, enabling fast navigation across multiple periods. With cumulative drilldown reports, results can be summarized across multiple periods, such as by quarter or fiscal year.

Summarization Hierarchy Reports

Summarization hierarchies allow you flexibility in setting up and displaying summarized data. A summarization hierarchy groups together manufacturing orders or product cost collectors at the lowest-level summarization nodes, which in turn are grouped together at higher-level nodes, to create a pyramid structure.

Each summarization level is set up manually in configuration. The hierarchy levels are presented as expandable and collapsible rows in the reports. Here is an example of hierarchy levels, starting at the top of the pyramid: Controlling area, profit center, plant, material group, and material number. Since you can display summarized data at each node, you may decide to define hierarchy levels based on responsibility at lower management levels, e. g., profit center, material groups, or order types. You may also decide to create an alternate summarization hierarchy with levels based on profitability reporting requirements, such as profit center, division, and sales document.

After you define the summarization hierarchy in configuration, you run a data collection transaction, which populates the hierarchy with current data.

During a data collection run, the following cost data is collected for all orders included in the run and rolled upwards through the hierarchy nodes and levels:

▶ Plan

▶ Target

▶ Actual

▶ Variances
▶ Work in process

Following the data collection run, the above cost data is available to be added as columns to the summarization report. You then run a summarization report, which displays the data summarized at each of the hierarchy levels. You may typically display the following cost data as columns at each level: Target, Actual, and Variance. This allows you to display total variance for a plant and then at each of the lower hierarchy levels, by expanding the levels as required. At the lowest level, you can display variance details of individual orders. You can then display a detailed report with cost element rows and drill down to line item reports and source documents.

Now that I've described how summarization hierarchy reports work, I'll describe in detail the three steps necessary to display the reports.

Configuration

This configuration step is required only once. You only need to change the configuration if you need an additional hierarchy or if you need to change an existing hierarchy.

Tip

You typically shouldn't need to make many changes to hierarchies, provided they are tested and reviewed by users before implementation in the production system. Testing and having users review results procedure for configuration implementation is good practice for any configuration changes, not just summarization hierarchies.

You maintain summarization hierarchies with transaction KKR0 or via menu path: **IMG • Controlling • Product Cost Controlling • Information System • Cost Object Controlling • Settings for Summarized Analysis/Order Selection • Maintain Summarization Hierarchies**. The screen shown in Figure 6.9 is displayed.

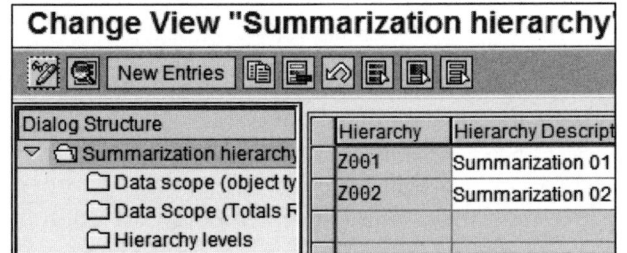

Figure 6.9 Change Summarization Hierarchy Initial Screen

This screen displays the existing **Hierarchy** list and allows you to define new hierarchies. Select an existing hierarchy and double-click on **Data scope (object types)** to display hierarchy details, as shown in Figure 6.10.

In this screen you specify which object types are summarized in the hierarchy. Read the **Description** in the row with the **Summarize** indicator selected to understand the purpose of the hierarchy.

You can also specify a status selection profile in the **Status sel.** column. Enter a status selection profile if you want to select only objects with a status that matches the selection criteria in the status selection profile. For example, you may be interested in only summarizing production orders with a status of fully delivered or technically complete. You can achieve this with a status selection profile.

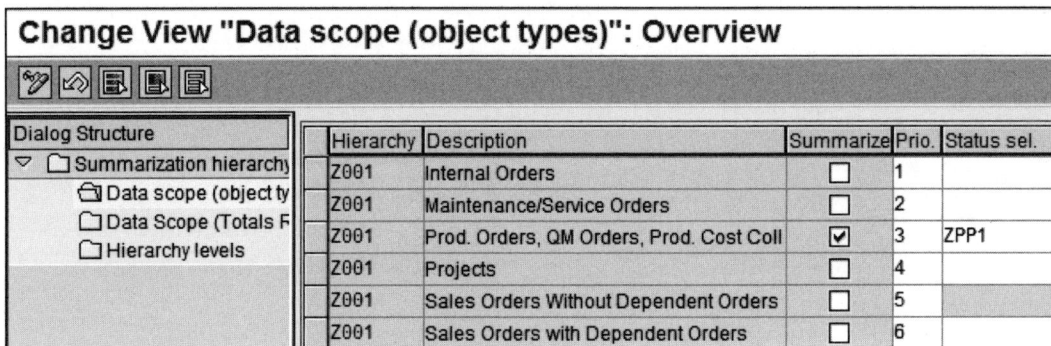

Figure 6.10 Change Data Scope Object Types Overview

To display further details of the hierarchy, double-click on **Hierarchy levels**. The screen shown in Figure 6.11 is displayed.

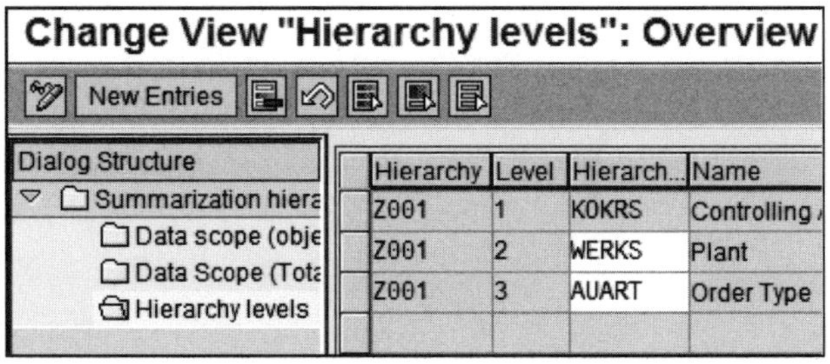

Change View "Hierarchy levels": Overview

Hierarchy	Level	Hierarch...	Name
Z001	1	KOKRS	Controlling /
Z001	2	WERKS	Plant
Z001	3	AUART	Order Type

Dialog Structure
▽ ☐ Summarization hiera
  ☐ Data scope (obje
  ☐ Data Scope (Tota
  ☐ Hierarchy levels

Figure 6.11 Change Hierarchy Levels

In this screen you specify the hierarchy levels of the summarization hierarchy. You can display a list of possible levels by right-clicking in any row in the **Hierarch...** (hierarchy field) column and clicking on **Possible Entries**. Some typical hierarchy levels are plant, order type, profit center, material, and order number. Note that long run times can result if order-number is included in the hierarchie.

Now that we've maintained a hierarchy, let's examine how to maintain a status selection profile to narrow the selection of summarized orders.

You maintain status selection profiles with transaction BS42 or via menu path: **IMG • Controlling • Product Cost Controlling • Information System • Cost Object Controlling • Settings for Summarized Analysis/Order Selection • Define Status Selection Profiles**. The screen shown in Figure 6.12 is displayed.

This screen shows the existing **SelProf** (selection profile) list and allows you to define new profiles. Select an existing selection profile and double-click on **Selection condition** to display selection profile details, as shown in Figure 6.13.

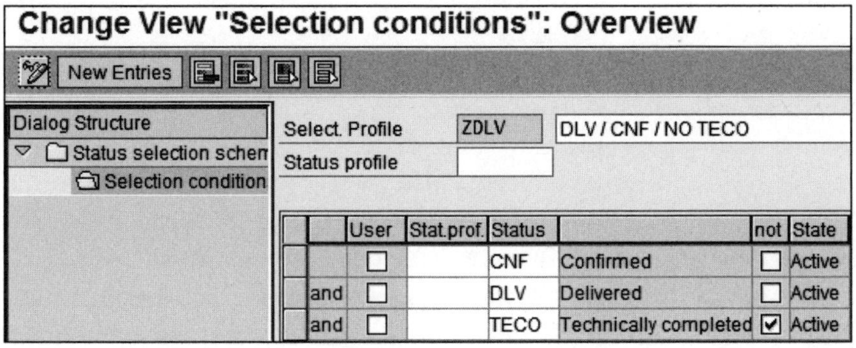

Change View "Status selection schema":

SelProf	Text
SAP001	Operations dispatched
SAP002	Operations not dispatched
SAP003	Split planned
SAP004	Split not planned

Dialog Structure
▽ ☐ Status selection schen
  ☐ Selection condition

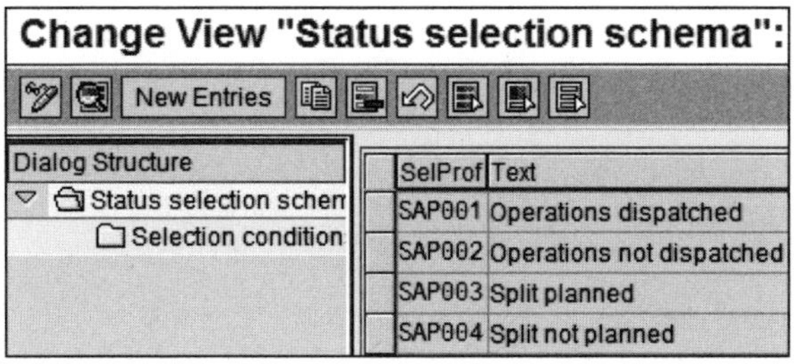

Figure 6.12 Status Selection Profile Overview Screen

This screen is where you define the **Status** of orders for selection. The selection conditions displayed in Figure 6.13 result in a selection of orders with a **Status of Confirmed and Delivered and not Technically completed**.

Now that we've defined the summarization hierarchy and looked at how to create a status selection profile, the next step is to populate the summarization hierarchy with data collection.

Data Collection

Summarization hierarchy reports access a dataset, which must first be populated during a data collection run and saved. You run data collection for summarization hierarchy reports with transaction KKRC or via menu path: **Accounting • Controlling • Product Cost Controlling • Cost Object Controlling • Product Cost by Period • Information System • Tools • Data Collection • For Summarization Hierarchy**. The screen shown in Figure 6.14 is displayed.

You normally run data collection following period-end closing for the current and previous period, since data on orders can change within open financial periods. If data collection has already been run, the system resets and recalculates all data within the summarization time frame

Change View "Selection conditions": Overview

Dialog Structure
▽ ☐ Status selection schen
  ☐ Selection condition

Select. Profile: ZDLV   DLV / CNF / NO TECO
Status profile:

	User	Stat.prof.	Status		not	State
	☐		CNF	Confirmed	☐	Active
and	☐		DLV	Delivered	☐	Active
and	☐		TECO	Technically completed	☑	Active

Figure 6.13 Selection Profile Selection Conditions Screen

of the new data collection run. Data outside the time frame is retained.

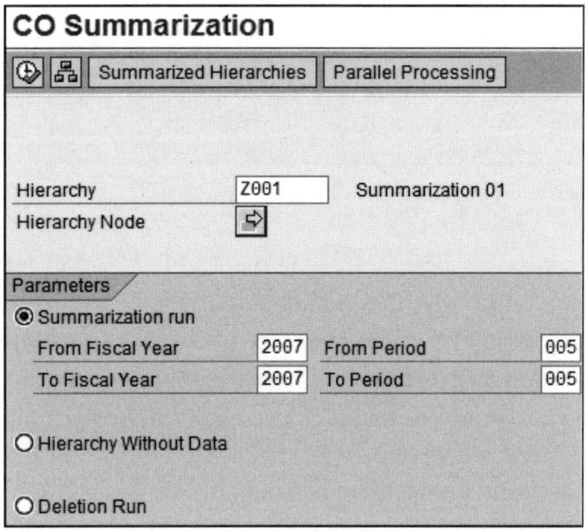

Figure 6.14 Data Collection for Summarization Reports

Complete the fields in Figure 6.14 and click on the **Hierarchy Node** (right-pointing arrow) icon. The screen shown in Figure 6.15 is displayed.

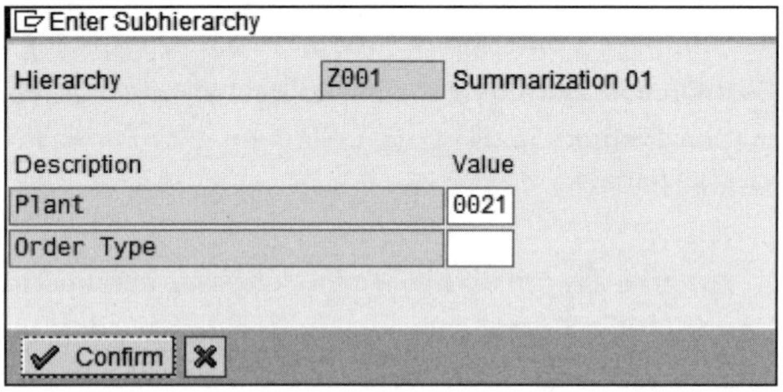

Figure 6.15 Hierarchy Node Screen

You can narrow the data collection run to specific objects by entering the object number in a **Value** field. Click on the **Confirm** button to return to the screen in Figure 6.14, and then click on the execute icon. A data collection results screen appears, indicating the number of records read.

Run Reports

Following data collection, you can execute summarization reports. You run summarization reports with transaction KKBC_HOE or via menu path: **Accounting • Controlling • Product Cost Controlling • Cost Object Con-**

trolling **• Product Cost by Period • Information System • Reports for Product Cost by Period • Summarized Analysis • With Defined Summarization Hierarchy**. The screen shown in Figure 6.16 is displayed.

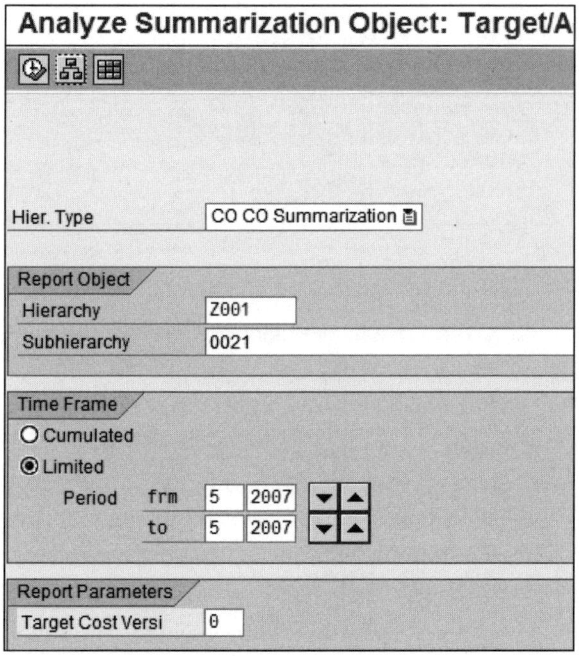

Figure 6.16 Summarization Report Selection Screen

You can run the report with a wide period range, or you can restrict the period range to improve performance if you only need to report on one period. Complete the fields and click on the hierarchy icon to display the report shown in Figure 6.17.

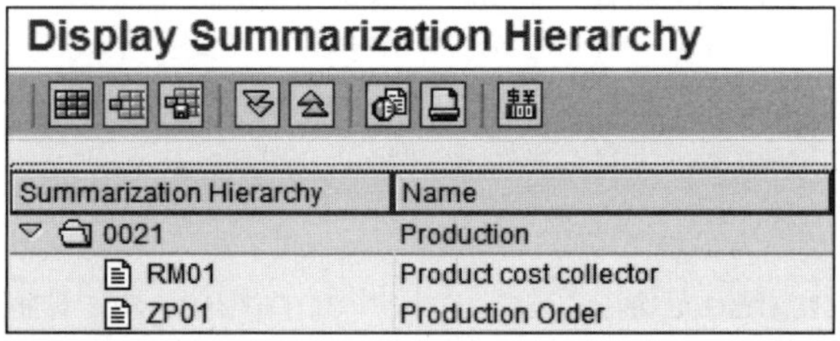

Figure 6.17 Display Summarization Hierarchy Screen

You can see the hierarchy levels we defined in the previous Configuration section, which are plant (**0021**) and order type (**RM01** and **ZP01**). To display the Target, Actual, and Variance columns in this report, follow menu path: **Settings • Layout • Choose** and click on the Target/Actual Comparison layout (not shown). The screen shown in Figure 6.18 is displayed.

Summarization ...	Total tgt costs	Actual debit	Target/actual var.
▽ 🗁 0021	9,063.34	3,317.24	5,746.10-
📄 RM01	9,063.34	3,317.24	5,746.10-

Figure 6.18 Target, Actual, and Variance Columns Displayed

This report indicates that the **Actual debit** for all orders of order type **RM01** is **3,317.24**. To see details of individual orders reporting to this node, click on node **RM01** and follow menu path: **Goto • Single Objects**. The screen shown in Figure 6.19 is displayed.

OTy	Object	ɛ	Actl	ɛ	Tgt	ɛ	Variance
ORD	786960		246,064.96		154,738.43		91,365.08
ORD	786855		110,826.72		90,673.79		65,850.97
ORD	786865		385,201.21		347,858.60		30,004.12
ORD	787063		292,255.35		235,662.70		27,700.51
ORD	786838		27,749.27		20,683.21		22,509.88

Figure 6.19 Single Objects Results Screen

In Figure 6.19, the **Variance** column is sorted in descending order. Sorting provides visibility to product cost collectors or orders with large variances during the time frame selected. Double-click on any line to display a cost element analysis report for the product cost collector or order. You can change the target cost version in the screen shown in Figure 6.19 by following menu path: **Settings • Target Cost Version**.

Alternate Summarization Hierarchies
An advantage of summarization reporting is that you can create multiple hierarchies. In the example hierarchy in the previous Configuration section, I chose plant and order type as hierarchy levels. You can create hierarchies with an additional level of order or material number and see more details directly in the results screen in Figure 6.17, without branching to the single objects screen in Figure 6.19. An advantage of the single objects report is that the columns are easily sorted and rearranged.

If you add more detail in hierarchy levels, you can create exception rules and display traffic light symbols in the results screen shown in Figure 6.17. This helps you quickly find nodes that require further analysis. To create exception rules, follow menu path: **IMG • Controlling • Prod-**

uct Cost Controlling • Information System • Cost Object Controlling • Settings for Summarized Analysis/Order Selection • Define Exception Rules**. You include exception rules during data collection with transaction KKRC and menu path: **Extras • Exception • Define Rule**.

6.2 Detailed Reports

If you use summarized analysis, you'll most often drill down to detailed reports. You can also display detailed reports directly if you know the material or manufacturing order to be analyzed. You typically run a detailed report directly if you identify a material with large variances during variance analysis. Since you can't drill down to line item details from the variance calculation output screen, you need to take note of the material number and run this report to drill down to line item reports and source documents.

Detailed reports are useful during variance analysis because they provide cost element details by row, and usually target, actual, and variance by column for an individual product cost collector or manufacturing order. You can display the costs for one or multiple periods, or cumulatively (all periods). The cost elements rows can be grouped together by similar business transactions, such as confirmations, goods issues, and goods receipts in the report.

This style of report is particularly useful when analyzing variance for an order. You simply search for the cost element with the largest variance and drill down (double-click) to line item details. You then sort the line item list and double-click on the line item with the largest value to display the source document. The source document generally contains all the information needed to find the cause of the largest variances.

You can display and analyze target vs. actual costs in detailed product cost collector reports with transaction PKBC_PKO or menu path: **Accounting • Controlling • Product Cost Controlling • Cost Object Controlling • Product Cost by Period • Information System • Reports for Product Cost by Period • Detailed Reports**. A selection screen is displayed, as shown in Figure 6.20. A similar report is also available for production and process orders with transaction PKBC_ORD.

Analyze Product Cost Collector: Cost trend

Report Object	
Material	
Plant	0021
Production proc.	

Time Frame			
○ Cumulated			
● Limited			
Period	frm	5	2007
	to	5	2007

Figure 6.20 Analyze Product Cost Collector Selection Screen

You can display costs for one period, a range of periods, or cumulatively (all periods). Complete the fields and click on the execute icon to display the screen shown in Figure 6.21.

BusTran.	Origin	Origin (Text)	Σ Total tgt	Σ Ttl actual
Confirmations	1650/RUN	Sewing / Run Time	4,706.44	15,127.19
	1650/SET	Sewing / Set Time	47.41	218.71
	1650/REW...	Sewing / Rework	0.00	14.41
	1660/RUN	Painting / Run Time	46.02	0.00
	1660/SET	Painting / Set Time	15.34	0.00

Figure 6.21 Analyze Product Cost Collector Results Screen

You are presented with a detailed report with cost elements as rows and **Total tgt** (total target), **Ttl actual** (total actual), and Variance (not shown) as columns. Sort a column in descending order and double-click on the row containing the largest value to display line item details, as shown in Figure 6.22.

In Figure 6.22, the **Quantity** column is sorted in descending order. This provides visibility to confirmations with the largest time bookings. By double-clicking on a line in the screen shown in Figure 6.22, you can drill down to individual activity confirmations and analyze the reasons for confirmations with the largest **Quantity**.

Now that I've explained how to run and analyze detailed reports for individual product cost collectors and manufacturing orders, let's look at line item reports. Although you nearly always drill down to line item reports from detailed reports, it's possible to display them directly. I'll now explain how to do that next.

Cost Elem.	CElem.name	Σ Val.in RC	Quantity	PUM	Off.acct	Offst.acct
690010	Labour	266.60	449.717	MIN		
690010	Labour	266.31	449.233	MIN		
690010	Labour	266.21	449.050	MIN		
690010	Labour	265.49	447.833	MIN		
690010	Labour	264.85	446.750	MIN		
690010	Labour	264.75	446.600	MIN		

Figure 6.22 Confirmation Line Items

6.3 Line Item Reports

You often drill down to line item reports for an individual object from summarized analysis and detailed reports. This is useful because there can be many thousands, or even millions, of line items. Just as summarization reports group together product cost collectors by characteristics for management variance reporting, detailed reports group together line items for production and management accounting reporting.

Analyzing a detailed report for a product cost collector and drilling down on the cost element with the largest variance is a much more efficient method of variance analysis than searching through possibly millions of line items directly. However, if you are in a situation where you need to display line items directly, the procedure is as follows.

Display and analyze line item reports with transaction KRMI or via menu path: **Accounting • Controlling • Product Cost Controlling • Cost Object Controlling • Product Cost by Period • Information System • Reports for Product Cost by Period • Line Items • Product Cost Collectors • Actual Costs**. A selection screen is displayed, as shown in Figure 6.23. A similar report is also available for production and process orders with transaction KOB1.

When displaying line items directly, it's important to restrict the **Posting Date** range sufficiently to avoid long runtimes, since there can be large numbers of line items. It's usually best to tightly restrict the **Posting Date** range initially, and then gradually increase it if required. Complete the fields and click on the execute icon. The screen shown in Figure 6.24 is displayed.

You typically sort line item lists by **Val.in RC** (value in reporting currency) or **Quantity** and analyze the lines with the largest and smallest values by double-clicking through to the source documents. In the case of confirmation line items, the source documents are activity confirmations. In the case of goods receipt and goods issue line items, the source documents are material documents.

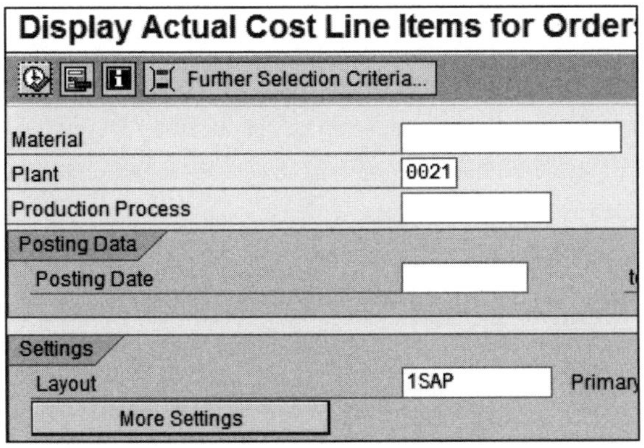

Display Actual Cost Line Items for Order

Material		
Plant	0021	
Production Process		
Posting Data		
Posting Date		t
Settings		
Layout	1SAP	Primary
More Settings		

Figure 6.23 Line Item Report Selection Screen

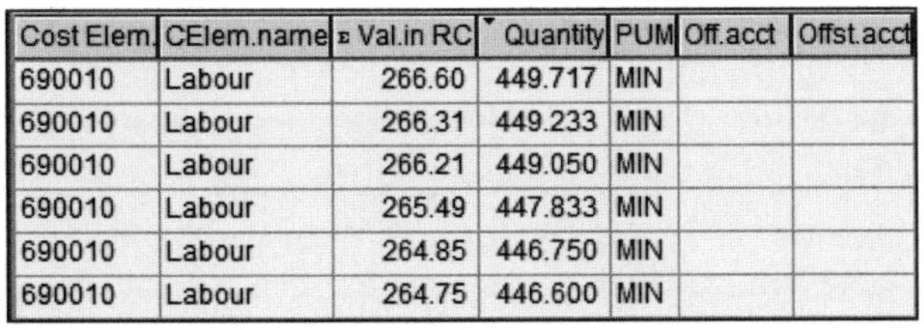

Cost Elem.	CElem.name	∑ Val.in RC	Quantity	PUM	Off.acct	Offst.acct
690010	Labour	266.60	449.717	MIN		
690010	Labour	266.31	449.233	MIN		
690010	Labour	266.21	449.050	MIN		
690010	Labour	265.49	447.833	MIN		
690010	Labour	264.85	446.750	MIN		
690010	Labour	264.75	446.600	MIN		

Figure 6.24 Confirmation Line Items

Now that I've explained how to run line item reports directly without drilling down from a detailed report, we've reached the end of this chapter, and of this Essentials Guide. In the following summary sections, I will present a summary of this chapter and also review some of the main take-home points that you should take note of, from the guide. These take-home points are in Section 6.6.

6.4 Summary

In this chapter I examined variance analysis from a management perspective, with the use of summarized analysis reports. These reports contain highly summarized data, which allows a plant manager to display and analyze plant manufacturing variances at a glance. The cost data in a summarized report is usually displayed as Target, Actual, and Variance columns. A manager can expand the hierarchy rows in the summarization report to display cost information at lower levels in the hierarchy. By navigating down through the hierarchy, you can narrow down the cause of a variance to an individual product cost collector or manufacturing order.

The two types of summarization reports are *product drilldown* and *summarization hierarchy* reports. Product drilldown reports require little, if any, configuration since the hierarchy is predefined. These reports provide sufficient summarized data for most circumstances. Summarization hierarchy reports allow you to define your own multiple hierarchies, if required. I explained in detail how to configure summarization reports, run data collection, and execute and analyze the reports.

Summarized reports allow selection of individual orders for further analysis. Variance on an individual order can be analyzed at a cost element level with detailed reports. Selecting the Material Origin indicator in the material master Costing 1 view results in the material number appearing in the Origin column of detailed reports, which assists in establishing the cause of the variance. When you double-click on a cost element, you are presented with a line item report. Line item reports can also be run directly, without drilling down, although this is often not necessary.

I presented a method to display line item reports directly, sort the rows based on value, and drill down on the largest values to examine the source documents, such as activity confirmations and material documents. Analyzing source documents often helps explain the cause of the variance.

In conclusion, standard reports provide excellent reporting functionality, sufficient to analyze variances for most companies. Product drilldown reports can be used with only a small amount of configuration and setup required. Summarization hierarchy reports allow you to create your own multiple hierarchies. With detailed reports, you can view all postings by cost element within a time frame and drill down to line item details.

6.5 Guide Summary

The Controlling process involves internal reporting for management to determine and reduce costs and improve profitability. The purpose of variance analysis is to assist in this process. Variance analysis involves comparing actual costs with standard costs, analyzing the difference, and taking corrective action.

The process of determining standard costs begins in the previous fiscal year, when sales plans are determined. You enter the sales plan into Sales and Operations Planning and convert it to a production plan. The production plan is then transferred to Long-Term Planning, where it is used to generate component Purchasing requirements and to transfer scheduled activity requirements to Cost Center Accounting.

You then create standard cost estimates to determine the standard cost. BOMs and routings provide quantity structure information, while material and activity prices provide valuation structure information, costing sheets provide overhead information, and the costing variant contains information on how a cost estimate calculates the standard price. Standard cost estimates are created, marked, and released to update the material master standard price. During release, inventory is revalued if there is stock.

Actual cost postings to product cost collectors and manufacturing orders occur during activity confirmations, goods receipts and issues, overhead calculation, and settlement.

During variance analysis, target and actual costs are compared. Target costs are based on the standard price and plan quantity, adjusted by quantity delivered to inventory. During variance calculation, the order balance is divided into variance categories, which assist in identifying the source of the variance. During settlement, the order receives a credit equal to the order balance, and postings are made to Financial Accounting and Profitability Analysis. Cost center and purchase price variance should also be considered during period-end variance analysis.

Scrap variance analysis involves master data settings to plan for scrap. These settings influence standard cost estimates. Actual scrap postings occur during activity confirmation, and, if actual scrap is confirmed as planned, there is no scrap variance. This reduces total variance, making the task of variance analysis easier.

Standard variance analysis reports include summarized, detailed, and line item reports. You can analyze plant manufacturing variances at a glance with summarized reports and quickly determine individual orders that are causing large variances by expanding the hierarchy levels. You can analyze individual orders at a cost element level with detailed reports and drill down to line item reports. By sorting on the Value column in line item reports, you can drill down on the largest values to source documents, which contain information to assist in determining the cause of the variance. You can then take corrective action.

6.6 Looking Ahead

Carrying out regular variance analysis and taking immediate corrective action as required can provide your company with a cost advantage over companies that wait to see a noticeable effect on the bottom line before taking corrective action. In industries with low profit margins, this can mean the difference between making a profit and a loss.

You should notice manufacturing, cost center, and purchase price variances decrease over time if you routinely carry out variance analysis and request production and purchasing personnel to explain variances in their cost centers at each period-end. This process involves a learning curve associated with understanding how variances occur and what action can be taken to reduce them in the future. However, it eventually results in constant improvements in production and purchasing efficiency and has the added benefit of improved communications between departments.

Variance analysis is an iterative process. You create sales, production, and cost center plans and analyze variances during the following fiscal year. As you gain a greater understanding of how variances occur, planning for the next fiscal year improves and variances decrease. This is not an easy process at first, and may initially create minor conflict between some users or departments as their understanding of the interaction and dependency between departments improves. Be assured that any conflict will be temporary and will result in a more efficient and profitable organization. And that is, of course, your ultimate goal.

Bibliography

SAP Training Course Guide: *AC505–Product Cost Planning–Release 470*. April 11, 2006.

SAP Training Course Guide: *AC412–Cost Center Accounting–Advanced Functions–Release 470*. April 11, 2006.

Glossary

Activity Type

An activity type identifies activities provided by a cost center to product cost collectors and manufacturing orders. The secondary cost element associated with an activity type identifies the activity costs on cost center and detailed reports.

Actual Costing

Actual costing determines what portion of the variance is debited to the next highest level using material consumption. All purchasing and manufacturing difference postings are allocated upward through the BOM to assemblies and finished goods. Variances can be rolled up over multiple production levels to the finished product.

Actual Costs

Actual costs debit a product cost collector or manufacturing order during business transactions such as general ledger account postings, inventory goods movements, internal activity allocations, and overhead calculation.

Assembly Scrap

Assembly scrap is the percentage of assembly quantity that does not meet required production quality standards. The plan quantity of the assembly is increased. Assembly scrap is an output scrap, since it affects the planned output quantity of items in the production process.

Bill of Material

A bill of material (BOM) is a structured hierarchy of components necessary to build an assembly. BOMs, together with purchasing info records or vendor quotations, provide cost estimates with the information necessary to calculate material costs of assemblies.

Component Scrap

Component scrap is the percentage of component quantity that does not meet required production quality standards before being inserted in the production process. The plan quantity of components is increased. Component scrap is an input scrap, since it is detected before use in the production process.

Cost Component

A cost component identifies costs of similar types, such as material, labor, and overhead costs, by grouping together cost elements in the cost component structure.

Cost Center

A cost center is master data that identifies where the cost occurred. There is usually a responsible person assigned to the cost center who analyzes and explains cost center variances at period-end.

Cost Element

A cost element is master data that identifies what the cost is. Primary cost elements correspond to Financial Accounting accounts and identify external costs. Secondary cost elements identify costs allocated within Controlling, such as activity allocations from cost centers to manufacturing orders.

Cost Estimate

A cost estimate calculates the plan cost to manufacture a product or purchase a component. It determines material costs by multiplying BOM quantities by material standard price, labor costs multiplying operation standard quantities by plan activity price, and overhead values by costing sheet configuration.

Costing Lot Size

The costing lot size in the material master Costing 1 view determines the quantity cost estimate calculations are based on. The costing lot size should be set as close as possible to actual purchase and production quantities to reduce lot size variance.

Costing Run

A costing run is a collective processing of cost estimates.

Costing Sheet

A costing sheet summarizes the rules for allocating overhead from cost centers to cost estimates, product cost collectors, and manufacturing orders. The components of a costing sheet are calculation base (group of cost elements), overhead rate (percentage rate applied to base), and credit key (cost center receiving credit).

Costing Type

The costing type is a component of the costing variant, and it determines if the cost estimate is able to update the standard price in the material master.

Costing Variant

The costing variant contains information on how a cost estimate calculates the standard price. For example, it determines if the purchasing info record price is used for purchased materials or if an estimated price is manually entered in the Planned price 1 field of the material master Costing 2 view.

Detailed Reports

Detailed reports display cost element details of manufacturing orders and product cost collectors. You can drill down on cost elements to display line item reports during variance analysis.

Input Variance

Variances on the input side are based on goods issues, internal activity allocations, overhead allocation, and general ledger account postings. The four input variances are: input price, resource-usage, input quantity, and remaining input variance.

Line Item Reports

Line item reports display a list of postings to a cost object within a time frame. You can sort the value or quantity columns to find the largest postings during variance analysis.

Long-Term Planning

Long-Term Planning allows you to enter medium- to longer-term production plans and simulate future production requirements with long-term Material Requirements Planning (MRP). You can determine future purchasing requirements for vendor requests for quotations and update purchasing info records prior to a costing run, and also transfer planned activity requirements to Cost Center Accounting.

Master Data

Master data is information that stays relatively constant over long periods of time. For example, purchasing info records contain vendor information, such as business name and address, which usually doesn't change.

Material Origin

The Material Origin indicator in the material master Costing 1 view determines if the material number is displayed in detailed reports. This is one of the single most important indicators in providing greater visibility to the causes of variances. If you have already created material master records without the Material Origin indicator selected, you can use report RKHKMAT0 to select the indicator.

Material Master

A material master contains all the information required to manage a material. Information is stored in views, each corresponding to a department or area of business responsibility. Views conveniently group information together for users in different departments, e.g., sales and purchasing.

Material Requirements Planning

Material Requirements Planning (MRP) guarantees material availability by monitoring stocks and generating planned orders for procurement and production.

Manufacturing Order
Manufacturing order is an umbrella term for production and process orders.

Moving Average Price
The moving average price (MAP) in the material master Costing 2 view determines the inventory valuation price if price control is set at moving average (V). The MAP is updated during goods receipt.

Operation Scrap
Operation scrap is the percentage of assembly quantity that does not meet required production quality standards. Operation scrap is an output scrap, since it reduces the planned output quantity in the production process.

Output Variance
Variances on the output side result from too little or too much of planned order quantity being delivered, or because the delivered quantity was valuated differently. Output variances are divided into the following categories during variance calculation: mixed price, output price, lot size, and remaining variance.

Planning Variance
Planning variance is a type of variance calculation based on the difference between costs on the preliminary cost estimate for the order and target costs based on the standard cost estimate and planned order quantity. You calculate planning variances with target cost version 2. Planning variances are for information only, and are not relevant for settlement.

Price Control
The price control field in the material master Costing 2 view indicates whether inventory is valuated at standard (S) or moving average (V) price.

Product Cost Collector
A product cost collector collects target and actual costs during the manufacture of an assembly. Product cost collectors are necessary for repetitive manufacturing and optional for order-related manufacturing.

Product Drilldown Reports
Product drilldown reports allow you to slice and dice data based on characteristics such as product group, material, plant, cost component, and period. Product drilldown reports use predefined summarization levels.

Production Variance
Production variance is a type of variance calculation based on the difference between net actual costs debited to the order and target costs based on the preliminary cost estimate and quantity delivered to inventory. You calculate production variances with target cost version 1. Production variances are for information only, and are not relevant for settlement.

Purchase Price Variance
When raw materials are valued at standard price, there will be a purchase price variance posting during goods receipt if the purchase price is different from the material standard price.

Purchasing Info Record
A purchasing info record stores all the information relevant to the procurement of a material from a vendor. It contains the purchase price field, which the standard cost usually search for when determining purchase material price.

Repetitive Manufacturing
Repetitive manufacturing eliminates the need for production or process orders in manufacturing environments with production lines and long production runs. It reduces the work involved in production control and simplifies confirmations and goods receipt postings.

Request for Quotation
This refers to the request made to a vendor to submit a quotation for materials or services.

Rework
Assemblies or components that do not meet quality standards may either become scrap or require rework. Depending on the problem, cheaper items may become scrap, while more costly assemblies may justify rework.

Routing

A routing is a list of tasks containing standard activity times required to perform operations to build an assembly. Routings, together with planned activity prices, provide cost estimates with the information necessary to calculate labor costs of products.

Sales and Operations Planning

This allows you to enter a sales plan, convert it to a production plan, and transfer it to Long-Term Planning.

Scale

A scale represents vendor quotations containing reduced prices for greater purchase quantities. Scales are entered in purchasing info records.

Settlement

Work in process and variances are transferred to Financial Accounting, Profit Center Accounting, and Profitability Analysis during settlement. Variance categories can also be transferred to value fields in Profitability Analysis.

Standard Price

The standard price in the material master Costing 2 view determines the inventory valuation price if price control is set at standard (S). The standard price is updated when a standard cost estimate is released. You normally value manufactured goods at standard price.

Summarization Hierarchy Reports

Summarization hierarchy reports are based on data collected at the levels and nodes of a summarization hierarchy. A summarization hierarchy groups together manufacturing orders or product cost collectors at the lowest-level summarization nodes, which in turn are grouped together at higher-level nodes, to create a pyramid structure. You can create your own multiple hierarchies in configuration.

Target Cost Version

The target cost version determines the basis for the calculation of target costs. Target cost version 0 calculates total variance and is used to explain the difference between actual debits and credits on an order. It is the only target cost version that can be settled to Financial Accounting, Profit Center Accounting, and Profitability Analysis.

Transfer Control

Transfer control is a costing variant component that requires a top-level cost estimate to use recently created standard cost estimates for all lower-level materials. Preliminary cost estimates for product cost collectors use transfer control.

Total Variance

Total variance is a type of variance calculation based on the difference between actual costs debited to the order and credits from deliveries to inventory. You calculate total variance with target cost version 0, which determines the basis for calculation of target costs.

Under/Over Absorption

Cost center balance, otherwise known as under/over absorption, represents the difference between cost center debits and credits during a period or range of periods. Cost center under/over absorption occurs due to differences between plan and actual debits, and plan and actual credits.

Variance Calculation

Variance calculation provides information to assist you during analysis of how the order balance occurred. In other words, it helps you determine the reason for the difference between order debits and credits. It does this by analyzing variance causes and assigning categories. The three main types of variance calculation are: total, production, and planning.

Valuation Class

The valuation class in the material master Costing 2 view determines which general ledger accounts are updated as a result of inventory movement or settlement.

Valuation Variant

The valuation variant is a costing variant component that allows different search strategies for materials, activity types, subcontracting, and external processing.

For example, the search strategy for materials typically searches first for a price from the purchasing info record.

Valuation Variant for Scrap and WIP

This valuation variant allows a choice of cost estimates to valuate scrap and work in process (WIP) in a WIP at target scenario. If the structure of a routing is changed after a costing run, WIP can still be valuated with the valuation variant for scrap and WIP.

Variance Categories

During variance calculation, the order balance is divided into categories on the input and output sides. Variance categories provide reasons for the cause of the variance, which you can use when deciding what corrective action to take.

Variance Key

This key ensures the manufacturing order or product cost collector is selected during variance calculation, and determines whether scrap costs are reported in a separate category. The variance key in the material master Costing 1 view defaults when creating product cost collectors and manufacturing orders.

Variance Variant

Variance variants determine which variance categories are calculated. If a variance category is not selected, variances of that category are assigned to remaining variances. Scrap variances are the only exception to this rule. If a scrap variance is not selected, these variances enter all other variances on the input side.

Work in Process

Work in process (WIP) represents production costs of incomplete assemblies. In order for balance sheet accounts to accurately reflect company assets at period-end, WIP costs are moved temporarily to WIP balance sheet and profit and loss accounts. WIP postings are canceled during period-end processing following delivery of associated assemblies or finished products to inventory.

WIP at Actual

Work in process (WIP) at actual is valuated based on actual debits to a manufacturing order or product cost collector.

WIP at Target

Work in process (WIP) at target is valuated based on a cost estimate.

Index

ISBN   978-1-59229-109-0

1st edition 2007

© 2007 by Galileo Press GmbH

SAP PRESS is an imprint of Galileo Press,

Boston (MA), USA

Bonn, Germany

Editor Jawahara Saidullah

Copy Editor Heather Meyers, UCG, Inc., Boston, MA

Cover Design Vera Brauner

Printed in Germany